The Editor

MICHAEL PATRICK GILLESPIE is Professor of English at Florida International University. He is the author of *Branding Oscar Wilde, Oscar Wilde and the Poetics of Ambiguity, The Picture of Dorian Gray: "What the World Thinks Me,"* and books on James Joyce, William Kennedy, literary theory, and film. His edited works include the Norton Critical Edition of *The Picture of Dorian Gray*.

NORTON CRITICAL EDITIONS
Victorian Era

BARRETT BROWNING, Aurora Leigh
C. BRONTË, Jane Eyre
E. BRONTË, Wuthering Heights
BROWNING, Robert Browning's Poetry
CARROLL, Alice in Wonderland
The Classic Fairy Tales
DARWIN, Darwin
DICKENS, Bleak House
DICKENS, David Copperfield
DICKENS, Great Expectations
DICKENS, Hard Times
DICKENS, Oliver Twist
DICKENS, A Tale of Two Cities
ELIOT, Middlemarch
ELIOT, The Mill on the Floss
GASKELL, Mary Barton
GASKELL, North and South
HARDY, Far from the Madding Crowd
HARDY, Jude the Obscure
HARDY, The Mayor of Casterbridge
HARDY, The Return of the Native
HARDY, Tess of the d'Urbervilles
KIPLING, Kim
MILL, The Spirit of the Age, On Liberty,
The Subjection of Women
STEVENSON, Strange Case of Dr. Jekyll and Mr. Hyde
STOKER, Dracula
TENNYSON, In Memoriam
TENNYSON, Tennyson's Poetry
THACKERAY, Vanity Fair
WELLS, The Time Machine
WILDE, The Importance of Being Earnest
WILDE, The Picture of Dorian Gray

For a complete list of Norton Critical Editions, visit
wwnorton.com/nortoncriticals

A NORTON CRITICAL EDITION

Oscar Wilde

THE IMPORTANCE OF BEING EARNEST

AUTHORITATIVE TEXT
BACKGROUNDS
CRITICISM

SECOND EDITION

Edited by

MICHAEL PATRICK GILLESPIE
FLORIDA INTERNATIONAL UNIVERSITY

W. W. NORTON & COMPANY
Independent Publishers Since 1923

W. W. Norton & Company has been independent since its founding in 1923, when William Warder Norton and Mary D. Herter Norton first published lectures delivered at the People's Institute, the adult education division of New York City's Cooper Union. The firm soon expanded its program beyond the Institute, publishing books by celebrated academics from America and abroad. By mid-century, the two major pillars of Norton's publishing program—trade books and college texts—were firmly established. In the 1950s, the Norton family transferred control of the company to its employees, and today—with a staff of five hundred and hundreds of trade, college, and professional titles published each year—W. W. Norton & Company stands as the largest and oldest publishing house owned wholly by its employees.

Copyright © 2023, 2006 by W. W. Norton & Company, Inc.

Manufacturing by Maple Press
Book design by Antonina Krass
Production manager: Brenda Manzanedo

Library of Congress Cataloging-in-Publication Data

Names: Wilde, Oscar, 1854–1900, author. | Gillespie, Michael Patrick, editor.
Title: The importance of being earnest : authoritative text, backgrounds,
    criticism / Oscar Wilde ; edited by Michael Patrick Gillespie, Florida
    International University.
Description: Second edition. | New York : W. W. Norton & Company, 2022. |
    Series: A Norton critical edition | Includes bibliographical references.
Identifiers: LCCN 2021026533 | **ISBN 9780393421972 (paperback)**
Subjects: LCSH: Wilde, Oscar, 1854–1900. Importance of being earnest. |
    Identity (Psychology)—Drama. | Foundlings—Drama. | England—Drama. |
    GSAFD: Comedies. | LCGFT: Drama.
Classification: LCC PR5818 .I4 2022 | DDC 822/.8—dc23
LC record available at https://lccn.loc.gov/2021026533

W. W. Norton & Company, Inc., 500 Fifth Avenue, New York, NY 10110
www.wwnorton.com
W. W. Norton & Company Ltd., 15 Carlisle Street, London W1D 3BS

1 2 3 4 5 6 7 8 9 0

This edition is dedicated to the memory of Chavalah Madeline Pilmaier, a precious child to all who knew and loved her.

Contents

Preface to the Second Edition

Let me begin with a statement that shows my keen grasp of the obvious. To one degree or another, consciously or not, all artists create out of their environment. They incorporate into their work the influences of the world in which they exist and simultaneously struggle against these forces to define an independent vision. Oscar Wilde was determinedly and flamboyantly a creature of and in opposition to his times. Therefore, an understanding of his work is greatly enhanced by first having some sense of the life from which it emerged.

Paradox defined Wilde's world from the time he was very young, and it can be no wonder that it formed the foundation of his social appeal and literary wit. Wilde was born in 1854 (though later in life he would claim 1856 as the year of his birth). He grew up in upper-middle-class, Protestant Dublin in a household full of physical and metaphysical contradictions. His father was small in stature, and his mother was a large, imposing woman. His father delighted in family life, yet had the well-deserved reputation of a notorious philanderer. His mother had been an ardent Irish nationalist as a young woman, yet she gloried in her title, Lady Wilde, after her husband was knighted by Queen Victoria.

Displacement also became a key element early in his life. Wilde began his formal education at the age of nine when his parents sent him to one of the oldest and most exclusive public schools in Ireland (that is to say what in America would be a private school), Portora Royal School in Enniskillen. (A half-century later Samuel Beckett was also a student there.) In 1871 he returned to Dublin on a Royal School scholarship to study at Trinity College. After three years there, he took a competitive examination and received a Demy-ship (the term Magdalen College uses to denote a scholarship) to study classics at Oxford. While he was at the university, Wilde distinguished himself academically, earning a rare double first[1] in his final exams. Artistically, he won the prestigious Newdigate Prize for his poem "Ravenna," and delighted friends and classmates by reciting it from memory at the awards ceremony. And socially, he became

---

1. A double first at Oxford recognizes the highest achievement a student can attain in two separate areas of study.

notorious around the campus for his imitation, and possibly his burlesque, of the "art for art's sake" credo espoused by, among others, his tutors Walter Pater and John Ruskin, at one point lamenting that "I find it harder and harder every day to live up to my blue china."

After completing his studies in 1878, Wilde toyed with the idea of staying at Oxford. However, his cavalier attitude while an undergraduate aroused a good deal of institutional hostility. (After the results of his exams were announced, he wrote to a friend with the news: "The dons are 'astonied' beyond words—the Bad Boy doing so well in the end") University administrators have notoriously long memories and little or no sense of humor, and Wilde could hardly have been surprised when his essay "The Rise of Historical Criticism" failed to win the Chancellor's Prize. That setback, in turn, precluded the possibility that Magdalen College would award him a fellowship. As a result, in 1879, Wilde moved permanently to London.

When he came to the city he was already fully formed, and by the early 1880s Wilde's charm and wit quickly made him a favorite at dinner parties and other society gatherings. Even before he had produced anything of literary consequence, he became famous for being famous, and his friendships with established figures in the art world and the theater—such as Lillie Langtry, James A. McNeill Whistler, Sarah Bernhardt, and Edward Burne-Jones—led to even broader celebrity. To his delight, he was repeatedly caricatured in the satirical journal *Punch* and lampooned in a series of theatrical productions culminating in the Gilbert and Sullivan operetta *Patience* (1881). This notoriety led in 1882 to a highly successful lecture tour of America. He devoted much of his time there to caricaturing the foibles of the British, and during complementary tours throughout the United Kingdom (1883–84) he reversed roles by poking fun at the mores of Americans.

In 1884 he married Constance Lloyd and set up house in Chelsea. Two sons, Cyril and Vyvyan, were born in quick succession. Although Wilde had still had not begun to enjoy wide success as a published writer, he had achieved a solid reputation as a lecturer. He gained further eminence as the editor of *Woman's World* (1887–89), notably in part for the celebrated figures he persuaded to contribute to the magazine. And, by the last years of the decade he had made a name for himself as an engaging author of fairy tales, short stories, and critical essays.

All this was a prelude to Wilde's greatest creative period, from 1890 to 1895. During that time, he composed his two best-known works, *The Picture of Dorian Gray* (1890–91) and *The Importance of Being Earnest* (1895), which bracketed a series of commercially and critically successful West End plays—*Lady Windermere's Fan* (1892), *A Woman of No Importance* (1893), and *An Ideal Husband*

(1895). He also wrote and published a stylized drama on the death of John the Baptist—*Salomé* (1892)—originally composed in French with the hope that Sarah Bernhardt would take the title role. Wilde's writings were in great demand, and his reputation was at its zenith. When *The Importance of Being Earnest*, premiered on Valentine's Day 1895 at the St. James's Theatre in London's West End, it achieved immediate critical and popular acclaim.

However, shortly after the opening of this last play, a series of catastrophic events produced a radical change in Wilde's personal life and in his professional career. Early in 1895 John Douglas, the Ninth Marquess of Queensberry and the father of Wilde's lover Lord Alfred "Bosie" Douglas, began vociferously and publicly attacking Wilde's character. Wilde initiated a libel suit against Queensberry, and the ill-considered action ultimately brought about Wilde's downfall. After a trial sensationalized in the popular press, Queensberry was acquitted, and Wilde was arrested for the homosexual offenses reported by witnesses tracked down by Queensberry's counsel. (Bosie, enjoying the protection generally extended to the aristocracy, was never directly implicated in any of these accounts.) Despite an initial mistrial, Wilde was eventually convicted and sentenced, on May 25, 1895, to two years at hard labor. This caused a premature cancellation of the run of *The Importance of Being Earnest*, triggered demands from creditors that led to bankruptcy, and precipitated the virtual disappearance of his writings from booksellers' stocks.

Upon conviction, Wilde was taken to Pentonville Prison, where he spent several months picking oakum. He was subsequently transferred to Reading Gaol, where he served the remainder of his sentence. During his incarceration there, Wilde wrote his prison letter, *De Profundis*, which was not published in full until it appeared in the 1962 *Letters of Oscar Wilde*, edited by Rupert Hart-Davis. Wilde was released on May 19, 1897; shortly after, he left England for the Continent.

For the next three years, Wilde lived a solitary, transient, and often impoverished life, mainly in France. During this time of financial strain, poor health, and social ostracism, Wilde's artistic abilities were at a near standstill; his only publication was the poem inspired by his experiences in prison, *The Ballad of Reading Gaol*, brought out by Leonard Smithers in 1898. He led a peripatetic existence in Europe, subsisting on the charity of friends. Wilde died in Paris on November 30, 1900, after receiving the Last Rites of the Catholic Church in an apparent deathbed conversion. He was first buried in the British cemetery in Bagneux, France, and then in 1909 Wilde's remains were moved to Père Lachaise Cemetery in Paris.

The sad circumstances of Wilde's final years have not prevented *The Importance of Being Earnest* from remaining one of the most frequently performed works in contemporary theatrical repertory. Although the play can appear at first glance both familiar and predictable, many productions have highlighted the subtle features of its structure. The 1993 revival of the play in London's West End, for example, offered a memorable instance of this elasticity. Maggie Smith's portrayal of Lady Bracknell as a woman whose domineering manner only partially masks her *nouvelle venue* insecurities brought to the foreground a sophisticated critique of the foibles of humanity, as relevant today as it was a century ago.

The play's humorous use of highly improbable plot situations, exaggerated characters, and slapstick elements has evoked justifiable praise of its lighthearted wit. Nonetheless, cataloging *The Importance of Being Earnest* as a charming farce and ignoring the intricacies of its structure overlooks its considerable insights into the human condition. Gently but persistently, *The Importance of Being Earnest* takes up large issues of class, gender, sexuality, identity, and other topics that engage the interest of contemporary readers. As with any great work of art, despite the specificity of its context, the rich and often sardonic representations of human nature allow the play to transcend its setting, era, and eccentricities, and to create broad resonance with its readers' and viewers' experiences.

One sees this trait neatly illustrated in the opening exchange of the play, between a smug and self-satisfied young man, Algernon Moncrieff, and his worldlywise servant Lane (see p. 6). Their discussion runs from Algernon's abilities as a pianist, to the amount of wine young men (and supposedly their servants), consume, to the state of married life. In every instance wit dominates, but a dark undercurrent gives deeper meaning to the dialogue. The flippancy of Algernon and the languor of Lane combine to comment profoundly on the complacency of the financially and socially secure, and on the casual callousness they enforce upon those who must make their own way in the world.

On the surface, both Algernon and Lane understand the game being played—the master and servant match wits with the implicit understanding that the master must always win the contest. However, the sophistication and cynicism of Lane's responses go well beyond Algernon's ability to comprehend fully the mores of the world that they both inhabit, even as they underscore their drastically different levels of accountability. Despite Lane's marked cultural disadvantage, he presents a deft repartee that does more than simply deflect and then undercut the attempted witticisms of his employer. Without trumpeting a heavy-handed didactic message, Lane's rejoinders to Algernon call attention to a range of social issues and class restraints that conditioned ordinary Victorian life, and to the ability of a nimble mind to subvert the clumsy attempts at domination, made all the more offensive by Algernon's obliviousness to their distasteful-ness. Such intricate exchanges animate every scene, extend interpre-tive possibilities, and ensure ongoing pleasure in repeated viewings and readings.

The structure of this Norton Critical Edition is fairly straight-forward, and generally follows the model of other works in the series. It begins with the three-act version set according to the edi-tion published by Smithers in 1899, for which Wilde corrected the proofs, with a few typographical errors silently corrected. Following the play are some of the excised portions of the original four-act ver-sion. They were removed at the insistence of George Alexander, manager of the St. James's Theatre and the first actor to play Jack Worthing (as such, doing the work of a producer and a director). The resulting three-act form of *The Importance of Being Earnest* now dominates productions and editions, but the juxtaposition of deleted scenes offers students the opportunity to judge for them-selves whether this approach is the best representation of the play.

Next, in "Backgrounds," several essays offer discussions of the context out of which Wilde's work emerged. Karl Beckson's summary of the central features of the London social and cultural world of the 1890s remains an important overview of the ethos surrounding Wilde's writing. Sharon Marcus's essay offers a refreshing reexami-nation of received opinions of Victorian drama, acknowledging its weaknesses but also proving perspectives for understanding its strengths. Although she places *The Importance of Being Earnest* outside this period, her overview gives readers useful insights into the cultural context from which Wilde's drama emerged. And Michael Patrick Gillespie's characterization of Wilde's self-marketing offers a concentrated view of the construction of Wilde's public persona. In discussing how Wilde's self-conscious branding shaped not only the way he wrote but how readers and audiences under-stood his ideas, the essay orients readers to an important interpretive perspective. Overall, these selections give students a grounding in the period, provide a sense of the significance of earnestness to the period, and suggest how the constructed nature of the author impacts both artist and audience.

"Early Reviews and Reactions" contains a selection of con-temporaneous responses to the play. It features prominent reviewers—among them William Archer, George Bernard Shaw, and H. G. Wells—reacting to the play's premiere. Most are posi-tive, though Shaw's well-known dissenting view gives a sense of how difficult it is to discern the complex narrative patterns of *Earnest* in a single viewing, particularly if you are yourself a playwright.

"Essays in Criticism" samples a variety of recent approaches to the work. These selections reflect changes in critical emphasis that have accrued over the past few years. In many instances while the approaches used in the critical studies included in the previous edition of this volume are not evoked directly, they are treated as *données*. To that end, many of the new interpretive essays build on rather than reiterate the gender, nationality, psychology, and broad culture studies found in the first Norton Critical Edition of the play. That of course does not mean disregarding all previous work, and illustrative of that I have kept is E. H. Mikhail's fine textual study, an overview of the original four-act version of Wilde's play.

The rest of the critical essays are new to this edition. Burkhard Niederhoff examines *The Importance of Being Earnest* from a slightly unusual perspective, emphasizing its parodic features rather than its satirical tone. Although this essay may initially seem a rather basic reading, it brings out the importance of how one's fundamental understanding of critical language, in this case paradox and parody, has a profound effect on any assessment of Wilde's play. Christopher S. Nassaar's point-by-point response to the Niederhoff essay underscores the idea that no reading is definitive and illustrates how the dialectic process, particularly when applied to the work of other critics, extends existing critical conclusions and produces insights that will be of use to all readers. Clifton Snider provides perspectives that are complementary and contrasting to those of Niederhoff by exploring Wilde's integration of the concept of trickster into the play. Brigitte Bastiat offers a good example of the polymorphic qualities of *The Importance of Being Earnest* through her representation of how the play challenges "the social norms, sexual stereotypes and gender representations of his time while pleasing aristocratic London socialites." Eibhear Walshe's essay examines gender and nation to underscore the important interpretive connections to issues addressed in the play that are not always obvious to some readers but that exerted strong influences on Wilde's process of composition. And Maneck Daruwala expands the scope of these inquiries to touch on Wilde's early intellectual life by addressing the impact of his classical education along with Darwin's influence on the composition of *The Importance of Being Earnest*.

A Chronology and Selected Bibliography close the edition, offering abbreviated information on the author and the scholarship his work has inspired. The Chronology presents a thumbnail sketch of Wilde's life. The Selected Bibliography focuses on more recent responses to the play, with particular attention to those growing out of older criticism.

To conclude the Preface, I would like to thank a number of people who have made material contributions to this project. Their support took various forms, but in every instance it was offered with generosity and insight. Whatever success this edition enjoys relates directly to their efforts.

I remain grateful to those who were so helpful in compiling the first edition: Brian Baker, Carol Bemis, Joseph Donohue, Darcy Dupree, A. Nicholas Fargnoli, Paula Gillespie, Warwick Gould, Richard Haslam, Merlin Holland, Tim Machan, Russell Maylone and the Special Collections staff at Northwestern Library, Michael McKinney, Donald Mead, Valerie Murrenus, Joan Navarre, Ben Reynolds, Albert Rivero, David Rose, and Joan Sommers and the Inter-Library Loan staff at Marquette University.

I would also like to thank those who made particular contributions to the second edition: Lisa Batista, Carol Bemis (as always), Maneck Daruwala, Yates Diaz, Emily Eels, Juan Espinosa, Tiffany Fajardo, Kenneth Furton (who offered both intellectual help and material assistance through a grant from the Provost's Office of Florida International University), David Gardner, Celeste Giglio, Ann Gillespie, Paula Gillespie, Christian Gomez, Rachel Goodman, Harry Haskell, Kenneth Johnson, Phillip Lapadula, Ana Luszczynska, Alana Meija, Ana Menendez, Asher Milbauer, Maureen Mulvihill, Erika Nakagawa, Anne Prestamo, and the Inter-Library Loan staff at Florida International University, Mary Jane Rochelson, Lyana Rodriguez, James Silas Rogers, Anais Rosales, David Rose, Ranijun Ruado, Dayana Soler, James Sutton, Roxanne Timon, George Wendell, Madison Whatley, and Kieron Williams.

The Text of
THE IMPORTANCE OF BEING EARNEST
A Trivial Comedy
for Serious People

To
Robert Baldwin Ross
In Appreciation
In Affection

The Persons of the Play

JOHN WORTHING, J.P.,[1] *of the Manor House, Woolton, Hertfordshire*
ALGERNON MONCRIEFF, *his friend*
REV. CANON CHASUBLE, D.D.,[2] *Rector of Woolton*
MERRIMAN, *butler to Mr. Worthing*
LANE, *Mr. Moncrieff's manservant*
LADY BRACKNELL
HON. GWENDOLEN FAIRFAX,[3] *her daughter*
CECILY CARDEW,[4] *John Worthing's ward*
MISS PRISM, *her governess*

The Scenes of the Play

Act I   *Algernon Moncrieff's Flat in Half-Moon Street, W.*
Act II   *The Garden at the Manor House, Woolton*
Act III *Morning-Room at the Manor House, Woolton*

Time: The Present

First Act

Scene—Morning-room in ALGERNON'S *flat in Half-Moon Street.*[1] *The room is luxuriously and artistically furnished. The sound of a piano is heard in the adjoining room.*

> (LANE *is arranging afternoon tea on the table, and after the music has ceased,* ALGERNON *enters.*)

ALGERNON   Did you hear what I was playing, Lane?

LANE   I didn't think it polite to listen, sir.

ALGERNON   I'm sorry for that, for your sake. I don't play accurately— anyone can play accurately—but I play with wonderful expression.

---

1. Justice of the Peace.
2. Doctor of Divinity.
3. Gwendolen uses her family's name, Fairfax, as her surname. Lady Bracknell uses the name associated with her husband's title. (Bracknell is a town in the county of Berkshire.) Lord Bracknell would have been a baron, for had he been a marquess or earl, Gwendolen would have been Lady Gwendolen Fairfax rather than the Honorable Gwendolen Fairfax.
4. Cecily is in love with "Ernest" before having seen him—unseeing love is blind love— and thus *Cecily* becomes in a reverse prosopopoeia *cécité*, French for blindness.
1. Located in the fashionable West End of London.

5

As far as the piano is concerned, sentiment is my forte.[2] I keep
science for Life.

LANE Yes, sir.

ALGERNON And, speaking of the science of Life, have you got the
cucumber sandwiches cut for Lady Bracknell?

LANE Yes, sir. (*Hands them on a salver.*[3])

ALGERNON (*Inspects them, takes two, and sits down on the
sofa.*) Oh!—by the way, Lane, I see from your book that on Thursday night, when Lord Shoreman and Mr. Worthing were dining
with me, eight bottles of champagne are entered as having been
consumed.

LANE Yes, sir; eight bottles and a pint.

ALGERNON Why is it that at a bachelor's establishment the servants
invariably drink the champagne? I ask merely for information.

LANE I attribute it to the superior quality of the wine, sir. I have
often observed that in married households the champagne is rarely
of a first-rate brand.

ALGERNON Good heavens! Is marriage so demoralizing as that?

LANE I believe it *is* a very pleasant state, sir. I have had very little
experience of it myself up to the present. I have only been married
once. That was in consequence of a misunderstanding between
myself and a young person.

ALGERNON (*Languidly.*) I don't know that I am much interested in
your family life, Lane.

LANE No, sir; it is not a very interesting subject. I never think of it
myself.

ALGERNON Very natural, I am sure. That will do, Lane, thank you.

LANE Thank you, sir. (LANE *goes out.*)

ALGERNON Lane's views on marriage seem somewhat lax. Really,
if the lower orders[4] don't set us a good example, what on earth is
the use of them? They seem, as a class, to have absolutely no sense
of moral responsibility.

(*Enter* LANE.)

LANE Mr. Ernest Worthing.

(*Enter* JACK.)

(LANE *goes out.*)

ALGERNON How are you, my dear Ernest? What brings you up to
town?

2. A forte is something at which one excels. The pun in the line turns on the name of the
instrument that Algernon is playing, a shortened form of fortepiano, a forerunner of
the grand piano.
3. A small tray commonly used for serving refreshments or for presenting letters, visiting
cards, or similar items.
4. A vague designation referring to anyone not included in the refined social circles in
which Algernon travels.

JACK   Oh, pleasure, pleasure! What else should bring one anywhere? Eating as usual, I see, Algy!

ALGERNON (*Stiffly.*)   I believe it is customary in good society to take some slight refreshment at five o'clock.[5] Where have you been since last Thursday?

JACK (*Sitting down on the sofa.*)   In the country.

ALGERNON   What on earth do you do there?

JACK (*Pulling off his gloves.*)   When one is in town one amuses oneself. When one is in the country one amuses other people. It is excessively boring.

ALGERNON   And who are the people you amuse?

JACK (*Airily.*)   Oh, neighbours, neighbours.

ALGERNON   Got nice neighbours in your part of Shropshire?[6]

JACK   Perfectly horrid! Never speak to one of them.

ALGERNON   How immensely you must amuse them! (*Goes over and takes sandwich.*) By the way, Shropshire is your county, is it not?

JACK   Eh? Shropshire? Yes, of course. Hallo! Why all these cups? Why cucumber sandwiches? Why such reckless extravagance in one so young? Who is coming to tea?

ALGERNON   Oh! merely Aunt Augusta and Gwendolen.

JACK   How perfectly delightful!

ALGERNON   Yes, that is all very well; but I am afraid Aunt Augusta won't quite approve of your being here.

JACK   May I ask why?

ALGERNON   My dear fellow, the way you flirt with Gwendolen is perfectly disgraceful. It is almost as bad as the way Gwendolen flirts with you.

JACK   I am in love with Gwendolen. I have come up to town expressly to propose to her.

ALGERNON   I thought you had come up for pleasure?—I call that business.

JACK   How utterly unromantic you are!

ALGERNON   I really don't see anything romantic in proposing. It is very romantic to be in love. But there is nothing romantic about a definite proposal. Why, one may be accepted. One usually is, I believe. Then the excitement is all over. The very essence of romance is uncertainty. If ever I get married, I'll certainly try to forget the fact.

JACK   I have no doubt about that, dear Algy. The Divorce Court[7] was specially invented for people whose memories are so curiously constituted.

---

5. Typically the time to take a light meal of tea and sandwiches or cakes.
6. A county in England located in the west Midlands.
7. Established in 1857, the Court for Divorce and Matrimonial Causes, based in London, heard pleas for divorce that had previously come before the church courts. At the time

ALGERNON   Oh! there is no use speculating on that subject. Divorces are made in Heaven—(JACK *puts out his hand to take a sandwich.* ALGERNON *at once interferes.*) Please don't touch the cucumber sandwiches. They are ordered specially for Aunt Augusta. (*Takes one and eats it.*)

JACK   Well, you have been eating them all the time.

ALGERNON   That is quite a different matter. She is my aunt. (*Takes plate from below.*) Have some bread and butter. The bread and butter is for Gwendolen. Gwendolen is devoted to bread and butter.

JACK (*Advancing to table and helping himself.*)   And very good bread and butter it is too.

ALGERNON   Well, my dear fellow, you need not eat as if you were going to eat it all. You behave as if you were married to her already. You are not married to her already, and I don't think you ever will be.

JACK   Why on earth do you say that?

ALGERNON   Well, in the first place girls never marry the men they flirt with. Girls don't think it right.

JACK   Oh, that is nonsense!

ALGERNON   It isn't. It is a great truth. It accounts for the extraordinary number of bachelors that one sees all over the place. In the second place, I don't give my consent.

JACK   Your consent!

ALGERNON   My dear fellow, Gwendolen is my first cousin. And before I allow you to marry her, you will have to clear up the whole question of Cecily. (*Rings bell.*)

JACK   Cecily! What on earth do you mean? What do you mean, Algy, by Cecily! I don't know anyone of the name of Cecily.   ↳nickname

(*Enter* LANE.)

ALGERNON   Bring me that cigarette case Mr. Worthing left in the smoking-room[8] the last time he dined here.

LANE   Yes, sir. (LANE *goes out.*)

JACK   Do you mean to say you have had my cigarette case all this time? I wish to goodness you had let me know. I have been writing frantic letters to Scotland Yard[9] about it. I was very nearly offering a large reward.

---

of the play, a wife's adultery was sufficient cause for a man to obtain a divorce, but a woman had to prove cruelty or desertion in addition to her husband's adultery to obtain a divorce.

8. Because of the lingering aroma of tobacco smoke, rooms in houses, hotels, and clubs were often set apart as places for smoking.

9. This is a shorthand designation for the location of the Metropolitan (i.e., London) Police headquarters and a synonym for the force. At the time of the play, Scotland Yard was located on a tiny street off Whitehall called New Scotland Yard; it occupied the entire street.

ALGERNON   Well, I wish you would offer one. I happen to be more than usually hard up.

JACK   There is no good offering a large reward now that the thing is found.

>   (*Enter* LANE *with the cigarette case on a salver.* ALGERNON *takes it at once.* LANE *goes out.*)

ALGERNON   I think that is rather mean of you, Ernest, I must say. (*Opens case and examines it.*) However, it makes no matter, for, now that I look at the inscription inside, I find that the thing isn't yours after all.

JACK   Of course it's mine. (*Moving to him.*) You have seen me with it a hundred times, and you have no right whatsoever to read what is written inside. It is a very ungentlemanly thing to read a private cigarette case.

ALGERNON   Oh! it is absurd to have a hard-and-fast rule about what one should read and what one shouldn't. More than half of modern culture depends on what one shouldn't read.

JACK   I am quite aware of the fact, and I don't propose to discuss modern culture. It isn't the sort of thing one should talk of in private. I simply want my cigarette case back.

ALGERNON   Yes; but this isn't your cigarette case. This cigarette case is a present from someone of the name of Cecily, and you said you didn't know anyone of that name.

JACK   Well, if you want to know, Cecily happens to be my aunt.

ALGERNON   Your aunt!

JACK   Yes. Charming old lady she is, too. Lives at Tunbridge Wells.[1] Just give it back to me, Algy.

ALGERNON (*Retreating to back of sofa.*)   But why does she call herself little Cecily if she is your aunt and lives at Tunbridge Wells? (*Reading.*) "From little Cecily with her fondest love."

JACK (*Moving to sofa and kneeling upon it.*)   My dear fellow, what on earth is there in that? Some aunts are tall, some aunts are not tall. That is a matter that surely an aunt may be allowed to decide for herself. You seem to think that every aunt should be exactly like your aunt! That is absurd! For Heaven's sake give me back my cigarette case. (*Follows* ALGERNON *round the room.*)

ALGERNON   Yes. But why does your aunt call you her uncle? "From little Cecily, with her fondest love to her dear Uncle Jack." There is no objection, I admit, to an aunt being a small aunt, but why an aunt, no matter what her size may be, should call her own nephew her uncle, I can't quite make out. Besides, your name isn't Jack at all; it is Ernest.

JACK   It isn't Ernest; it's Jack.

---

1. Located in the county of Kent, Tunbridge Wells is southeast of London.

ALGERNON   You have always told me it was Ernest. I have introduced
  you to everyone as Ernest. You answer to the name of Ernest. You
  look as if your name was Ernest. You are the most earnest looking person I ever saw in my life. It is perfectly absurd your saying
  that your name isn't Ernest. It's on your cards. Here is one of them.
  (*Taking it from case.*) "Mr. Ernest Worthing, B. 4, The Albany."[2]
  I'll keep this as a proof that your name is Ernest if ever you attempt
  to deny it to me, or to Gwendolen, or to anyone else. (*Puts the card
  in his pocket.*)
JACK   Well, my name is Ernest in town and Jack in the country, and
  the cigarette case was given to me in the country.
ALGERNON   Yes, but that does not account for the fact that your
  small Aunt Cecily, who lives at Tunbridge Wells, calls you her dear
  uncle. Come, old boy, you had much better have the thing out at
  once.
JACK   My dear Algy, you talk exactly as if you were a dentist. It is
  very vulgar to talk like a dentist when one isn't a dentist. It produces a false impression.[3]
ALGERNON   Well, that is exactly what dentists always do. Now, go
  on! Tell me the whole thing. I may mention that I have always suspected you of being a confirmed and secret Bunburyist; and I am
  quite sure of it now.
JACK   Bunburyist? What on earth do you mean by a Bunburyist?
ALGERNON   I'll reveal to you the meaning of that incomparable
  expression as soon as you are kind enough to inform me why you
  are Ernest in town and Jack in the country.
JACK   Well, produce my cigarette case first.
ALGERNON   Here it is. (*Hands cigarette case.*) Now produce your
  explanation, and pray make it improbable. (*Sits on sofa.*)
JACK   My dear fellow, there is nothing improbable about my explanation at all. In fact it's perfectly ordinary. Old Mr. Thomas
  Cardew, who adopted me when I was a little boy, made me in his
  will guardian to his granddaughter, Miss Cecily Cardew. Cecily,
  who addresses me as her uncle from motives of respect that you
  could not possibly appreciate, lives at my place in the country
  under the charge of her admirable governess, Miss Prism.
ALGERNON   Where is that place in the country, by the way?
JACK   That is nothing to you, dear boy. You are not going to
  be invited.—I may tell you candidly that the place is not in
  Shropshire.

---

2. A three-story mansion completed in Piccadily in 1776 and divided into apartments in
   1802. It was in Wilde's time and continues to be a most exclusive address.
3. A pun on an impression taken in dental work: a negative imprint of the hard and soft
   tissues in the mouth from which a positive reproduction can be formed.

ALGERNON   I suspected that, my dear fellow! I have Bunburyed all over Shropshire on two separate occasions. Now, go on. Why are you Ernest in town and Jack in the country?

JACK   My dear Algy, I don't know whether you will be able to understand my real motives. You are hardly serious enough. When one is placed in the position of guardian, one has to adopt a very high moral tone on all subjects. It's one's duty to do so. And as a high moral tone can hardly be said to conduce very much to either one's health or one's happiness, in order to get up to town I have always pretended to have a younger brother of the name of Ernest, who lives in the Albany, and gets into the most dreadful scrapes. That, my dear Algy, is the whole truth pure and simple.

ALGERNON   The truth is rarely pure and never simple. Modern life would be very tedious if it were either, and modern literature a complete impossibility!

JACK   That wouldn't be at all a bad thing.

ALGERNON   Literary criticism is not your forte my dear fellow. Don't try it. You should leave that to people who haven't been at a University. They do it so well in the daily papers. What you really are is a Bunburyist. I was quite right in saying you were a Bunburyist. You are one of the most advanced Bunburyists I know.

JACK   What on earth do you mean?

ALGERNON   You have invented a very useful younger brother called Ernest, in order that you may be able to come up to town as often as you like. I have invented an invaluable permanent invalid called Bunbury, in order that I may be able to go down into the country whenever I choose. Bunbury is perfectly invaluable. If it wasn't for Bunbury's extraordinary bad health, for instance, I wouldn't be able to dine with you at Willis's[4] tonight, for I have been really engaged to Aunt Augusta for more than a week.

JACK   I haven't asked you to dine with me anywhere to-night.

ALGERNON   I know. You are absurdly careless about sending out invitations. It is very foolish of you. Nothing annoys people so much as not receiving invitations.

JACK   You had much better dine with your Aunt Augusta.

ALGERNON   I haven't the smallest intention of doing anything of the kind. To begin with, I dined there on Monday, and once a week is quite enough to dine with one's own relations. In the second place, whenever I do dine there I am always treated as a member of the family, and sent down[5] with either no woman at all, or two. In the third place, I know perfectly well whom she will place me next

4. A shortened form of Willis's Rooms, a fashionable London restaurant where one could see celebrities dining.
5. Processing formally to dinner.

to, tonight. She will place me next Mary Farquhar, who always flirts with her own husband across the dinner-table. That is not very pleasant. Indeed, it is not even decent—and that sort of thing is enormously on the increase. The amount of women in London who flirt with their own husbands is perfectly scandalous. It looks so bad. It is simply washing one's clean linen in public. Besides, now that I know you to be a confirmed Bunburyist I naturally want to talk to you about Bunburying. I want to tell you the rules.

JACK   I'm not a Bunburyist at all. If Gwendolen accepts me, I am going to kill my brother, indeed I think I'll kill him in any case. Cecily is a little too much interested in him. It is rather a bore. So I am going to get rid of Ernest. And I strongly advise you to do the same with Mr.—with your invalid friend who has the absurd name.

ALGERNON   Nothing will induce me to part with Bunbury, and if you ever get married, which seems to me extremely problematic, you will be very glad to know Bunbury. A man who marries without knowing Bunbury has a very tedious time of it.

JACK   That is nonsense. If I marry a charming girl like Gwendolen, and she is the only girl I ever saw in my life that I would marry, I certainly won't want to know Bunbury.

ALGERNON   Then your wife will. You don't seem to realize, that in married life three is company and two is none.

JACK (*Sententiously*)   That, my dear young friend, is the theory that the corrupt French Drama has been propounding for the last fifty years.

ALGERNON   Yes; and that the happy English home has proved in half the time.

JACK   For heaven's sake, don't try to be cynical. It's perfectly easy to be cynical.

ALGERNON   My dear fellow, it isn't easy to be anything nowadays. There's such a lot of beastly competition about. (*The sound of an electric bell is heard.*) Ah! that must be Aunt Augusta. Only relatives, or creditors, ever ring in that Wagnerian[6] manner. Now, if I get her out of the way for ten minutes, so that you can have an opportunity for proposing to Gwendolen, may I dine with you tonight at Willis's?

JACK   I suppose so, if you want to.

ALGERNON   Yes, but you must be serious about it. I hate people who are not serious about meals. It is so shallow of them.

(*Enter* LANE.)

---

6. Relating to the German operatic composer Richard Wagner (1813–1883), his music, and his theories of musical and dramatic composition. Wagner's music had a reputation for being bombastic and overblown.

LANE   Lady Bracknell and Miss Fairfax.

   (ALGERNON *goes forward to meet them. Enter* LADY BRACKNELL
   and GWENDOLEN.)

LADY BRACKNELL   Good afternoon, dear Algernon, I hope you are
   behaving very well.

ALGERNON   I'm feeling very well, Aunt Augusta.

LADY BRACKNELL   That's not quite the same thing. In fact the two
   things rarely go together. (*Sees* JACK *and bows to him with icy
   coldness.*)

ALGERNON (*To* GWENDOLEN.)   Dear me, you are smart!

GWENDOLEN   I am always smart! Aren't I, Mr. Worthing?

JACK   You're quite perfect, Miss Fairfax.

GWENDOLEN   Oh! I hope I am not that. It would leave no room for
   developments, and I intend to develop in many directions. (GWEN-
   DOLEN *and* JACK *sit down together in the corner.*)

LADY BRACKNELL   I'm sorry if we are a little late, Algernon, but I
   was obliged to call on dear Lady Harbury. I hadn't been there since
   her poor husband's death. I never saw a woman so altered; she
   looks quite twenty years younger. And now I'll have a cup of tea,
   and one of those nice cucumber sandwiches you promised me.

ALGERNON   Certainly, Aunt Augusta. (*Goes over to tea-table.*)

LADY BRACKNELL   Won't you come and sit here, Gwendolen?

GWENDOLEN   Thanks, mamma, I'm quite comfortable where I am.

ALGERNON (*Picking up empty plate in horror.*)   Good heavens!
   Lane! Why are there no cucumber sandwiches? I ordered them
   specially.

LANE (*Gravely.*)   There were no cucumbers in the market this
   morning, sir. I went down twice.

ALGERNON   No cucumbers!

LANE   No, sir. Not even for ready money.[7]

ALGERNON   That will do, Lane, thank you.

LANE   Thank you, sir. (*Goes out.*)

ALGERNON   I am greatly distressed, Aunt Augusta, about there being
   no cucumbers, not even for ready money.

LADY BRACKNELL   It really makes no matter, Algernon. I had some
   crumpets[8] with Lady Harbury, who seems to me to be living entirely
   for pleasure now.

ALGERNON   I hear her hair has turned quite gold from grief.

LADY BRACKNELL   It certainly has changed its colour. From what
   cause I, of course, cannot say. (ALGERNON *crosses and hands tea.*)

---

7. The term denotes cash available for immediate payment for anything bought. Lane
   sardonically indicates that he would have gone so far as actually to pay for the cucumbers rather than acquire them through credit.

8. A soft, round cake made of flour, beaten egg, milk, and barm or baking powder, mixed
   into batter, and baked on a griddle, and usually eaten toasted with butter.

Thank you. I've quite a treat for you tonight, Algernon. I am going
to send you down with Mary Farquhar. She is such a nice woman,
and so attentive to her husband. It's delightful to watch them.

ALGERNON   I am afraid, Aunt Augusta, I shall have to give up the
pleasure of dining with you tonight after all.

LADY BRACKNELL (*Frowning.*)   I hope not, Algernon. It would put
my table completely out. Your uncle would have to dine upstairs.
Fortunately he is accustomed to that.

ALGERNON   It is a great bore, and, I need hardly say, a terrible disappointment to me, but the fact is I have just had a telegram to
say that my poor friend Bunbury is very ill again. (*Exchanges
glances with* JACK.) They seem to think I should be with him.

LADY BRACKNELL   It is very strange. This Mr. Bunbury seems to suf-
fer from curiously bad health.

ALGERNON   Yes; poor Bunbury is a dreadful invalid.

LADY BRACKNELL   Well, I must say, Algernon, that I think it is high
time that Mr. Bunbury made up his mind whether he was going
to live or to die. This shilly-shallying with the question is absurd.
Nor do I in any way approve of the modern sympathy with inva-
lids. I consider it morbid. Illness of any kind is hardly a thing to
be encouraged in others. Health is the primary duty of life. I am
always telling that to your poor uncle, but he never seems to take
much notice—as far as any improvement in his ailment goes. I
should be much obliged if you would ask Mr. Bunbury, from me,
to be kind enough not to have a relapse on Saturday, for I rely on
you to arrange my music for me. It is my last reception, and one
wants something that will encourage conversation, particularly at
the end of the season when everyone has practically said whatever they had to say, which, in most cases, was probably not much.

ALGERNON   I'll speak to Bunbury, Aunt Augusta, if he is still conscious, and I think I can promise you he'll be all right by Saturday. Of course the music is a great difficulty. You see, if one plays
good music, people don't listen, and if one plays bad music people
don't talk. But I'll run over the programme I've drawn out, if you
will kindly come into the next room for a moment.

LADY BRACKNELL   Thank you, Algernon. It is very thoughtful of you.
(*Rising, and following* ALGERNON.) I'm sure the programme will be
delightful, after a few expurgations. French songs I cannot possibly allow. People always seem to think that they are improper,
and either look shocked, which is vulgar, or laugh, which is worse.
But German sounds a thoroughly respectable language, and
indeed, I believe is so. Gwendolen, you will accompany me.

GWENDOLEN   Certainly, mamma.

> (LADY BRACKNELL *and* ALGERNON *go into the music-room,*
> GWENDOLEN *remains behind.*)

JACK   Charming day it has been, Miss Fairfax.

GWENDOLEN   Pray don't talk to me about the weather, Mr. Worthing. Whenever people talk to me about the weather, I always feel quite certain that they mean something else. And that makes me so nervous.

JACK   I do mean something else.

GWENDOLEN   I thought so. In fact, I am never wrong.

JACK   And I would like to be allowed to take advantage of Lady Bracknell's temporary absence—

GWENDOLEN   I would certainly advise you to do so. Mamma has a way of coming back suddenly into a room that I have often had to speak to her about.

JACK (*Nervously.*)   Miss Fairfax, ever since I met you I have admired you more than any girl—I have ever met since—I met you.

GWENDOLEN   Yes, I am quite well aware of the fact. And I often wish that in public, at any rate, you had been more demonstrative. For me you have always had an irresistible fascination. Even before I met you I was far from indifferent to you. (JACK *looks at her in amazement.*) We live, as I hope you know, Mr. Worthing, in an age of ideals. The fact is constantly mentioned in the more expensive monthly magazines, and has reached the provincial pulpits I am told: and my ideal has always been to love someone of the name of Ernest. There is something in that name that inspires absolute confidence. The moment Algernon first mentioned to me that he had a friend called Ernest, I knew I was destined to love you.

JACK   You really love me, Gwendolen?

GWENDOLEN   Passionately!

JACK   Darling! You don't know how happy you've made me.

GWENDOLEN   My own Ernest!

JACK   But you don't really mean to say that you couldn't love me if my name wasn't Ernest?

GWENDOLEN   But your name is Ernest.

JACK   Yes, I know it is. But supposing it was something else? Do you mean to say you couldn't love me then?

GWENDOLEN (*Glibly.*)   Ah! that is clearly a metaphysical speculation, and like most metaphysical speculations has very little reference at all to the actual facts of real life, as we know them.

JACK   Personally, darling, to speak quite candidly, I don't much care about the name of Ernest—I don't think the name suits me at all.

GWENDOLEN   It suits you perfectly. It is a divine name. It has a music of its own. It produces vibrations.

JACK   Well, really, Gwendolen, I must say that I think there are lots of other much nicer names. I think Jack, for instance, a charming name.

GWENDOLEN   Jack?—No, there is very little music in the name Jack, if any at all, indeed. It does not thrill. It produces absolutely no vibrations.—I have known several Jacks, and they all, without exception, were more than usually plain. Besides, Jack is a notorious domesticity for John! And I pity any woman who is married to a man called John. She would probably never be allowed to know the entrancing pleasure of a single moment's solitude. The only really safe name is Ernest.

JACK   Gwendolen, I must get christened at once—I mean we must get married at once. There is no time to be lost.

GWENDOLEN   Married, Mr. Worthing?

JACK (*Astounded.*)   Well—surely. You know that I love you, and you led me to believe, Miss Fairfax, that you were not absolutely indifferent to me.

GWENDOLEN   I adore you. But you haven't proposed to me yet. Nothing has been said at all about marriage. The subject has not even been touched on.

JACK   Well—may I propose to you now?

GWENDOLEN   I think it would be an admirable opportunity. And to spare you any possible disappointment. Mr. Worthing, I think it only fair to tell you quite frankly beforehand that I am fully determined to accept you.

JACK   Gwendolen!

GWENDOLEN   Yes, Mr. Worthing, what have you got to say to me?

JACK   You know what I have got to say to you.

GWENDOLEN   Yes, but you don't say it.

JACK   Gwendolen, will you marry me? (*Goes on his knees.*)

GWENDOLEN   Of course I will, darling. How long you have been about it! I am afraid you have had very little experience in how to propose.

JACK   My own one, I have never loved anyone in the world but you.

GWENDOLEN   Yes, but men often propose for practice. I know my brother Gerald does. All my girl friends tell me so. What wonderfully blue eyes you have, Ernest! They are quite, quite blue. I hope you will always look at me just like that, especially when there are other people present.

(*Enter* LADY BRACKNELL.)

LADY BRACKNELL   Mr. Worthing! Rise, sir, from this semi-recumbent posture. It is most indecorous.

GWENDOLEN   Mamma! (*He tries to rise; she restrains him.*) I must beg you to retire. This is no place for you. Besides, Mr. Worthing has not quite finished yet.

LADY BRACKNELL   Finished what, may I ask?

GWENDOLEN   I am engaged to Mr. Worthing, mamma. (*They rise together.*)

LADY BRACKNELL   Pardon me, you are not engaged to anyone. When you do become engaged to some one, I, or your father, should his health permit him, will inform you of the fact. An engagement should come on a young girl as a surprise, pleasant or unpleasant, as the case may be. It is hardly a matter that she could be allowed to arrange for herself.—And now I have a few questions to put to you, Mr. Worthing. While I am making these inquiries, you, Gwendolen, will wait for me below in the carriage.

GWENDOLEN (*Reproachfully.*)   Mamma!

LADY BRACKNELL   In the carriage, Gwendolen! (GWENDOLEN *goes to the door. She and* JACK *blow kisses to each other behind* LADY BRACKNELL'S *back.* LADY BRACKNELL *looks vaguely about as if she could not understand what the noise was. Finally turns around.*) Gwendolen, the carriage!

GWENDOLEN   Yes, mamma. (*Goes out, looking back at* JACK.)

LADY BRACKNELL (*Sitting down.*)   You can take a seat, Mr. Worthing. (*Looks in her pocket for notebook and pencil.*)

JACK   Thank you, Lady Bracknell, I prefer standing.

LADY BRACKNELL (*Pencil and notebook in hand.*)   I feel bound to tell you that you are not down on my list of eligible young men, although I have the same list as the dear Duchess of Bolton has. We work together, in fact. However, I am quite ready to enter your name, should your answers be what a really affectionate mother requires. Do you smoke?

JACK   Well, yes, I must admit I smoke.

LADY BRACKNELL   I am glad to hear it. A man should always have an occupation of some kind. There are far too many idle men in London as it is. How old are you?

JACK   Twenty-nine.

LADY BRACKNELL   A very good age to be married at. I have always been of the opinion that a man who desires to get married should know either everything or nothing. Which do you know?

JACK (*After some hesitation.*)   I know nothing, Lady Bracknell.

LADY BRACKNELL   I am pleased to hear it. I do not approve of anything that tampers with natural ignorance. Ignorance is like a delicate exotic fruit; touch it and the bloom is gone. The whole theory of modern education is radically unsound. Fortunately in England, at any rate, education produces no effect whatsoever. If it did, it would prove a serious danger to the upper classes, and probably lead to acts of violence in Grosvenor Square.[9] What is your income?

JACK   Between seven and eight thousand a year.[1]

---

9. Located in the fashionable West End of London.
1. Using the Consumer Price Index as a basis for comparison, this would be well over $1,000,000 today.

LADY BRACKNELL (*Makes a note in her book.*)   In land, or in investments?

JACK   In investments, chiefly.

LADY BRACKNELL   That is satisfactory. What between the duties expected of one during one's lifetime, and the duties[2] exacted from one after one's death, land has ceased to be either a profit or a pleasure. It gives one position, and prevents one from keeping it up. That's all that can be said about land.

JACK   I have a country house with some land, of course, attached to it, about fifteen hundred acres, I believe; but I don't depend on that for my real income. In fact, as far as I can make out, the poachers are the only people who make anything out of it.

LADY BRACKNELL   A country house! How many bedrooms? Well, that point can be cleared up afterwards. You have a town house, I hope? A girl with a simple, unspoiled nature, like Gwendolen, could hardly be expected to reside in the country.

JACK   Well, I own a house in Belgrave Square,[3] but it is let by the year to Lady Bloxham. Of course, I can get it back whenever I like, at six months' notice.

LADY BRACKNELL   Lady Bloxham? I don't know her.

JACK   Oh, she goes about very little. She is a lady considerably advanced in years.

LADY BRACKNELL   Ah, nowadays that is no guarantee of respectability of character. What number in Belgrave Square?

JACK   149.

LADY BRACKNELL (*Shaking her head.*)   The unfashionable side. I thought there was something. However, that could easily be altered.

JACK   Do you mean the fashion, or the side?

LADY BRACKNELL (*Sternly.*)   Both, if necessary, I presume. What are your politics?

JACK   Well, I am afraid I really have none. I am a Liberal Unionist.[4]

LADY BRACKNELL   Oh, they count as Tories.[5] They dine with us. Or come in the evening,[6] at any rate. Now to minor matters. Are your parents living?

JACK   I have lost both my parents.

LADY BRACKNELL   Both?—To lose one parent, Mr. Worthing, may be regarded as a misfortune—to lose *both* looks like carelessness.[7]

---

2. Taxes imposed on the estate of the deceased.
3. Located in the fashionable West End of London.
4. This name was given to any member of the party formed by those Liberals who refused to support Gladstone's measure of Irish Home Rule in 1886.
5. Members of the Conservative Party. As a formal party name, "Tory" was superseded c. 1830 by Conservative, but "Tory" is still retained colloquially today.
6. This is a subtle form of class distinction. They may not be suitable to have in for dinner, but they can provide amusing conversation afterwards.
7. "To lose . . . carelessness" is the sentence that Wilde originally wrote. In the 1899 edition, Wilde abbreviated this line to read as follows: "That seems like carelessness."

Who was your father? He was evidently a man of some wealth. Was he born in what the Radical papers call the purple of commerce, or did he rise from the ranks of the aristocracy?

JACK I am afraid I really don't know. The fact is, Lady Bracknell, I said I had lost my parents. It would be nearer the truth to say that my parents seem to have lost me—I don't actually know who I am by birth. I was—well, I was found.

LADY BRACKNELL Found!

JACK The late Mr. Thomas Cardew, an old gentleman of a very charitable and kindly disposition, found me, and gave me the name of Worthing, because he happened to have a first-class ticket for Worthing[8] in his pocket at the time. Worthing is a place in Sussex.[9] It is a seaside resort.

LADY BRACKNELL Where did the charitable gentleman who had a first-class ticket for this seaside resort find you?

JACK (*Gravely.*) In a handbag.

LADY BRACKNELL A handbag?

JACK (*Very seriously.*) Yes, Lady Bracknell. I was in a handbag—a somewhat large, black leather handbag, with handles to it—an ordinary handbag in fact.

LADY BRACKNELL In what locality did this Mr. James, or Thomas, Cardew come across this ordinary handbag?

JACK In the cloakroom at Victoria Station.[1] It was given to him in mistake for his own.

LADY BRACKNELL The cloakroom at Victoria Station?

JACK Yes. The Brighton line.[2]

LADY BRACKNELL The line is immaterial. Mr. Worthing, I confess I feel somewhat bewildered by what you have just told me. To be born, or at any rate bred, in a handbag, whether it had handles or not, seems to me to display a contempt for the ordinary decencies of family life that reminds one of the worst excesses of the French Revolution. And I presume you know what that unfortunate movement led to? As for the particular locality in which the handbag was found, a cloakroom at a railway station might serve

This edition follows what has become common practice in deviating from the Smithers text to retain the wittier version.

8. From the eighteenth century, when it was made popular by George III (1738–1820; reigned 1760–1820). Worthing has been a favorite seaside resort for the royal, the rich, and the fashionable. Wilde spent the summer and autumn of 1894 there writing *The Importance of Being Earnest.*

9. A county located south of London.

1. One of London's largest railway stations, located southwest of Westminster Cathedral.

2. According to Peter Cunningham's *Hand-Book of London* from 1850, the Brighton Line was "[b]egun in 1837, projected by Sir John Rennie, executed by Mr. Rastrick, and opened 21st of September 1841. Its cost up to the 31st December 1844, has been 2,640,000*l.* out of which the law expenses have been nearly 200,000*l.* The first mile and a half runs side by side with the Greenwich Railway. For the next eight miles the Croydon Railway is used."

to conceal a social indiscretion—has probably, indeed, been used for that purpose before now—but it could hardly be regarded as an assured basis for a recognized position in good society.

JACK   May I ask you then what you would advise me to do? I need hardly say I would do anything in the world to ensure Gwendolen's happiness.

LADY BRACKNELL   I would strongly advise you, Mr. Worthing, to try and acquire some relations as soon as possible, and to make a definite effort to produce at any rate one parent, of either sex, before the season is quite over.

JACK   Well, I don't see how I could possibly manage to do that. I can produce the handbag at any moment. It is in my dressingroom at home. I really think that should satisfy you, Lady Bracknell.

LADY BRACKNELL   Me, sir! What has it to do with me? You can hardly imagine that I and Lord Bracknell would dream of allowing our only daughter—a girl brought up with the utmost care—to marry into a cloakroom and form an alliance with a parcel? Good morning, Mr. Worthing!

(LADY BRACKNELL *sweeps out in majestic indignation.*)

JACK   Good morning! (ALGERNON, *from the other room, strikes up the Wedding March.*[3] JACK *looks perfectly furious, and goes to the door.*) For goodness' sake don't play that ghastly tune, Algy. How idiotic you are!

(*The music stops and* ALGERNON *enters cheerily.*)

ALGERNON   Didn't it go off all right, old boy? You don't mean to say Gwendolen refused you? I know it is a way she has. She is always refusing people. I think it is most ill-natured of her.

JACK   Oh, Gwendolen is as right as a trivet. As far as she is concerned, we are engaged. Her mother is perfectly unbearable. Never met such a Gorgon—I don't really know what a Gorgon[4] is like, but I am quite sure that Lady Bracknell is one. In any case, she is a monster, without being a myth, which is rather unfair—I beg your pardon, Algy, I suppose I shouldn't talk about your own aunt in that way before you.

ALGERNON   My dear boy, I love hearing my relations abused. It is the only thing that makes me put up with them at all. Relations are simply a tedious pack of people, who haven't got the remotest knowledge of how to live, nor the smallest instinct about when to die.

JACK   Oh, that is nonsense!

---

3. One of the incidental pieces in Felix Mendelsson's music to Shakespeare's *A Midsummer Night's Dream* is frequently played at wedding ceremonies.
4. From Greek mythology any of three females, with snakes for hair, whose gaze turned the onlooker to stone. The best-known, and the only mortal, Medusa was slain by Perseus. He gave the head of Medusa to the goddess Athena, who fixed it on her shield. The term has come to denote a very acerbic or ugly person.

ALGERNON   It isn't!

JACK   Well, I won't argue about the matter. You always want to argue about things.

ALGERNON   That is exactly what things were originally made for.

JACK   Upon my word, if I thought that, I'd shoot myself—(*A pause.*) You don't think there is any chance of Gwendolen becoming like her mother in about a hundred and fifty years, do you Algy?

ALGERNON   All women become like their mothers. That is their tragedy. No man does. That's his.

JACK   Is that clever?

ALGERNON   It is perfectly phrased! and quite as true as any observation in civilized life should be.

JACK   I am sick to death of cleverness. Everybody is clever nowadays. You can't go anywhere without meeting clever people. The thing has become an absolute public nuisance. I wish to goodness we had a few fools left.

ALGERNON   We have.

JACK   I should extremely like to meet them. What do they talk about?

ALGERNON   The fools? Oh! about the clever people, of course.

JACK   What fools!

ALGERNON   By the way, did you tell Gwendolen the truth about your being Ernest in town, and Jack in the country?

JACK (*In a very patronizing manner.*)   My dear fellow, the truth isn't quite the sort of thing one tells to a nice sweet refined girl. What extraordinary ideas you have about the way to behave to a woman!

ALGERNON   The only way to behave to a woman is to make love to her if she is pretty, and to someone else, if she is plain.

JACK   Oh, that is nonsense.

ALGERNON   What about your brother? What about the profligate Ernest?

JACK   Oh, before the end of the week I shall have got rid of him. I'll say he died in Paris of apoplexy.[5] Lots of people die of apoplexy, quite suddenly, don't they?

ALGERNON   Yes, but it's hereditary, my dear fellow. It's a sort of thing that runs in families. You had much better say a severe chill.

JACK   You are sure a severe chill isn't hereditary, or anything of that kind?

ALGERNON   Of course it isn't!

JACK   Very well, then. My poor brother Ernest is carried off suddenly in Paris, by a severe chill. That gets rid of him.

---

5. A sudden physical seizure that arrests more or less completely the powers of sense and motion; it is usually caused by an effusion of blood or serum in the brain and preceded by giddiness or partial loss of muscular power.

ALGERNON   But I thought you said that—Miss Cardew was a little too much interested in your poor brother Ernest? Won't she feel his loss a good deal?

JACK   Oh, that is all right. Cecily is not a silly romantic girl, I am glad to say. She has got a capital appetite, goes on long walks, and pays no attention at all to her lessons.

ALGERNON   I would rather like to see Cecily.

JACK   I will take very good care you never do. She is excessively pretty, and she is only just eighteen.

ALGERNON   Have you told Gwendolen yet that you have an excessively pretty ward who is only just eighteen?

JACK   Oh! one doesn't blurt these things out to people. Cecily and Gwendolen are perfectly certain to be extremely great friends. I'll bet you anything you like that half an hour after they have met, they will be calling each other sister.

ALGERNON   Women only do that when they have called each other a lot of other things first. Now, my dear boy, if we want to get a good table at Willis's, we really must go and dress. Do you know it is nearly seven?

JACK (*Irritably.*)   Oh! It always is nearly seven.

ALGERNON   Well, I'm hungry.

JACK   I never knew you when you weren't—

ALGERNON   What shall we do after dinner? Go to a theatre?

JACK   Oh, no! I loathe listening.

ALGERNON   Well, let us go to the Club?

JACK   Oh, no! I hate talking.

ALGERNON   Well, we might trot round to the Empire[6] at ten?

JACK   Oh, no! I can't bear looking at things. It is so silly.

ALGERNON   Well, what shall we do?

JACK   Nothing!

ALGERNON   It is awfully hard work doing nothing. However, I don't mind hard work where there is no definite object of any kind.
   (*Enter* LANE.)

LANE   Miss Fairfax.
   (*Enter* GWENDOLEN, LANE *goes out.*)

ALGERNON   Gwendolen, upon my word!

GWENDOLEN   Algy, kindly turn your back. I have something very particular to say to Mr. Worthing.

ALGERNON   Really, Gwendolen, I don't think I can allow this at all.

GWENDOLEN   Algy, you always adopt a strictly immoral attitude towards life. You are not quite old enough to do that. (ALGERNON *retires to the fireplace.*)

---

6. Referring to the Empire Theatre of Varieties in Leicester Square. It originally opened as a theater in 1884 and became a music hall in 1887.

JACK   My own darling!

GWENDOLEN   Ernest, we may never be married. From the expression on mamma's face I fear we never shall. Few parents nowadays pay any regard to what their children say to them. The old-fashioned respect for the young is fast dying out. Whatever influence I ever had over mamma, I lost at the age of three. But although she may prevent us from becoming man and wife, and I may marry someone else, and marry often, nothing that she can possibly do can alter my eternal devotion to you.

JACK   Dear Gwendolen!

GWENDOLEN   The story of your romantic origin, as related to me by mamma, with unpleasing comments, has naturally stirred the deeper fibres of my nature. Your Christian name[7] has an irresistible fascination. The simplicity of your character makes you exquisitely incomprehensible to me. Your town address at the Albany I have. What is your address in the country?

JACK   The Manor House, Woolton, Hertfordshire.[8]

(ALGERNON, *who has been carefully listening, smiles to himself, and writes the address on his shirt cuff. Then picks up the Railway Guide.[9]*)

GWENDOLEN   There is a good postal service, I suppose? It may be necessary to do something desperate. That of course will require serious consideration. I will communicate with you daily.

JACK   My own one!

GWENDOLEN   How long do you remain in town?

JACK   Till Monday.

GWENDOLEN   Good! Algy, you may turn round now.

ALGERNON   Thanks, I've turned round already.

GWENDOLEN   You may also ring the bell.

JACK   You will let me see you to your carriage, my own darling?

GWENDOLEN   Certainly.

JACK (*To* LANE, *who now enters.*)   I will see Miss Fairfax out.

LANE   Yes, sir. (JACK *and* GWENDOLEN *go off.*)

(LANE *presents several letters on a salver to* ALGERNON. *It is to be surmised that they are bills, as* ALGERNON, *after looking at the envelopes, tears them up.*)

ALGERNON   A glass of sherry, Lane.

LANE   Yes, sir.

ALGERNON   Tomorrow, Lane, I'm going Bunburying.

---

7. In the play's Victorian society, which privileged the dominant culture, this was an alternative form for designating one's first, or given, name.
8. Woolton is located in Merseyside, in the northwest of England. Hertfordshire is known for its Roman ruins, the childhood home of Queen Elizabeth I (1533–1603; reigned 1558–1603) (Hatfield House), and the home of the Irish playwright George Bernard Shaw, a contemporary of Wilde's.
9. A train timetable.

LANE   Yes, sir.

ALGERNON   I shall probably not be back till Monday. You can put up[1] my dress clothes, my smoking jacket,[2] and all the Bunbury suits—

IANE   Yes, sir. (*Handing sherry.*)

ALGERNON   I hope tomorrow will be a fine day, Lane.

LANE   It never is, sir.

ALGERNON   Lane, you're a perfect pessimist.

LANE   I do my best to give satisfaction, sir.
    (*Enter* JACK. LANE *goes off.*)

JACK   There's a sensible, intellectual girl! the only girl I ever cared for in my life. (ALGERNON *is laughing immoderately.*) What on earth are you so amused at?

ALGERNON   Oh, I'm a little anxious about poor Bunbury, that is all.

JACK   If you don't take care, your friend Bunbury will get you into a serious scrape some day.

ALGERNON   I love scrapes. They are the only things that are never serious.

JACK   Oh, that's nonsense, Algy. You never talk anything but nonsense.

ALGERNON   Nobody ever does.
    (JACK *looks indignantly at him, and leaves the room.* ALGERNON *lights a cigarette, reads his shirt cuff, and smiles.*)

ACT-DROP

Second Act

Scene—Garden at the Manor House. A flight of grey stone steps leads up to the house. The garden, an old-fashioned one, full of roses. Time of year, July. Basket chairs, and a table covered with books, are set under a large yew tree.

    (MISS PRISM *discovered seated at the table.* CECILY *is at the back watering flowers.*)

MISS PRISM[1] (*Calling.*)   Cecily, Cecily! Surely such a utilitarian occupation as the watering of flowers is rather Moulton's duty than yours? Especially at a moment when intellectual pleasures await you. Your German grammar is on the table. Pray open it at page fifteen. We will repeat yesterday's lesson.

---

1. Pack.
2. A man's evening jacket, often made of a fine fabric, elaborately trimmed, and usually worn at home and intended to protect other clothes from the smell of tobacco smoke.
1. *Prism*: a device for breaking light into bands of color.

CECILY (*Coming over very slowly.*) But I don't like German. It isn't at all a becoming language. I know perfectly well that I look quite plain after my German lesson.

MISS PRISM Child, you know how anxious your guardian is that you should improve yourself in every way. He laid particular stress on your German, as he was leaving for town yesterday. Indeed, he always lays stress on your German when he is leaving for town.

CECILY Dear Uncle Jack is so very serious! Sometimes he is so serious that I think he cannot be quite well.

MISS PRISM (*Drawing herself up.*) Your guardian enjoys the best of health, and his gravity of demeanour is especially to be commended in one so comparatively young as he is. I know no one who has a higher sense of duty and responsibility.

CECILY I suppose that is why he often looks a little bored when we three are together.

MISS PRISM Cecily! I am surprised at you. Mr. Worthing has many troubles in his life. Idle merriment and triviality would be out of place in his conversation. You must remember his constant anxiety about that unfortunate young man his brother.

CECILY I wish Uncle Jack would allow that unfortunate young man, his brother, to come down here sometimes. We might have a good influence over him, Miss Prism. I am sure you certainly would. You know German, and geology, and things of that kind influence a man very much. (CECILY *begins to write in her diary.*)

MISS PRISM (*Shaking her head.*) I do not think that even I could produce any effect on a character that according to his own brother's admission is irretrievably weak and vacillating. Indeed I am not sure that I would desire to reclaim him. I am not in favour of this modern mania for turning bad people into good people at a moment's notice. As a man sows so let him reap.[2] You must put away your diary, Cecily. I really don't see why you should keep a diary at all.

CECILY I keep a diary in order to enter the wonderful secrets of my life. If I didn't write them down I should probably forget all about them.

MISS PRISM Memory, my dear Cecily, is the diary that we all carry about with us.

CECILY Yes, but it usually chronicles the things that have never happened, and couldn't possibly have happened. I believe that Memory is responsible for nearly all the three-volume novels that Mudie[3] sends us.

2. A paraphrase of Galatians 6:7–8: "Be not deceived; God is not mocked: for whatsoever a man soweth, that shall he also reap."
3. An abbreviated form of the name of the circulating library opened by Charles Mudie in London.

MISS PRISM   Do not speak slightingly of the three-volume novel, Cecily. I wrote one myself in earlier days.

CECILY   Did you really, Miss Prism? How wonderfully clever you are! I hope it did not end happily? I don't like novels that end happily. They depress me so much.

MISS PRISM   The good ended happily, and the bad unhappily. That is what Fiction means.

CECILY   I suppose so. But it seems very unfair. And was your novel ever published?

MISS PRISM   Alas! no. The manuscript unfortunately was abandoned. I use the word in the sense of lost or mislaid. To your work, child, these speculations are profitless.

CECILY (*Smiling.*)   But I see dear Dr. Chasuble coming up through the garden.

MISS PRISM (*Rising and advancing.*)   Dr. Chasuble! This is indeed a pleasure.

(*Enter* CANON[4] CHASUBLE.[5])

CHASUBLE   And how are we this morning? Miss Prism, you are, I trust, well?

CECILY   Miss Prism has just been complaining of a slight headache. I think it would do her so much good to have a short stroll with you in the Park, Dr. Chasuble.

MISS PRISM   Cecily, I have not mentioned anything about a headache.

CECILY   No, dear Miss Prism, I know that, but I felt instinctively that you had a headache. Indeed I was thinking about that, and not about my German lesson, when the Rector[6] came in.

CHASUBLE   I hope, Cecily, you are not inattentive.

CECILY   Oh, I am afraid I am.

CHASUBLE   That is strange. Were I fortunate enough to be Miss Prism's pupil, I would hang upon her lips. (MISS PRISM *glares.*) I spoke metaphorically.—My metaphor was drawn from bees. Ahem! Mr. Worthing, I suppose, has not returned from town yet?

MISS PRISM   We do not expect him till Monday afternoon.

CHASUBLE   Ah yes, he usually likes to spend his Sunday in London. He is not one of those whose sole aim is enjoyment, as, by all accounts, that unfortunate young man his brother seems to be. But I must not disturb Egeria[7] and her pupil any longer.

MISS PRISM   Egeria? My name is Laetitia, Doctor.

---

4. A member of certain religious communities living under a common rule and bound by vows. It is not clear from the context if this title fits Dr. Chasuble.
5. Chasuble's name echoes that of a cloak-like ecclesiastical vestment worn over the alb and stole by the celebrant at Mass or the Eucharist.
6. A cleric in charge of, and who derives tithes from, a Church of England parish.
7. A goddess from Roman mythology, supposed to be the instructress of Numa Pompilius, and regarded as the giver of life. Hence, an idealized designation for an educator.

CHASUBLE (*Bowing.*)   A classical allusion merely, drawn from the Pagan authors. I shall see you both no doubt at Evensong?[8]

MISS PRISM   I think, dear Doctor, I will have a stroll with you. I find I have a headache after all, and a walk might do it good.

CHASUBLE   With pleasure, Miss Prism, with pleasure. We might go as far as the schools and back.

MISS PRISM   That would be delightful. Cecily, you will read your Political Economy in my absence. The chapter on the Fall of the Rupee[9] you may omit. It is somewhat too sensational. Even these metallic problems have their melodramatic side. (*Goes down the garden with Dr.* CHASUBLE.)

CECILY (*Picks up books and throws them back on table.*)   Horrid Political Economy! Horrid Geography! Horrid, horrid German!
   (*Enter* MERRIMAN *with a card on a salver.*)

MERRIMAN   Mr. Ernest Worthing has just driven over from the station. He has brought his luggage with him.

CECILY (*Takes the card and reads it.*)   "Mr. Ernest Worthing, B. 4 The Albany, W." Uncle Jack's brother! Did you tell him Mr. Worthing was in town?

MERRIMAN   Yes, Miss. He seemed very much disappointed. I mentioned that you and Miss Prism were in the garden. He said he was anxious to speak to you privately for a moment.

CECILY   Ask Mr. Ernest Worthing to come here. I suppose you had better talk to the housekeeper about a room for him.

MERRIMAN   Yes, Miss. (MERRIMAN *goes off.*)

CECILY   I have never met any really wicked person before. I feel rather frightened. I am so afraid he will look just like everyone else. (*Enter* ALGERNON, *very gay and debonair.*) He does!

ALGERNON (*Raising his hat.*)   You are my little cousin Cecily, I'm sure.

CECILY   You are under some strange mistake. I am not little. In fact, I believe I am more than usually tall for my age. (ALGERNON *is rather taken aback.*) But I am your cousin Cecily. You, I see from your card, are Uncle Jack's brother, my cousin Ernest, my wicked cousin Ernest.

ALGERNON   Oh! I am not really wicked at all, Cousin Cecily. You mustn't think that I am wicked.

CECILY   If you are not, then you have certainly been deceiving us all in a very inexcusable manner. I hope you have not been

---

8. A prayer service usually celebrated shortly before sunset, being the sixth of the seven "canonical hours" of the Western Church. In the Church of England it is also known as the "Evening Prayer."
9. The monetary unit of India, represented by a cupro-nickel (formerly silver) coin and equivalent to 100 paise.

leading a double life, pretending to be wicked and being really good all the time. That would be hypocrisy.

ALGERNON (*Looks at her in amazement.*)   Oh! Of course I have been rather reckless.

CECILY   I am glad to hear it.

ALGERNON   In fact, now you mention the subject, I have been very bad in my own small way.

CECILY   I don't think you should be so proud of that, though I am sure it must have been very pleasant.

ALGERNON   It is much pleasanter being here with you.

CECILY   I can't understand how you are here at all. Uncle Jack won't be back till Monday afternoon.

ALGERNON   That is a great disappointment. I am obliged to go up by the first train on Monday morning. I have a business appointment that I am anxious—to miss.

CECILY   Couldn't you miss it anywhere but in London?

ALGERNON   No: the appointment is in London.

CECILY   Well, I know, of course, how important it is not to keep a business engagement, if one wants to retain any sense of the beauty of life, but still I think you had better wait till Uncle Jack arrives. I know he wants to speak to you about your emigrating.

ALGERNON   About my what?

CECILY   Your emigrating. He has gone up to buy your outfit.

ALGERNON   I certainly wouldn't let Jack buy my outfit. He has no taste in neckties at all.

CECILY   I don't think you will require neckties. Uncle Jack is sending you to Australia.

ALGERNON   Australia! I'd sooner die.

CECILY   Well, he said at dinner on Wednesday night, that you would have to choose between this world, the next world, and Australia.

ALGERNON   Oh, well! The accounts I have received of Australia and the next world are not particularly encouraging. This world is good enough for me, Cousin Cecily.

CECILY   Yes, but are you good enough for it?

ALGERNON   I'm afraid I'm not that. That is why I want you to reform me. You might make that your mission, if you don't mind, cousin Cecily.

CECILY   I'm afraid I've no time, this afternoon.

ALGERNON   Well, would you mind my reforming myself this afternoon?

CECILY   It is rather Quixotic[1] of you. But I think you should try.

ALGERNON   I will. I feel better already.

---

1. A term applied to one with the idealism and clouded sense of perceptions of Don Quixote, the eponymous hero of *Don Quixote* (1605 and 1615), written by Miguel de Cervantes (1547–1616).

CECILY   You are looking a little worse.

ALGERNON   That is because I am hungry.

CECILY   How thoughtless of me. I should have remembered that when one is going to lead an entirely new life, one requires regular and wholesome meals. Won't you come in?

ALGERNON   Thank you. Might I have a button-hole[2] first? I never have any appetite unless I have a button-hole first.

CECILY   A Maréchal Niel?[3] (*Picks up scissors.*)

ALGERNON   No, I'd sooner have a pink rose.

CECILY   Why? (*Cuts a flower.*)

ALGERNON   Because you are like a pink rose, Cousin Cecily.

CECILY   I don't think it can be right for you to talk to me like that. Miss Prism never says such things to me.

ALGERNON   Then Miss Prism is a short-sighted old lady. (CECILY *puts the rose in his button-hole.*) You are the prettiest girl I ever saw.

CECILY   Miss Prism says that all good looks are a snare.

ALGERNON   They are a snare that every sensible man would like to be caught in.

CECILY   Oh, I don't think I would care to catch a sensible man. I shouldn't know what to talk to him about.

> (*They pass into the house.* MISS PRISM *and* Dr. CHASUBLE *return.*)

MISS PRISM   You are too much alone, dear Dr. Chasuble. You should get married. A misanthrope I can understand—a woman-thrope, never!

CHASUBLE (*With a scholar's shudder.*)   Believe me, I do not deserve so neologistic a phrase. The precept as well as the practice of the Primitive Church[4] was distinctly against matrimony.

MISS PRISM (*Sententiously.*)   That is obviously the reason why the Primitive Church has not lasted up to the present day. And you do not seem to realize, dear Doctor, that by persistently remaining single, a man converts himself into a permanent public temptation. Men should be more careful; this very celibacy leads weaker vessels astray.

CHASUBLE   But is a man not equally attractive when married?

MISS PRISM   No married man is ever attractive except to his wife.

CHASUBLE   And often, I've been told, not even to her.

MISS PRISM   That depends on the intellectual sympathies of the woman. Maturity can always be depended on. Ripeness can be trusted. Young women are green. (*Dr.* CHASUBLE *starts.*) I spoke

---

2. A shortened form of the term *button-hole flower*, a decorative ornament worn in the lapel of a man's jacket.
3. A variety of climbing rose introduced in 1864, bearing large, fragrant, yellow flowers.
4. A designation for the early Christian Church, with the implication that it reflected the purest level of practice.

horticulturally. My metaphor was drawn from fruits. But where is Cecily?

CHASUBLE   Perhaps she followed us to the schools.

(*Enter* JACK *slowly from the back of the garden. He is dressed in the deepest mourning, with crape hat-band and black gloves.*)

MISS PRISM   Mr. Worthing!

CHASUBLE   Mr. Worthing?

MISS PRISM   This is indeed a surprise. We did not look for you till Monday afternoon.

JACK (*Shakes* MISS PRISM's *hand in a tragic manner.*)   I have returned sooner than I expected. Dr. Chasuble, I hope you are well?

CHASUBLE   Dear Mr. Worthing, I trust this garb of woe does not betoken some terrible calamity?

JACK   My brother.

MISS PRISM   More shameful debts and extravagance?

CHASUBLE   Still leading his life of pleasure?

JACK (*Shaking his head.*)   Dead!

CHASUBLE   Your brother Ernest dead?

JACK   Quite dead.

MISS PRISM   What a lesson for him! I trust he will profit by it.

CHASUBLE   Mr. Worthing, I offer you my sincere condolence. You have at least the consolation of knowing that you were always the most generous and forgiving of brothers.

JACK   Poor Ernest! He had many faults, but it is a sad, sad blow.

CHASUBLE   Very sad indeed. Were you with him at the end?

JACK   No. He died abroad; in Paris, in fact. I had a telegram last night from the manager of the Grand Hotel.

CHASUBLE   Was the cause of death mentioned?

JACK   A severe chill, it seems.

MISS PRISM   As a man sows, so shall he reap.[5]

CHASUBLE (*Raising his hand.*)   Charity, dear Miss Prism, charity! None of us are perfect. I myself am peculiarly susceptible to draughts. Will the interment take place here?

JACK   No. He seems to have expressed a desire to be buried in Paris.

CHASUBLE   In Paris! (*Shakes his head.*) I fear that hardly points to any very serious state of mind at the last. You would no doubt wish me to make some slight allusion to this tragic domestic affliction next Sunday. (JACK *presses his hand convulsively.*) My sermon on the meaning of the manna[6] in the wilderness can be adapted to

5. St. Paul's letter to the Galatians 6:7–8.
6. Identified in the Bible (Exodus 16) as a substance miraculously provided each day as food for the Israelites in the wilderness after their departure from Egypt. It has come to mean spiritual nourishment, especially God-given, or simply something beneficial or pleasing (originally food) appearing or being provided unexpectedly or opportunely.

almost any occasion, joyful, or, as in the present case, distressing. (*All sigh.*) I have preached it at harvest celebrations, christenings, confirmations, on days of humiliation and festal days. The
last time I delivered it was in the Cathedral, as a charity sermon
on behalf of the Society for the Prevention of Discontent among
the Upper Orders. The Bishop, who was present, was much struck
by some of the analogies I drew.

JACK   Ah! that reminds me, you mentioned christenings I think,
Dr. Chasuble? I suppose you know how to christen all right?
(*Dr.* CHASUBLE *looks astounded.*) I mean, of course, you are con-
tinually christening, aren't you?

MISS PRISM   It is, I regret to say, one of the Rector's most constant
duties in this parish. I have often spoken to the poorer classes on
the subject. But they don't seem to know what thrift is.

CHASUBLE   But is there any particular infant in whom you are interested, Mr. Worthing? Your brother was, I believe, unmarried, was
he not?

JACK   Oh yes.

MISS PRISM (*Bitterly.*)   People who live entirely for pleasure usually
are.

JACK   But it is not for any child, dear Doctor. I am very fond of
children. No! the fact is, I would like to be christened myself, this
afternoon, if you have nothing better to do.

CHASUBLE   But surely, Mr. Worthing, you have been christened
already?

JACK   I don't remember anything about it.

CHASUBLE   But have you any grave doubts on the subject?

JACK   I certainly intend to have. Of course I don't know if the thing
would bother you in any way, or if you think I am a little too old
now.

CHASUBLE   Not at all. The sprinkling, and, indeed, the immersion
of adults is a perfectly canonical practice.

JACK   Immersion!

CHASUBLE   You need have no apprehensions. Sprinkling is all that
is necessary, or indeed I think advisable. Our weather is so change-
able. At what hour would you wish the ceremony performed?

JACK   Oh, I might trot round about five if that would suit you.

CHASUBLE   Perfectly, perfectly! In fact I have two similar ceremonies to perform at that time. A case of twins that occurred recently
in one of the outlying cottages on your own estate. Poor Jenkins
the carter,[7] a most hard-working man.

JACK   Oh! I don't see much fun in being christened along with other
babies. It would be childish. Would half-past five do?

7. One who drives carts or wagons.

CHASUBLE   Admirably! Admirably! (*Takes out watch.*) And now, dear Mr. Worthing, I will not intrude any longer into a house of sorrow. I would merely beg you not to be too much bowed down by grief. What seem to us bitter trials are often blessings in disguise.

MISS PRISM   This seems to me a blessing of an extremely obvious kind. (*Enter* CECILY *from the house.*)

CECILY   Uncle Jack! Oh, I am pleased to see you back. But what horrid clothes you have got on! Do go and change them.

MISS PRISM   Cecily!

CHASUBLE   My child! my child! (CECILY *goes towards* JACK; *he kisses her brow in a melancholy manner.*)

CECILY   What is the matter, Uncle Jack? Do look happy! You look as if you had toothache, and I have got such a surprise for you. Who do you think is in the dining-room? Your brother!

JACK   Who?

CECILY   Your brother Ernest. He arrived about half an hour ago.

JACK   What nonsense! I haven't got a brother.

CECILY   Oh, don't say that. However badly he may have behaved to you in the past he is still your brother. You couldn't be so heartless as to disown him. I'll tell him to come out. And you will shake hands with him, won't you, Uncle Jack? (*Runs back into the house.*)

CHASUBLE   These are very joyful tidings.

MISS PRISM   After we had all been resigned to his loss, his sudden return seems to me peculiarly distressing.

JACK   My brother is in the dining-room? I don't know what it all means. I think it is perfectly absurd.

(*Enter* ALGERNON *and* CECILY *hand in hand. They come slowly up to* JACK.)

JACK   Good heavens! (*Motions* ALGERNON *away.*)

ALGERNON   Brother John, I have come down from town to tell you that I am very sorry for all the trouble I have given you, and that I intend to lead a better life in the future. (JACK *glares at him and does not take his hand.*)

CECILY   Uncle Jack, you are not going to refuse your own brother's hand?

JACK   Nothing will induce me to take his hand. I think his coming down here disgraceful. He knows perfectly well why.

CECILY   Uncle Jack, do be nice. There is some good in everyone. Ernest has just been telling me about his poor invalid friend Mr. Bunbury whom he goes to visit so often. And surely there must be much good in one who is kind to an invalid, and leaves the pleasures of London to sit by a bed of pain.

JACK   Oh! he has been talking about Bunbury, has he?

CECILY   Yes, he has told me all about poor Mr. Bunbury, and his terrible state of health.

JACK Bunbury! Well, I won't have him talk to you about Bunbury or about anything else. It is enough to drive one perfectly frantic.

ALGERNON Of course I admit that the faults were all on my side. But I must say that I think that Brother John's coldness to me is peculiarly painful. I expected a more enthusiastic welcome, especially considering it is the first time I have come here.

CECILY Uncle Jack, if you don't shake hands with Ernest I will never forgive you.

JACK Never forgive me?

CECILY Never, never, never!

JACK Well, this is the last time I shall ever do it. (*Shakes with* ALGERNON *and glares.*)

CHASUBLE It's pleasant, is it not, to see so perfect a reconciliation? I think we might leave the two brothers together.

MISS PRISM Cecily, you will come with us.

CECILY Certainly, Miss Prism. My little task of reconciliation is over.

CHASUBLE You have done a beautiful action today, dear child.

MISS PRISM We must not be premature in our judgments.

CECILY I feel very happy.
(*They all go off.*)

JACK You young scoundrel, Algy, you must get out of this place as soon as possible. I don't allow any Bunburying here.
(*Enter* MERRIMAN.)

MERRIMAN I have put Mr. Ernest's things in the room next to yours, sir. I suppose that is all right?

JACK What?

MERRIMAN Mr. Ernest's luggage, sir. I have unpacked it and put it in the room next to your own.

JACK His luggage?

MERRIMAN Yes, sir. Three portmanteaus,[8] a dressing-case,[9] two hat-boxes,[1] and a large luncheon-basket.[2]

ALGERNON I am afraid I can't stay more than a week this time.

JACK Merriman, order the dog-cart[3] at once. Mr. Ernest has been suddenly called back to town.

MERRIMAN Yes, sir. (*Goes back into the house.*)

ALGERNON What a fearful liar you are, Jack. I have not been called back to town at all.

8. Cases or bags used for carrying clothing and other necessaries when traveling. Originally of a form suitable for carrying on horseback; now applied to oblong stiff leather cases, which open like books, with hinges in the middle of the back.
9. A case used to carry toiletries.
1. Large boxes intended to house one's hat safely.
2. A box for holding one's food; a picnic basket.
3. An open, horse-drawn vehicle with two back-to-back seats. In early versions of the cart, the seat further back shut to form a box for dogs.

JACK   Yes, you have.

ALGERNON   I haven't heard anyone call me.

JACK   Your duty as a gentleman calls you back.

ALGERNON   My duty as a gentleman has never interfered with my pleasures in the smallest degree.

JACK   I can quite understand that.

ALGERNON   Well, Cecily is a darling.

JACK   You are not to talk of Miss Cardew like that. I don't like it.

ALGERNON   Well, I don't like your clothes. You look perfectly ridiculous in them. Why on earth don't you go up and change? It is perfectly childish to be in deep mourning for a man who is actually staying for a whole week with you in your house as a guest. I call it grotesque.

JACK   You are certainly not staying with me for a whole week as a guest or anything else. You have got to leave—by the four-five train.

ALGERNON   I certainly won't leave you so long as you are in mourning. It would be most unfriendly. If I were in mourning you would stay with me, I suppose. I should think it very unkind if you didn't.

JACK   Well, will you go if I change my clothes?

ALGERNON   Yes, if you are not too long. I never saw anybody take so long to dress, and with such little result.

JACK   Well, at any rate, that is better than being always overdressed as you are.

ALGERNON   If I am occasionally a little overdressed, I make up for it by being always immensely overeducated.

JACK   Your vanity is ridiculous, your conduct an outrage, and your presence in my garden utterly absurd. However, you have got to catch the four-five, and I hope you will have a pleasant journey back to town. This Bunburying, as you call it, has not been a great success for you. (*Goes into the house.*)

ALGERNON   I think it has been a great success. I'm in love with Cecily, and that is everything. (*Enter* CECILY *at the back of the garden. She picks up the can and begins to water the flowers.*) But I must see her before I go, and make arrangements for another Bunbury. Ah, there she is.

CECILY   Oh, I merely came back to water the roses. I thought you were with Uncle Jack.

ALGERNON   He's gone to order the dog-cart for me.

CECILY   Oh, is he going to take you for a nice drive?

ALGERNON   He's going to send me away.

CECILY   Then have we got to part?

ALGERNON   I am afraid so. It's a very painful parting.

CECILY   It is always painful to part from people whom one has known for a very brief space of time. The absence of old friends one can endure with equanimity. But even a momentary separation from anyone to whom one has just been introduced is almost unbearable.

ALGERNON   Thank you.

(*Enter* MERRIMAN.)

MERRIMAN   The dog-cart is at the door, sir. (ALGERNON *looks appealingly at* CECILY.)

CECILY   It can wait, Merriman—for—five minutes.

MERRIMAN   Yes, Miss.   (*Exit* MERRIMAN.)

ALGERNON   I hope, Cecily, I shall not offend you if I state quite frankly and openly that you seem to me to be in every way the visible personification of absolute perfection.

CECILY   I think your frankness does you great credit, Ernest. If you will allow me I will copy your remarks into my diary. (*Goes over to table and begins writing in diary.*)

ALGERNON   Do you really keep a diary? I'd give anything to look at it. May I?

CECILY   Oh no. (*Puts her hand over it.*) You see, it is simply a very young girl's record of her own thoughts and impressions, and consequently meant for publication. When it appears in volume form I hope you will order a copy. But pray, Ernest, don't stop. I delight in taking down from dictation. I have reached "absolute perfection." You can go on. I am quite ready for more.

ALGERNON (*Somewhat taken aback.*)   Ahem! Ahem!

CECILY   Oh, don't cough, Ernest. When one is dictating one should speak fluently and not cough. Besides, I don't know how to spell a cough. (*Writes as* ALGERNON *speaks.*)

ALGERNON (*Speaking very rapidly.*)   Cecily, ever since I first looked upon your wonderful and incomparable beauty, I have dared to love you wildly, passionately, devotedly, hopelessly.

CECILY   I don't think that you should tell me that you love me wildly, passionately, devotedly, hopelessly. Hopelessly doesn't seem to make much sense, does it?

ALGERNON   Cecily!

(*Enter* MERRIMAN.)

MERRIMAN   The dog-cart is waiting, sir.

ALGERNON   Tell it to come round next week, at the same hour.

MERRIMAN (*Looks at* CECILY, *who makes no sign.*)   Yes, sir. (MERRIMAN *retires.*)

CECILY   Uncle Jack would be very much annoyed if he knew you were staying on till next week, at the same hour.

ALGERNON   Oh, I don't care about Jack. I don't care for anybody in the whole world but you. I love you, Cecily. You will marry me, won't you?

CECILY   You silly boy! Of course. Why, we have been engaged for the last three months.

ALGERNON   For the last three months?

CECILY   Yes, it will be exactly three months on Thursday.

ALGERNON   But how did we become engaged?

CECILY   Well, ever since dear Uncle Jack first confessed to us that
  he had a younger brother who was very wicked and bad, you of
  course have formed the chief topic of conversation between myself
  and Miss Prism. And of course a man who is much talked about
  is always very attractive. One feels there must be something in
  him after all. I daresay it was foolish of me, but I fell in love with
  you, Ernest.

ALGERNON   Darling! And when was the engagement actually
  settled?

CECILY   On the 14th of February last. Worn out by your entire ignorance of my existence, I determined to end the matter one way or
  the other, and after a long struggle with myself I accepted you
  under this dear old tree here. The next day I bought this little ring
  in your name, and this is the little bangle[4] with the true lovers'
  knot I promised you always to wear.

ALGERNON   Did I give you this? It's very pretty, isn't it?

CECILY   Yes, you've wonderfully good taste, Ernest. It's the excuse
  I've always given for your leading such a bad life. And this is the
  box in which I keep all your dear letters. (*Kneels at table, opens
  box, and produces letters tied up with blue ribbon.*)

ALGERNON   My letters! But my own sweet Cecily, I have never written you any letters.

CECILY   You need hardly remind me of that, Ernest. I remember
  only too well that I was forced to write your letters for you. I wrote
  always three times a week, and sometimes oftener.

ALGERNON   Oh, do let me read them, Cecily!

CECILY   Oh, I couldn't possibly. They would make you far too conceited. (*Replaces box.*) The three you wrote me after I had broken
  off the engagement are so beautiful, and so badly spelled, that
  even now I can hardly read them without crying a little.

ALGERNON   But was our engagement ever broken off?

CECILY   Of course it was. On the 22nd of last March. You can see
  the entry if you like. (*Shows diary.*) "Today I broke off my engagement with Ernest. I feel it is better to do so. The weather still
  continues charming."

ALGERNON   But why on earth did you break it off? What had I done?
  I had done nothing at all. Cecily, I am very much hurt indeed
  to hear you broke it off. Particularly when the weather was so
  charming.

4. A rigid bracelet.

CECILY   It would hardly have been a really serious engagement if it
   hadn't been broken off at least once. But I forgave you before the
   week was out.
ALGERNON (*Crossing to her, and kneeling.*)   What a perfect angel you
   are, Cecily.
CECILY   You dear romantic boy. (*He kisses her, she puts her fingers
   through his hair.*) I hope your hair curls naturally, does it?
ALGERNON   Yes, darling, with a little help from others.
CECILY   I am so glad.
ALGERNON   You'll never break off our engagement again, Cecily?
CECILY   I don't think I could break it off now that I have actually
   met you. Besides, of course, there is the question of your name.
ALGERNON   Yes, of course. (*Nervously.*)
CECILY   You must not laugh at me, darling, but it had always been
   a girlish dream of mine to love someone whose name was Ernest.
   (ALGERNON *rises,* CECILY *also.*) There is something in that name
   that seems to inspire absolute confidence. I pity any poor married
   woman whose husband is not called Ernest.
ALGERNON   But, my dear child, do you mean to say you could not
   love me if I had some other name?
CECILY   But what name?
ALGERNON   Oh, any name you like—Algernon—for instance—
CECILY   But I don't like the name of Algernon.
ALGERNON   Well, my own dear, sweet, loving little darling, I really
   can't see why you should object to the name of Algernon. It is
   not at all a bad name. In fact, it is rather an aristocratic name.
   Half of the chaps who get into the Bankruptcy Court[5] are called
   Algernon. But seriously, Cecily—(*Moving to her.*)—if my name
   was Algy, couldn't you love me?
CECILY (*Rising.*)   I might respect you, Ernest, I might admire your
   character, but I fear that I should not be able to give you my undi-
   vided attention.
ALGERNON   Ahem! Cecily! (*Picking up hat.*) Your Rector here is, I
   suppose, thoroughly experienced in the practice of all the rites and
   ceremonials of the Church?
CECILY   Oh, yes. Dr. Chasuble is a most learned man. He has never
   written a single book, so you can imagine how much he knows.
ALGERNON   I must see him at once on a most important christening—
   I mean on most important business.

5. The bankruptcy court in London is now located in Carey Street. According to Peter
   Cunningham's *Hand-Book of London* (1849), "The business of the court is managed by
   two judges, and five commissioners. Number of Bankrupts in 1845—1028; in 1846—
   1326. The bankrupt is a trader, the insolvent not necessarily so. The bankrupt, when
   discharged, is discharged not only as to his person, but as to future acquired property;
   while the insolvent is discharged only as to his person, and not as to future acquired
   property."

CECILY   Oh!

ALGERNON   I shan't be away more than half an hour.

CECILY   Considering that we have been engaged since February the 14th, and that I only met you to-day for the first time, I think it is rather hard that you should leave me for so long a period as half an hour. Couldn't you make it twenty minutes?

ALGERNON   I'll be back in no time. (*Kisses her and rushes down the garden.*)

CECILY   What an impetuous boy he is! I like his hair so much. I must enter his proposal in my diary.
      (*Enter* MERRIMAN.)

MERRIMAN   A Miss Fairfax has just called to see Mr. Worthing. On very important business, Miss Fairfax states.

CECILY   Isn't Mr. Worthing in his library?

MERRIMAN   Mr. Worthing went over in the direction of the Rectory some time ago.

CECILY   Pray ask the lady to come out here; Mr. Worthing is sure to be back soon. And you can bring tea.

MERRIMAN   Yes, Miss. (*Goes out.*)

CECILY   Miss Fairfax! I suppose one of the many good elderly women who are associated with Uncle Jack in some of his philanthropic work in London. I don't quite like women who are interested in philanthropic work. I think it is so forward of them.
      (*Enter* MERRIMAN.)

MERRIMAN   Miss Fairfax.
      (*Enter* GWENDOLEN.)

                                          (*Exit* MERRIMAN.)

CECILY (*Advancing to meet her.*)   Pray let me introduce myself to you. My name is Cecily Cardew.

GWENDOLEN   Cecily Cardew? (*Moving to her and shaking hands.*) What a very sweet name! Something tells me that we are going to be great friends. I like you already more than I can say. My first impressions of people are never wrong.

CECILY   How nice of you to like me so much after we have known each other such a comparatively short time. Pray sit down.

GWENDOLEN (*Still standing up.*)   I may call you Cecily, may I not?

CECILY   With pleasure!

GWENDOLEN   And you will always call me Gwendolen, won't you?

CECILY   If you wish.

GWENDOLEN   Then that is all quite settled, is it not?

CECILY   I hope so. (*A pause. They both sit down together.*)

GWENDOLEN   Perhaps this might be a favourable opportunity for my mentioning who I am. My father is Lord Bracknell. You have never heard of papa, I suppose?

CECILY   I don't think so.

GWENDOLEN   Outside the family circle, papa, I am glad to say, is entirely unknown. I think that is quite as it should be. The home seems to me to be the proper sphere for the man. And certainly once a man begins to neglect his domestic duties he becomes painfully effeminate, does he not? And I don't like that. It makes men so very attractive. Cecily, mamma, whose views on education are remarkably strict, has brought me up to be extremely short-sighted; it is part of her system; so do you mind my looking at you through my glasses?

CECILY   Oh! not at all, Gwendolen. I am very fond of being looked at.

GWENDOLEN   (*After examining* CECILY *carefully through a lorgnette.*[6])   You are here on a short visit, I suppose.

CECILY   Oh no! I live here.

GWENDOLEN   (*Severely.*)   Really? Your mother, no doubt, or some female relative of advanced years, resides here also?

CECILY   Oh no! I have no mother, nor, in fact, any relations.

GWENDOLEN   Indeed?

CECILY   My dear guardian, with the assistance of Miss Prism, has the arduous task of looking after me.

GWENDOLEN   Your guardian?

CECILY   Yes, I am Mr. Worthing's ward.

GWENDOLEN   Oh! It is strange he never mentioned to me that he had a ward. How secretive of him! He grows more interesting hourly. I am not sure, however, that the news inspires me with feelings of unmixed delight. (*Rising and going to her.*) I am very fond of you, Cecily; I have liked you ever since I met you! But I am bound to state that now that I know that you are Mr. Worthing's ward, I cannot help expressing a wish you were—well, just a little older than you seem to be—and not quite so very alluring in appearance. In fact, if I may speak candidly—

CECILY   Pray do! I think that whenever one has anything unpleasant to say, one should always be quite candid.

GWENDOLEN   Well, to speak with perfect candour, Cecily, I wish that you were fully forty-two, and more than usually plain for your age. Ernest has a strong upright nature. He is the very soul of truth and honour. Disloyalty would be as impossible to him as deception. But even men of the noblest possible moral character are extremely susceptible to the influence of the physical charms of others. Modern, no less than Ancient History, supplies us with many most painful examples of what I refer to. If it were not so, indeed, History would be quite unreadable.

CECILY   I beg your pardon, Gwendolen, did you say Ernest?

6. A pair of eyeglasses usually affixed to a metal, ivory, or tortoiseshell handle.

GWENDOLEN   Yes.

CECILY   Oh, but it is not Mr. Ernest Worthing who is my guardian. It is his brother—his elder brother.

GWENDOLEN (*Sitting down again.*)   Ernest never mentioned to me that he had a brother.

CECILY   I am sorry to say they have not been on good terms for a long time.

GWENDOLEN   Ah! that accounts for it. And now that I think of it I have never heard any man mention his brother. The subject seems distasteful to most men. Cecily, you have lifted a load from my mind. I was growing almost anxious. It would have been terrible if any cloud had come across a friendship like ours, would it not? Of course you are quite, quite sure that it is not Mr. Ernest Worthing who is your guardian?

CECILY   Quite sure. (*A pause.*) In fact, I am going to be his.

GWENDOLEN (*Enquiringly.*)   I beg your pardon?

CECILY (*Rather shy and confidingly.*)   Dearest Gwendolen, there is no reason why I should make a secret of it to you. Our little county newspaper is sure to chronicle the fact next week. Mr. Ernest Worthing and I are engaged to be married.

GWENDOLEN (*Quite politely, rising.*)   My darling Cecily, I think there must be some slight error. Mr. Ernest Worthing is engaged to me. The announcement will appear in the *Morning Post*[7] on Saturday at the latest.

CECILY (*Very politely, rising.*)   I am afraid you must be under some misconception. Ernest proposed to me exactly ten minutes ago. (*Shows diary.*)

GWENDOLEN (*Examines diary through her lorgnette carefully.*)   It is certainly very curious, for he asked me to be his wife yesterday afternoon at 5:30. If you would care to verify the incident, pray do so. (*Produces diary of her own.*) I never travel without my diary. One should always have something sensational to read in the train. I am so sorry, dear Cecily, if it is any disappointment to you, but I am afraid I have the prior claim.

CECILY   It would distress me more than I can tell you, dear Gwendolen, if it caused you any mental or physical anguish, but I feel bound to point out that since Ernest proposed to you he clearly has changed his mind.

GWENDOLEN (*Meditatively.*)   If the poor fellow has been entrapped into any foolish promise I shall consider it my duty to rescue him at once, and with a firm hand.

---

7. A popular and well-known London newspaper that ran upper-class marriage announcements.

CECILY (*Thoughtfully and sadly.*)   Whatever unfortunate entanglement my dear boy may have got into, I will never reproach him
with it after we are married.

GWENDOLEN   Do you allude to me, Miss Cardew, as an entanglement? You are presumptuous. On an occasion of this kind it
becomes more than a moral duty to speak one's mind. It becomes
a pleasure.

CECILY   Do you suggest, Miss Fairfax, that I entrapped Ernest into
an engagement? How dare you? This is no time for wearing the
shallow mask of manners. When I see a spade I call it a spade.

GWENDOLEN (*Satirically.*)   I am glad to say that I have never seen a
spade. It is obvious that our social spheres have been widely
different.

> (*Enter* MERRIMAN, *followed by the* FOOTMAN. *He carries a sal-
> ver, table cloth, and plate stand.* CECILY *is about to retort. The
> presence of the servants exercises a restraining influence, under
> which both girls chafe.*)

MERRIMAN   Shall I lay tea here as usual, miss?

CECILY (*Sternly, in a calm voice.*)   Yes, as usual. (MERRIMAN *begins
to clear table and lay cloth. A long pause.* CECILY *and* GWENDOLEN
glare at each other.)

GWENDOLEN   Are there many interesting walks in the vicinity, Miss
Cardew?

CECILY   Oh! yes! a great many. From the top of one of the hills quite
close one can see five counties.

GWENDOLEN   Five counties! I don't think I should like that; I hate
crowds.

CECILY (*Sweetly.*)   I suppose that is why you live in town? (GWENDO-
LEN *bites her lips, and beats her foot nervously with her parasol.*)

GWENDOLEN (*Looking round.*)   Quite a well-kept garden this is, Miss
Cardew.

CECILY   So glad you like it, Miss Fairfax.

GWENDOLEN   I had no idea there were any flowers in the country.

CECILY   Oh, flowers are as common[8] here, Miss Fairfax, as people
are in London.

GWENDOLEN   Personally I cannot understand how anybody manages to exist in the country, if anybody who is anybody does. The
country always bores me to death.

CECILY   Ah! This is what the newspapers call agricultural depression, is it not? I believe the aristocracy are suffering very much
from it just at present. It is almost an epidemic amongst them, I
have been told. May I offer you some tea, Miss Fairfax?

---

8. In this context, the term refers to something of inferior quality, and by extension to
people who are low-class, vulgar, or unrefined.

GWENDOLEN (*With elaborate politeness.*)   Thank you. (*Aside.*) Detestable girl! But I require tea!

CECILY (*Sweetly.*)   Sugar?

GWENDOLEN (*Superciliously.*)   No, thank you. Sugar is not fashionable any more. (CECILY *looks angrily at her, takes up the tongs and puts four lumps of sugar into the cup.*)

CECILY (*Severely.*)   Cake or bread and butter?

GWENDOLEN (*In a bored manner.*)   Bread and butter, please. Cake is rarely seen at the best houses nowadays.

CECILY (*Cuts a very large slice of cake, and puts it on the tray.*)   Hand that to Miss Fairfax.

> (MERRIMAN *does so, and goes out with* FOOTMAN. GWENDOLEN *drinks the tea and makes a grimace. Puts down cup at once, reaches out her hand to the bread and butter, looks at it, and finds it is cake. Rises in indignation.*)

GWENDOLEN   You have filled my tea with lumps of sugar, and though I asked most distinctly for bread and butter, you have given me cake. I am known for the gentleness of my disposition, and the extraordinary sweetness of my nature, but I warn you, Miss Cardew, you may go too far.

CECILY (*Rising.*)   To save my poor, innocent, trusting boy from the machinations of any other girl there are no lengths to which I would not go.

GWENDOLEN   From the moment I saw you I distrusted you. I felt that you were false and deceitful. I am never deceived in such matters. My first impressions of people are invariably right.

CECILY   It seems to me, Miss Fairfax, that I am trespassing on your valuable time. No doubt you have many other calls of a similar character to make in the neighbourhood.

> (*Enter* JACK.)

GWENDOLEN (*Catching sight of him.*)   Ernest! My own Ernest!

JACK   Gwendolen! Darling! (*Offers to kiss her.*)

GWENDOLEN (*Draws back.*)   A moment! May I ask if you are engaged to be married to this young lady? (*Points to* CECILY.)

JACK (*Laughing.*)   To dear little Cecily! Of course not! What could have put such an idea into your pretty little head?

GWENDOLEN   Thank you. You may! (*Offers her cheek.*)

CECILY (*Very sweetly.*)   I knew there must be some misunderstanding, Miss Fairfax. The gentleman whose arm is at present round your waist is my guardian, Mr. John Worthing.

GWENDOLEN   I beg your pardon?

CECILY   This is Uncle Jack.

GWENDOLEN (*Receding.*)   Jack! Oh!

> (*Enter* ALGERNON.)

CECILY   Here is Ernest.

ALGERNON (*Goes straight over to* CECILY *without noticing anyone else.*)   My own love! (*Offers to kiss her.*)

CECILY (*Drawing back.*)   A moment, Ernest! May I ask you—are you engaged to be married to this young lady?

ALGERNON (*Looking round.*)   To what young lady? Good heavens! Gwendolen!

CECILY   Yes! to good heavens, Gwendolen, I mean to Gwendolen.

ALGERNON (*Laughing.*)   Of course not! What could have put such an idea into your pretty little head?

CECILY   Thank you. (*Presenting her cheek to be kissed.*) You may. (ALGERNON *kisses her.*)

GWENDOLEN   I felt there was some slight error, Miss Cardew. The gentleman who is now embracing you is my cousin, Mr. Algernon Moncrieff.

CECILY (*Breaking away from* ALGERNON.)   Algernon Moncrieff! Oh! (*The two girls move towards each other and put their arms round each other's waists as if for protection.*)

CECILY   Are you called Algernon?

ALGERNON   I cannot deny it.

CECILY   Oh!

GWENDOLEN   Is your name really John?

JACK (*Standing rather proudly.*)   I could deny it if I liked. I could deny anything if I liked. But my name certainly is John. It has been John for years.

CECILY (*To* GWENDOLEN.)   A gross deception has been practised on both of us.

GWENDOLEN   My poor wounded Cecily!

CECILY   My sweet wronged Gwendolen!

GWENDOLEN (*Slowly and seriously.*)   You will call me sister, will you not? (*They embrace.* JACK *and* ALGERNON *groan and walk up and down.*)

CECILY (*Rather brightly.*)   There is just one question I would like to be allowed to ask my guardian.

GWENDOLEN   An admirable idea! Mr. Worthing, there is just one question I would like to be permitted to put to you. Where is your brother Ernest? We are both engaged to be married to your brother Ernest, so it is a matter of some importance to us to know where your brother Ernest is at present.

JACK (*Slowly and hesitatingly.*)   Gwendolen—Cecily—it is very painful for me to be forced to speak the truth. It is the first time in my life that I have ever been reduced to such a painful position, and I am really quite inexperienced in doing anything of the kind. However I will tell you quite frankly that I have no brother

Ernest. I have no brother at all. I never had a brother in my life, and I certainly have not the smallest intention of ever having one in the future.

CECILY (*Surprised.*)   No brother at all?

JACK (*Cheerily.*)   None!

GWENDOLEN (*Severely.*)   Had you never a brother of any kind?

JACK (*Pleasantly.*)   Never. Not even of any kind.

GWENDOLEN   I am afraid it is quite clear, Cecily, that neither of us is engaged to be married to anyone.

CECILY   It is not a very pleasant position for a young girl suddenly to find herself in. Is it?

GWENDOLEN   Let us go into the house. They will hardly venture to come after us there.

CECILY   No, men are so cowardly, aren't they?

(*They retire into the house with scornful looks.*)

JACK   This ghastly state of things is what you call Bunburying, I suppose?

ALGERNON   Yes, and a perfectly wonderful Bunbury it is. The most wonderful Bunbury I have ever had in my life.

JACK   Well, you've no right whatsoever to Bunbury here.

ALGERNON   That is absurd. One has a right to Bunbury anywhere one chooses. Every serious Bunburyist knows that.

JACK   Serious Bunburyist! Good heavens!

ALGERNON   Well, one must be serious about something, if one wants to have any amusement in life. I happen to be serious about Bunburying. What on earth you are serious about I haven't got the remotest idea. About everything, I should fancy. You have such an absolutely trivial nature.

JACK   Well, the only small satisfaction I have in the whole of this wretched business is that your friend Bunbury is quite exploded. You won't be able to run down to the country quite so often as you used to do, dear Algy. And a very good thing too.

ALGERNON   Your brother is a little off colour, isn't he, dear Jack? You won't be able to disappear to London quite so frequently as your wicked custom was. And not a bad thing either.

JACK   As for your conduct towards Miss Cardew, I must say that your taking in a sweet, simple, innocent girl like that is quite inexcusable. To say nothing of the fact that she is my ward.

ALGERNON   I can see no possible defence at all for your deceiving a brilliant, clever, thoroughly experienced young lady like Miss Fairfax. To say nothing of the fact that she is my cousin.

JACK   I wanted to be engaged to Gwendolen, that is all. I love her.

ALGERNON   Well, I simply wanted to be engaged to Cecily. I adore her.

JACK   There is certainly no chance of your marrying Miss Cardew.

ALGERNON   I don't think there is much likelihood, Jack, of you and Miss Fairfax being united.

JACK   Well, that is no business of yours.

ALGERNON   If it was my business, I wouldn't talk about it. (*Begins to eat muffins.*) It is very vulgar to talk about one's business. Only people like stockbrokers do that, and then merely at dinner parties.

JACK   How you can sit there, calmly eating muffins when we are in this horrible trouble, I can't make out. You seem to me to be perfectly heartless.

ALGERNON   Well, I can't eat muffins in an agitated manner. The butter would probably get on my cuffs. One should always eat muffins quite calmly. It is the only way to eat them.

JACK   I say it's perfectly heartless your eating muffins at all, under the circumstances.

ALGERNON   When I am in trouble, eating is the only thing that consoles me. Indeed, when I am in really great trouble, as anyone who knows me intimately will tell you, I refuse everything except food and drink. At the present moment I am eating muffins because I am unhappy. Besides, I am particularly fond of muffins. (*Rising.*)

JACK (*Rising.*)   Well, that is no reason why you should eat them all in that greedy way.

(*Takes muffins from* ALGERNON.)

ALGERNON (*Offering tea-cake.*)   I wish you would have tea-cake instead. I don't like tea-cake.

JACK   Good heavens! I suppose a man may eat his own muffins in his own garden.

ALGERNON   But you have just said it was perfectly heartless to eat muffins.

JACK   I said it was perfectly heartless of you, under the circumstances. That is a very different thing.

ALGERNON   That may be. But the muffins are the same. (*He seizes the muffin-dish from* JACK.)

JACK   Algy, I wish to goodness you would go.

ALGERNON   You can't possibly ask me to go without having some dinner. It's absurd. I never go without my dinner. No one ever does, except vegetarians and people like that. Besides I have just made arrangements with Dr. Chasuble to be christened at a quarter to six under the name of Ernest.

JACK   My dear fellow, the sooner you give up that nonsense the better. I made arrangements this morning with Dr. Chasuble to be christened myself at 5:30, and I naturally will take the name of Ernest. Gwendolen would wish it. We can't both be christened

Ernest. It's absurd. Besides, I have a perfect right to be christened if I like. There is no evidence at all that I have ever been christened by anybody. I should think it extremely probable I never was, and so does Dr. Chasuble. It is entirely different in your case. You have been christened already.

ALGERNON   Yes, but I have not been christened for years.

JACK   Yes, but you have been christened. That is the important thing.

ALGERNON   Quite so. So I know my constitution can stand it. If you are not quite sure about your ever having been christened, I must say I think it rather dangerous your venturing on it now. It might make you very unwell. You can hardly have forgotten that someone very closely connected with you was very nearly carried off this week in Paris by a severe chill.

JACK   Yes, but you said yourself that a severe chill was not hereditary.

ALGERNON   It usen't to be, I know—but I daresay it is now. Science is always making wonderful improvements in things.

JACK   (*Picking up the muffin-dish.*)   Oh, that is nonsense; you are always talking nonsense.

ALGERNON   Jack, you are at the muffins again! I wish you wouldn't. There are only two left. (*Takes them.*) I told you I was particularly fond of muffins.

JACK   But I hate tea-cake.

ALGERNON   Why on earth then do you allow tea-cake to be served up for your guests? What ideas you have of hospitality!

JACK   Algernon! I have already told you to go. I don't want you here. Why don't you go!

ALGERNON   I haven't quite finished my tea yet! and there is still one muffin left. (JACK *groans, and sinks into a chair.* ALGERNON *still continues eating.*)

ACT-DROP

Third Act

Scene—Morning-room at the Manor House.

(GWENDOLEN *and* CECILY *are at the window, looking out into the garden.*)

GWENDOLEN   The fact that they did not follow us at once into the house, as anyone else would have done, seems to me to show that they have some sense of shame left.

CECILY   They have been eating muffins. That looks like repentance.

GWENDOLEN (*After a pause.*)   They don't seem to notice us at all. Couldn't you cough?

CECILY   But I haven't got a cough.

GWENDOLEN   They're looking at us. What effrontery!

CECILY   They're approaching. That's very forward of them.

GWENDOLEN   Let us preserve a dignified silence.

CECILY   Certainly. It's the only thing to do now.

(*Enter* JACK *followed by* ALGERNON. *They whistle some dreadful popular air from a British Opera.*[1])

GWENDOLEN   This dignified silence seems to produce an unpleasant effect.

CECILY   A most distasteful one.

GWENDOLEN   But we will not be the first to speak.

CECILY   Certainly not.

GWENDOLEN   Mr. Worthing, I have something very particular to ask you. Much depends on your reply.

CECILY   Gwendolen, your common sense is invaluable. Mr. Moncrieff, kindly answer me the following question. Why did you pretend to be my guardian's brother?

ALGERNON   In order that I might have an opportunity of meeting you.

CECILY (*To* GWENDOLEN.)   That certainly seems a satisfactory explanation, does it not?

GWENDOLEN   Yes, dear, if you can believe him.

CECILY   I don't. But that does not affect the wonderful beauty of his answer.

GWENDOLEN   True. In matters of grave importance, style, not sincerity is the vital thing. Mr. Worthing, what explanation can you offer to me for pretending to have a brother? Was it in order that you might have an opportunity of coming up to town to see me as often as possible?

JACK   Can you doubt it, Miss Fairfax?

GWENDOLEN   I have the gravest doubts upon the subject. But I intend to crush them. This is not the moment for German skepticism.[2] (*Moving to* CECILY.) Their explanations appear to be quite satisfactory, especially Mr. Worthing's. That seems to me to have the stamp of truth upon it.

CECILY   I am more than content with what Mr. Moncrieff said. His voice alone inspires one with absolute credulity.

GWENDOLEN   Then you think we should forgive them?

1. Wilde is undoubtedly referring to a musical number by Sir William S. Gilbert (1836–1911) and Sir Arthur Sullivan (1842–1900), the famous British lyricist and composer, who lampooned him in their comic opera *Patience, or Bunthorne's Bride* (1881).
2. A broad reference to a perceived inclination to doubt the truth of some assertion or supposed fact, often extending to general mistrustfulness.

CECILY Yes. I mean no.

GWENDOLEN True! I had forgotten. There are principles at stake that one cannot surrender. Which of us should tell them? The task is not a pleasant one.

CECILY Could we not both speak at the same time?

GWENDOLEN An excellent idea! I nearly always speak at the same time as other people. Will you take the time from me?

CECILY Certainly. (GWENDOLEN *beats time with uplifted finger.*)

GWENDOLEN *and* CECILY (*Speaking together.*) Your Christian names are still an insuperable barrier. That is all!

JACK *and* ALGERNON (*Speaking together.*) Our Christian names! Is that all? But we are going to be christened this afternoon.

GWENDOLEN (*To* JACK.) For my sake you are prepared to do this terrible thing?

JACK I am.

CECILY (*To* ALGERNON.) To please me you are ready to face this fearful ordeal?

ALGERNON I am!

GWENDOLEN How absurd to talk of the equality of the sexes! Where questions of self-sacrifice are concerned, men are infinitely beyond us.

JACK We are. (*Clasps hands with* ALGERNON.)

CECILY They have moments of physical courage of which we women know absolutely nothing.

GWENDOLEN (*To* JACK.) Darling!

ALGERNON (*To* CECILY.) Darling! (*They fall into each other's arms.*)
    (*Enter* MERRIMAN. *When he enters he coughs loudly, seeing the situation.*)

MERRIMAN Ahem! Ahem! Lady Bracknell!

JACK Good heavens!
    (*Enter* LADY BRACKNELL. *The couples separate in alarm. Exit* MERRIMAN.)

LADY BRACKNELL Gwendolen! What does this mean?

GWENDOLEN Merely that I am engaged to be married to Mr. Worthing, mamma.

LADY BRACKNELL Come here. Sit down. Sit down immediately. Hesitation of any kind is a sign of mental decay in the young, of physical weakness in the old. (*Turns to* JACK.) Apprised, sir, of my daughter's sudden flight by her trusty maid, whose confidence I purchased by means of a small coin, I followed her at once by a luggage train.[3] Her unhappy father is, I am glad to say, under the impression that she is attending a more than usually lengthy

---

3. A cross-country train, as opposed to one making commuter stops.

lecture by the University Extension Scheme[4] on the Influence of a permanent income on Thought. I do not propose to undeceive him. Indeed I have never undeceived him on any question. I would consider it wrong. But of course, you will clearly understand that all communication between yourself and my daughter must cease immediately from this moment. On this point, as indeed on all points, I am firm.

JACK   I am engaged to be married to Gwendolen, Lady Bracknell!

LADY BRACKNELL   You are nothing of the kind, sir. And now, as regards Algernon!—Algernon!

ALGERNON   Yes, Aunt Augusta.

LADY BRACKNELL   May I ask if it is in this house that your invalid friend Mr. Bunbury resides?

ALGERNON (*Stammering.*)   Oh! No! Bunbury doesn't live here. Bunbury is somewhere else at present. In fact, Bunbury is dead.

LADY BRACKNELL   Dead! When did Mr. Bunbury die? His death must have been extremely sudden.

ALGERNON (*Airily.*)   Oh! I killed Bunbury this afternoon. I mean poor Bunbury died this afternoon.

LADY BRACKNELL   What did he die of?

ALGERNON   Bunbury? Oh, he was quite exploded.

LADY BRACKNELL   Exploded! Was he the victim of a revolutionary outrage? I was not aware that Mr. Bunbury was interested in social legislation. If so, he is well punished for his morbidity.

ALGERNON   My dear Aunt Augusta, I mean he was found out! The doctors found out that Bunbury could not live, that is what I mean—so Bunbury died.

LADY BRACKNELL   He seems to have had great confidence in the opinion of his physicians. I am glad, however, that he made up his mind at the last to some definite course of action, and acted under proper medical advice. And now that we have finally got rid of this Mr. Bunbury, may I ask, Mr. Worthing, who is that young person whose hand my nephew Algernon is now holding in what seems to me a peculiarly unnecessary manner?

JACK   That lady is Miss Cecily Cardew, my ward. (LADY BRACKNELL *bows coldly to* CECILY.)

ALGERNON   I am engaged to be married to Cecily, Aunt Augusta.

LADY BRACKNELL   I beg your pardon?

CECILY   Mr. Moncrieff and I are engaged to be married, Lady Bracknell.

LADY BRACKNELL (*With a shiver, crossing to the sofa and sitting down.*)   I do not know whether there is anything peculiarly

---

4. An effort to extend the scope of the universities by offering lectures and examinations to nonresident students.

exciting in the air of this particular part of Hertfordshire, but the number of engagements that go on seems to me considerably above the proper average that statistics have laid down for our guidance. I think some preliminary inquiry on my part would not be out of place. Mr. Worthing, is Miss Cardew at all connected with any of the larger railway stations in London? I merely desire information. Until yesterday I had no idea that there were any families or persons whose origin was a Terminus.[5] (JACK *looks perfectly furious, but restrains himself.*)

JACK (*In a clear, cold voice.*)   Miss Cardew is the granddaughter of the late Mr. Thomas Cardew of 149 Belgrave Square, S.W.; Gervase Park, Dorking, Surrey; and the Sporran, Fifeshire, N.B.[6]

LADY BRACKNELL   That sounds not unsatisfactory. Three addresses always inspire confidence, even in tradesmen. But what proof have I of their authenticity?

JACK   I have carefully preserved the Court Guides[7] of the period. They are open to your inspection, Lady Bracknell.

LADY BRACKNELL (*Grimly.*)   I have known strange errors in that publication.

JACK   Miss Cardew's family solicitors are Messrs. Markby, Markby, and Markby.

LADY BRACKNELL   Markby, Markby, and Markby? A firm of the very highest position in their profession. Indeed I am told that one of the Mr. Markbys is occasionally to be seen at dinner parties. So far I am satisfied.

JACK (*Very irritably.*)   How extremely kind of you, Lady Bracknell! I have also in my possession, you will be pleased to hear, certificates of Miss Cardew's birth, baptism, whooping cough, registration, vaccination, confirmation, and the measles; both the German and the English variety.

LADY BRACKNELL   Ah! A life crowded with incident, I see; though perhaps somewhat too exciting for a young girl. I am not myself in favour of premature experiences. (*Rises, looks at her watch.*) Gwendolen! the time approaches for our departure. We have not a moment to lose. As a matter of form, Mr. Worthing, I had better ask you if Miss Cardew has any little fortune?

JACK   Oh! about a hundred and thirty thousand pounds[8] in the Funds.[9] That is all. Good-bye, Lady Bracknell. So pleased to have seen you.

---

5. The end of a line of a railway, or the station at that end.
6. Fifeshire is a maritime peninsular county of east-central Scotland.
7. The title of a directory containing the names and addresses of the nobility, gentry, and people in "society," the theory being that it contains the names of all persons who have been presented at court.
8. This would amount to nearly $18,000,000 today.
9. Investments backed by the Bank of England.

LADY BRACKNELL (*Sitting down again.*)   A moment, Mr. Worthing. A hundred and thirty thousand pounds! And in the Funds! Miss Cardew seems to me a most attractive young lady, now that I look at her. Few girls of the present day have any really solid qualities, any of the qualities that last, and improve with time. We live, I regret to say, in an age of surfaces. (*To* CECILY.) Come over here, dear. (CECILY *goes across.*) Pretty child! your dress is sadly simple, and your hair seems almost as Nature might have left it. But we can soon alter all that. A thoroughly experienced French maid produces a really marvellous result in a very brief space of time. I remember recommending one to young Lady Lancing, and after three months her own husband did not know her.

JACK (*Aside.*)   And after six months nobody knew her.[1]

LADY BRACKNELL (*Glares at* JACK *for a few moments. Then bends, with a practised smile, to* CECILY.) Kindly turn round, sweet child. (CECILY *turns completely round.*) No, the side view is what I want. (CECILY *presents her profile.*) Yes, quite as I expected. There are distinct social possibilities in your profile. The two weak points in our age are its want of principle and its want of profile. The chin a little higher, dear. Style largely depends on the way the chin is worn. They are worn very high, just at present. Algernon!

ALGERNON   Yes, Aunt Augusta!

LADY BRACKNELL   There are distinct social possibilities in Miss Cardew's profile.

ALGERNON   Cecily is the sweetest, dearest, prettiest girl in the whole world. And I don't care twopence[2] about social possibilities.

LADY BRACKNELL   Never speak disrespectfully of Society, Algernon. Only people who can't get into it do that. (*To* CECILY.) Dear child, of course you know that Algernon has nothing but his debts to depend upon. But I do not approve of mercenary marriages. When I married Lord Bracknell I had no fortune of any kind. But I never dreamed for a moment of allowing that to stand in my way. Well, I suppose I must give my consent.

ALGERNON   Thank you, Aunt Augusta.

LADY BRACKNELL   Cecily, you may kiss me!

CECILY (*Kisses her.*)   Thank you, Lady Bracknell.

LADY BRACKNELL   You may also address me as Aunt Augusta for the future.

CECILY   Thank you, Aunt Augusta.

LADY BRACKNELL   The marriage, I think, had better take place quite soon.

---

1. Jack suggests that Lady Lancing's character so degenerated under the tutelage of her French maid that people in polite society refused to associate with her.
2. An insignificant sum.

ALGERNON Thank you, Aunt Augusta.

CECILY Thank you, Aunt Augusta.

LADY BRACKNELL To speak frankly, I am not in favour of long engagements. They give people the opportunity of finding out each other's character before marriage, which I think is never advisable.

JACK I beg your pardon for interrupting you, Lady Bracknell, but this engagement is quite out of the question. I am Miss Cardew's guardian, and she cannot marry without my consent until she comes of age. That consent I absolutely decline to give.

LADY BRACKNELL Upon what grounds may I ask? Algernon is an extremely, I may almost say an ostentatiously, eligible young man. He has nothing, but he looks everything. What more can one desire?

JACK It pains me very much to have to speak frankly to you, Lady Bracknell, about your nephew, but the fact is that I do not approve at all of his moral character. I suspect him of being untruthful. (ALGERNON *and* CECILY *look at him in indignant amazement.*)

LADY BRACKNELL Untruthful! My nephew Algernon? Impossible! He is an Oxonian.[3]

JACK I fear there can be no possible doubt about the matter. This afternoon during my temporary absence in London on an important question of romance, he obtained admission to my house by means of the false pretence of being my brother. Under an assumed name he drank, I've just been informed by my butler, an entire pint bottle of my Perrier-Jouet, Brut, '89;[4] a wine I was specially reserving for myself. Continuing his disgraceful deception, he succeeded in the course of the afternoon in alienating the affections of my only ward. He subsequently stayed to tea, and devoured every single muffin. And what makes his conduct all the more heartless is, that he was perfectly well aware from the first that I have no brother, that I never had a brother, and that I don't intend to have a brother, not even of any kind. I distinctly told him so myself yesterday afternoon.

LADY BRACKNELL Ahem! Mr. Worthing, after careful consideration I have decided entirely to overlook my nephew's conduct to you.

JACK That is very generous of you, Lady Bracknell. My own decision, however, is unalterable. I decline to give my consent.

LADY BRACKNELL (*To* CECILY.) Come here, sweet child. (CECILY *goes over.*) How old are you, dear?

---

3. The designation indicates that Algy has attended Oxford University.
4. A champagne produced by the firm of Perrier-Jouët of Epernay.

CECILY   Well, I am really only eighteen, but I always admit to twenty when I go to evening parties.

LADY BRACKNELL   You are perfectly right in making some slight alteration. Indeed, no woman should ever be quite accurate about her age. It looks so calculating.—(In a meditative manner.) Eighteen, but admitting to twenty at evening parties. Well, it will not be very long before you are of age and free from the restraints of tutelage. So I don't think your guardian's consent is, after all, a matter of any importance.

JACK   Pray excuse me, Lady Bracknell, for interrupting you again, but it is only fair to tell you that according to the terms of her grandfather's will Miss Cardew does not come legally of age till she is thirty-five.

LADY BRACKNELL   That does not seem to me to be a grave objection. Thirty-five is a very attractive age. London society is full of women of the very highest birth who have, of their own free choice, remained thirty-five for years. Lady Dumbleton is an instance in point. To my own knowledge she has been thirty-five ever since she arrived at the age of forty, which was many years ago now. I see no reason why our dear Cecily should not be even still more attractive at the age you mention than she is at present. There will be a large accumulation of property.

CECILY   Algy, could you wait for me till I was thirty-five?

ALGERNON   Of course I could, Cecily. You know I could.

CECILY   Yes, I felt it instinctively, but I couldn't wait all that time. I hate waiting even five minutes for anybody. It always makes me rather cross. I am not punctual myself, I know, but I do like punctuality in others, and waiting, even to be married, is quite out of the question.

ALGERNON   Then what is to be done, Cecily?

CECILY   I don't know, Mr. Moncrieff.

LADY BRACKNELL   My dear Mr. Worthing, as Miss Cardew states positively that she cannot wait till she is thirty-five—a remark which I am bound to say seems to me to show a somewhat impatient nature—I would beg of you to reconsider your decision.

JACK   But my dear Lady Bracknell, the matter is entirely in your own hands. The moment you consent to my marriage with Gwendolen, I will most gladly allow your nephew to form an alliance with my ward.

LADY BRACKNELL   (Rising and drawing herself up.)   You must be quite aware that what you propose is out of the question.

JACK   Then a passionate celibacy is all that any of us can look forward to.

LADY BRACKNELL   That is not the destiny I propose for Gwendolen. Algernon, of course, can choose for himself. (Pulls out her watch.)

Come, dear; (GWENDOLEN *rises*.) we have already missed five, if not six, trains. To miss any more might expose us to comment on the platform.

(*Enter Dr.* CHASUBLE.)

CHASUBLE   Everything is quite ready for the christenings.

LADY BRACKNELL   The christenings, sir! Is not that somewhat premature?

CHASUBLE (*Looking rather puzzled, and pointing to* JACK *and* ALGERNON.)   Both these gentlemen have expressed a desire for immediate baptism.

LADY BRACKNELL   At their age? The idea is grotesque and irreligious! Algernon, I forbid you to be baptized. I will not hear of such excesses. Lord Bracknell would be highly displeased if he learned that that was the way in which you wasted your time and money.

CHASUBLE   Am I to understand then that there are to be no christenings at all this afternoon?

JACK   I don't think that, as things are now, it would be of much practical value to either of us, Dr. Chasuble.

CHASUBLE   I am grieved to hear such sentiments from you, Mr. Worthing. They savour of the heretical views of the Anabaptists,[5] views that I have completely refuted in four of my unpublished sermons. However, as your present mood seems to be one peculiarly secular, I will return to the church at once. Indeed, I have just been informed by the pew-opener[6] that for the last hour and a half Miss Prism has been waiting for me in the vestry.

LADY BRACKNELL (*Starting.*)   Miss Prism! Did I hear you mention a Miss Prism?

CHASUBLE   Yes, Lady Bracknell. I am on my way to join her.

LADY BRACKNELL   Pray allow me to detain you for a moment. This matter may prove to be one of vital importance to Lord Bracknell and myself. Is this Miss Prism a female of repellent aspect, remotely connected with education?

CHASUBLE (*Somewhat indignantly.*)   She is the most cultivated of ladies, and the very picture of respectability.

LADY BRACKNELL   It is obviously the same person. May I ask what position she holds in your household?

CHASUBLE (*Severely.*)   I am a celibate, madam.

JACK (*Interposing.*)   Miss Prism, Lady Bracknell, has been for the last three years Miss Cardew's esteemed governess and valued companion.

---

5. A Protestant sect that emerged in the fifteenth century. Anabaptists believe that baptism is valid only when the candidate acknowledges Christ and asks to be baptized.
6. An usher in a church.

LADY BRACKNELL   In spite of what I hear of her, I must see her at once. Let her be sent for.

CHASUBLE (*Looking off.*)   She approaches; she is nigh.

    (*Enter* MISS PRISM *hurriedly.*)

MISS PRISM   I was told you expected me in the vestry, dear Canon. I have been waiting for you there for an hour and three-quarters. (*Catches sight of* LADY BRACKNELL *who has fixed her with a stony glare.* MISS PRISM *grows pale and quails. She looks anxiously round as if desirous to escape.*)

LADY BRACKNELL (*In a severe, judicial voice.*)   Prism! (MISS PRISM *bows her head in shame.*) Come here, Prism! (MISS PRISM *approaches in a humble manner.*) Prism! Where is that baby? (*General consternation. The* CANON *starts back in horror.* ALGERNON *and* JACK *pretend to be anxious to shield* CECILY *and* GWENDOLEN *from hearing the details of a terrible public scandal.*) Twenty-eight years ago, Prism, you left Lord Bracknell's house, Number 104, Upper Grosvenor Street, in charge of a perambulator[7] that contained a baby, of the male sex. You never returned. A few weeks later, through the elaborate investigations of the Metropolitan police,[8] the perambulator was discovered at midnight, standing by itself in a remote corner of Bayswater.[9] It contained the manuscript of a three-volume novel of more than usually revolting sentimentality. (MISS PRISM *starts in involuntary indignation.*) But the baby was not there! (*Everyone looks at* MISS PRISM.) Prism! Where is that baby? (*A pause.*)

MISS PRISM   Lady Bracknell, I admit with shame that I do not know. I only wish I did. The plain facts of the case are these. On the morning of the day you mention, a day that is for ever branded on my memory, I prepared as usual to take the baby out in its perambulator. I had also with me a somewhat old, but capacious handbag in which I had intended to place the manuscript of a work of fiction that I had written during my few unoccupied hours. In a moment of mental abstraction, for which I never can forgive myself, I deposited the manuscript in the basinette,[1] and placed the baby in the handbag.

---

7. A carriage with three or four wheels for one or two young children, pushed from behind.
8. The sector of Scotland Yard associated with the city of London.
9. From Charles Dickens, Jr.'s *Dickens's Dictionary of London*, 1879: "Bayswater lies to the west of Tyburnia, and possesses much the same characteristics. It has, however, rather a specialty for good shops at lower prices than are usual at this end of the town. There are some enormous houses about Lancaster-gate at proportionately enormous prices, but rents are here beginning to lower a little in comparison with those in Tyburnia, and a fairly comfortable house can be got for £150 to £200 a year. It is well, however, to bear in mind that this is merely a comparative drop in prices, and that good houses in this neighbourhood, as in most other parts of the West-end, are steadily rising in value from year to year."
1. This can be an oblong wickerwork basket, with a hood over one end, used as a cradle for babies, or, as in this instance, a form of child's perambulator of the same shape.

JACK (*Who has been listening attentively.*)   But where did you deposit the handbag?

MISS PRISM   Do not ask me, Mr. Worthing.

JACK   Miss Prism, this is a matter of no small importance to me. I insist on knowing where you deposited the handbag that contained that infant.

MISS PRISM   I left it in the cloakroom of one of the larger railway stations in London.

JACK   What railway station?

MISS PRISM (*Quite crushed.*)   Victoria. The Brighton line. (*Sinks into a chair.*)

JACK   I must retire to my room for a moment. Gwendolen, wait here for me.

GWENDOLEN   If you are not too long, I will wait here for you all my life.

(*Exit JACK in great excitement.*)

CHASUBLE   What do you think this means, Lady Bracknell?

LADY BRACKNELL   I dare not even suspect, Dr. Chasuble. I need hardly tell you that in families of high position strange coincidences are not supposed to occur. They are hardly considered the thing.

(*Noises heard overhead as if someone was throwing trunks about. Everyone looks up.*)

CECILY   Uncle Jack seems strangely agitated.

CHASUBLE   Your guardian has a very emotional nature.

LADY BRACKNELL   This noise is extremely unpleasant. It sounds as if he was having an argument. I dislike arguments of any kind. They are always vulgar, and often convincing.

CHASUBLE (*Looking up.*)   It has stopped now. (*The noise is redoubled.*)

LADY BRACKNELL   I wish he would arrive at some conclusion.

GWENDOLEN   This suspense is terrible. I hope it will last.

(*Enter JACK with a handbag of black leather in his hand.*)

JACK (*Rushing over to MISS PRISM.*)   Is this the handbag, Miss Prism? Examine it carefully before you speak. The happiness of more than one life depends on your answer.

MISS PRISM (*Calmly.*)   It seems to be mine. Yes, here is the injury it received through the upsetting of a Gower Street[2] omnibus[3] in younger and happier days. Here is the stain on the lining caused by the explosion of a temperance beverage,[4] an incident that

2. Located in the borough of Camden.
3. A public vehicle carrying passengers by road, running on a fixed route and typically requiring payment of a fare.
4. A nonalcoholic beverage as approved by a Temperance Society, that is, a society that believes in abstinence from alcohol.

occurred at Leamington.[5] And here, on the lock, are my initials. I had forgotten that in an extravagant mood I had had them placed there. The bag is undoubtedly mine. I am delighted to have it so unexpectedly restored to me. It has been a great inconvenience being without it all these years.

JACK (*In a pathetic voice.*)   Miss Prism, more is restored to you than this handbag. I was the baby you placed in it.

MISS PRISM (*Amazed.*)   You?

JACK (*Embracing her.*)   Yes—mother!

MISS PRISM (*Recoiling in indignant astonishment.*)   Mr. Worthing! I am unmarried.

JACK   Unmarried! I do not deny that is a serious blow. But after all, who has the right to cast a stone[6] against one who has suffered? Cannot repentance wipe out an act of folly? Why should there be one law for men, and another for women? Mother, I forgive you. (*Tries to embrace her again.*)

MISS PRISM (*Still more indignant.*)   Mr. Worthing, there is some error. (*Pointing to* LADY BRACKNELL.)   There is the lady who can tell you who you really are.

JACK (*After a pause.*)   Lady Bracknell, I hate to seem inquisitive, but would you kindly inform me who I am?

LADY BRACKNELL   I am afraid that the news I have to give you will not altogether please you. You are the son of my poor sister, Mrs. Moncrieff, and consequently Algernon's elder brother.

JACK   Algy's elder brother! Then I have a brother after all. I knew I had a brother! I always said I had a brother! Cecily,—how could you have ever doubted that I had a brother. (*Seizes hold of* ALGERNON.) Dr. Chasuble, my unfortunate brother. Miss Prism, my unfortunate brother. Gwendolen, my unfortunate brother. Algy, you young scoundrel, you will have to treat me with more respect in the future. You have never behaved to me like a brother in all your life.

ALGERNON   Well, not till today, old boy, I admit. I did my best, however, though I was out of practice. (*Shakes hands.*)

GWENDOLEN (*To* JACK.)   My own! But what own are you? What is your Christian name, now that you have become someone else?

JACK   Good heavens!—I had quite forgotten that point. Your decision on the subject of my name is irrevocable, I suppose?

GWENDOLEN   I never change, except in my affections.

CECILY   What a noble nature you have, Gwendolen!

---

5. Located in central England in Warwickshire, Leamington was famous in the nineteenth century for its health spa, the Royal Leamington Spa.
6. A variation on Christ's admonition, recorded in the Gospel of Saint John, to those planning to stone to death an adulterous woman: "Let him who is without sin cast the first stone" (8.7).

JACK   Then the question had better be cleared up at once. Aunt
   Augusta, a moment. At the time when Miss Prism left me in the
   handbag, had I been christened already?

LADY BRACKNELL   Every luxury that money could buy, including
   christening, had been lavished on you by your fond and doting
   parents.

JACK   Then I was christened! That is settled. Now, what name was
   I given? Let me know the worst.

LADY BRACKNELL   Being the eldest son you were naturally christened after your father.

JACK (*Irritably.*)   Yes, but what was my father's Christian name?

LADY BRACKNELL (*Meditatively.*)   I cannot at the present moment
   recall what the General's Christian name was. But I have no doubt
   he had one. He was eccentric, I admit. But only in later years. And
   that was the result of the Indian climate, and marriage, and indi-
   gestion, and other things of that kind.

JACK   Algy! Can't you recollect what our father's Christian name
   was?

ALGERNON   My dear boy, we were never even on speaking terms.
   He died before I was a year old.

JACK   His name would appear in the Army Lists[7] of the period, I
   suppose, Aunt Augusta?

LADY BRACKNELL   The General was essentially a man of peace,
   except in his domestic life. But I have no doubt his name would
   appear in any military directory.

JACK   The Army Lists of the last forty years are here. These delightful records should have been my constant study. (*Rushes to book-
   case and tears the books out.*) M. Generals—Mallam, Maxbohm,
   Magley, what ghastly names they have—Markby, Migsby, Mobbs,
   Moncrieff! Lieutenant 1840, Captain, Lieutenant-Colonel, Colonel, General 1869, Christian names, Ernest John. (*Puts book very
   quietly down and speaks quite calmly.*) I always told you, Gwendolen, my name was Ernest, didn't I? Well, it is Ernest after all. I
   mean it naturally is Ernest.

LADY BRACKNELL   Yes, I remember now that the General was called
   Ernest, I knew I had some particular reason for disliking the
   name.

GWENDOLEN   Ernest! My own Ernest! I felt from the first that you
   could have no other name!

JACK   Gwendolen, it is a terrible thing for a man to find out suddenly that all his life he has been speaking nothing but the truth.
   Can you forgive me?

---

7. A publication containing the official list of all the commissioned officers of the British
   Army.

GWENDOLEN   I can. For I feel that you are sure to change.

JACK   My own one!

CHASUBLE (*To* MISS PRISM.)   Laetitia! (*Embraces her.*)

MISS PRISM (*Enthusiastically.*)   Frederick! At last!

ALGERNON   Cecily! (*Embraces her.*) At last!

JACK   Gwendolen! (*Embraces her.*) At last!

LADY BRACKNELL   My nephew, you seem to be displaying signs of triviality.

JACK   On the contrary, Aunt Augusta, I've now realised for the first time in my life the vital Importance of Being Earnest.

TABLEAU

CURTAIN

Some Excised Portions of the Play

The Gribsby Episode from the Manuscript Draft[†]

The following sequence is transcribed from the manuscript draft of Act Two (New York Public Library), as reproduced in Sarah Augusta Dickson, *The Importance of Being Earnest—As Originally Written by Oscar Wilde* (New York, 2 volumes, 1956). The portion reprinted here corresponds to ff. 49–67 of the manuscript, and begins on p. 33 of the Second Act in the present edition.

MERRIMAN   Mr. Ernest's luggage, sir. I have unpacked it and put it in the room next to your own.

ALGY   I am afraid I can't stay more than a week, Jack, this time.

CECILY   A week? Will you really be able to stay over Monday?

ALGY   I think I can manage to stop over Monday, now.

CECILY   I am so glad.

MERRIMAN (*To* ERNEST.)   I beg your pardon, sir. There is an elderly gentleman wishes to see you. He has just co[m]e in a cab from the station. (*Holds card on salver.*)

ALGY   To see me?

MERRIMAN   Yes, sir.

ALGY (*Reads card.*)   Parker and Gribsby, Solicitors. I don't know anything about them. Who are they?

JACK (*Takes card.*)   Parker and Gribsby: I wonder who they can be[?] I expect Ernest they have come about some business for your friend Bunbury. Perhaps Bunbury wants to make his will, and wishes you to be executor. (*To* MERRIMAN.) Show Messrs. Parker and Gribsby in at once.

MERRIMAN   There is only one gentleman in the hall, sir.

JACK   Show either Mr. Parker or Mr. Gribsby in.

MERRIMAN   Yes, sir. (*Exit.*)

JACK   I hope, Ernest, that I may rely on the statement you made to me last week when I finally settled all your bills for you. I hope you have no outstanding accounts of any kind.

ALGY   I haven't any debts at all, dear Jack. Thanks to your generosity, I don't owe a penny, except for a few neckties I believe.

JACK   I am sincerely glad to hear it.

   (*Enter* MERRIMAN.)

MERRIMAN   Mr. Gribsby.

   (*Enter* GRIBSBY. *Exit* MERRIMAN.)

GRIBSBY (*To* CANON CHASUBLE.)   Mr. Ernest Worthing?

PRISM (*Indicating* ALGY.)   This is Mr. Ernest Worthing.

GRIBSBY   Mr. Ernest Worthing?

ALGY   Yes.

GRIBSBY   Of B.4, The Albany—?

ALGY   Yes, that is my address—

GRIBSBY   I am very sorry, Mr Worthing, but we have a writ of attachment for 20 days against you at the suit of the Savoy Hotel Co. Limited for £762. 14. 2.

ALGY   What perfect nonsense! I never dine at the Savoy at my own expense. I always dine at Willis's. It is far more expensive. I don't owe a penny to the Savoy.

GRIBSBY   The writ is marked as having been [served] on you personally at the Albany on May the 27th. Judgement was given in default against you on the fifth of June—Since then we have written to you no less than thirteen times, without receiving any reply. In the interest of our clients we had no option but to obtain an order for committal of your person. But, no doubt, Mr. Worthing, you will be able to settle the account, without any further unpleasantness. Seven and six should be added to the bill of costs for the expense of the cab which was hired for your convenience in case of any necessity of removal, but that I am sure is a contingency that is not likely to occur.

ALGY   Removal! What on earth do you mean by removal? I haven't the smallest intention of going away. I am staying here for a week. I am staying with my brother. (*Points to* JACK.)

GRIBSBY (*To* JACK.)   Pleased to meet you, sir.

ALGY (*To* GRIBSBY.)   If you imagine I am going up to town the moment I arrive you are extremely mistaken.

GRIBSBY   I am merely a Solicitor myself. I do not employ personal violence of any kind. The officer of the Court whose function it is to seize the person of the debtor is waiting in the fly outside. He has considerable experience in these matters. In the point of fact he has arrested in the course of his duties nearly all the younger sons of the aristocracy, as well as several eldest sons, besides of course a good many members of the House of Lords. His style and manner are considered extremely good. Indeed, he looks more like a betting man than a court official. That is why we always employ him. But no doubt you will prefer to pay the bill.

ALGY Pay it? How on earth am I going to do that? You don't suppose I have got any money? How perfectly silly you are. No gentleman ever has any money.

GRIBSBY My experience is that it is usually relations who pay.

JACK Kindly allow me to see this bill, Mr. Gribsby—(*Turns over
immense folio*)—£762. 14. 2 since last October. I am bound to say
I never saw such reckless extravagance in all my life. (*Hands it to
Dr.* CHASUBLE.)

PRISM £762 for eating! How grossly materialistic! There can be
little good in any young man who eats so much, and so often.

CHASUBLE It certainly is a painful proof of the disgraceful luxury
of the age. We are far away from Wordsworth's plain living and
high thinking.

JACK Now, Dr. Chasuble[,] do you consider that I am in any way
called upon to pay this monstrous account for my brother?

CHASUBLE I am bound to say that I do not think so. It would be
encouraging his profligacy.

PRISM As a man sows, so let him reap. The proposed incarceration
might be most salutary. It is to be regretted that it is only for 20 days.

JACK I am quite of your opinion.

ALGY My dear fellow, how ridiculous you are! You know perfectly
well that the bill is really yours.

JACK Mine[?]

ALGY Yes: you know it is.

CHASUBLE Mr. Worthing, if this is a jest, it is out of place.

PRISM It is gross effrontery. Just what I expected from him.

CECILY It is ingratitude. I didn't expect that.

JACK Never mind what he says. This is the way he always goes on.
(*To* ALGY.) You mean to say that you are not Ernest Worthing,
residing at B.4, The Albany[?] I wonder, as you are at it, that you
don't deny being my brother at all. Why don't you?

ALGY Oh! I am not going to do that, my dear fellow, it would be
absurd. Of course, I'm your brother. And that is why you should
pay this bill for me. What is the use of having a brother, if he
doesn't pay one's bills for one?

JACK Personally, if you ask me, I don't see *any* use in having a
brother. As for paying your bill I have not the smallest intention
of doing anything of the kind. Dr. Chasuble, the worthy Rector
of this parish, and Miss Prism[,] in whose admirable and sound
judgement I place great reliance[,] are both of opinion that incarceration would do you a great deal of good. And I think so too.

GRIBSBY (*Pulls out watch.*) I am sorry to disturb this pleasant family
meeting, but time presses. We have to be at Holloway not later
than four o'clock; otherwise it is difficult to obtain admission. The
rules are very strict.

ALGY   Holloway!

GRIBSBY   It is at Holloway that detentions of this character take place always.

ALGY   Well, I really am not going to be imprisoned in the suburbs for having dined in the West End. It is perfectly ridiculous.

GRIBSBY   The bill is for suppers, not for dinners.

ALGY   I really don't care. All I say is that I am not going to be imprisoned in the suburbs.

GRIBSBY   The surroundings I admit are middle class: but the gaol[1] itself is fashionable and well-aired: and there are ample opportunities of taking exercise at certain stated hours of the day. In the case of a medical certificate[,] which is always easy to obtain[,] the hours can be extended.

ALGY   Exercise! Good God! no gentleman ever takes exercise. You don't seem to understand what a gentleman is.

GRIBSBY   I have met so many of them, sir, that I am afraid I don't. There are the most curious varieties of them. The result of cultivation, no doubt. Will you kindly come now, sir, if it will not be inconvenient to you.

ALGY (*Appealingly.*)   Jack!

PRISM   Pray be firm, Mr. Worthing.

CHASUBLE   This is an occasion on which any weakness would be out of place. It would be a form of self-deception.

JACK   I am quite firm: and I don't know what weakness or deception of any kind is.

CECILY   Uncle Jack! I think you have a little money of mine haven't you? Let me pay this bill. I wouldn't like your own brother to be in prison.

JACK   Oh! you can't pay it, Cecily, that is nonsense.

CECILY   Then you will, won't you? I think you would be sorry if you thought your own brother was shut up. Of course, I am quite disappointed with him.

JACK   You won't speak to him again, Cecily, will you?

CECILY   Certainly not. Unless, of course[,] he speaks to me first[;] it would be very rude not to answer him.

JACK   Well, I'll take care he doesn't speak to you. I'll take care he doesn't speak to any body in this house. The man should be cut. Mr. Gribsby—

GRIBSBY   Yes, sir.

JACK   I'll pay this bill for my brother. It is the last bill I shall ever pay for him too. How much is it?

GRIBSBY   £762. 14. 2. May I ask your full name, sir?

---

1. English variant for "jail."

JACK   Mr. John Worthing, J.P., the Manor House, Woolton. Does that satisfy you?

GRIBSBY   Oh! certainly, sir, certainly. It was a mere formality. (*To* MISS PRISM.) Handsome place. Ah! the cab will be 5/9 extra: hired for the convenience of the client.

JACK   All right.

PRISM   I must say that I think such generosity quite foolish. Especially paying the cab.

CHASUBLE (*With a wave of the hand.*)   The heart has its wisdom as well as the head, Miss Prism.

JACK   Payable to Gribsby and Parker I suppose?

GRIBSBY   Yes, sir. Kindly don't cross the cheque. Thank you.

JACK   You are Gribsby aren't you? What is Parker like?

GRIBSBY   I am both, sir. Gribsby when I am on unpleasant business, Parker on occasions of a less severe kind.

JACK   The next time I see you I hope you will be Parker.

GRIBSBY   I hope so, sir. (*To Dr.* CHASUBLE.) Good day. (*Dr.* CHASUBLE *bows coldly.*) Good day. (MISS PRISM *bows coldly.*) Hope I shall have the pleasure of meeting you again. (*To* ALGY.)

ALGY   I sincerely hope not. What ideas you have of the sort of society a gentleman wants to mix in. No gentleman ever wants to know a Solicitor, who wants to imprison one in the suburbs.

GRIBSBY   Quite so, quite so.

ALGY   By the way, Gribsby. Gribsby, you are not to go back to the station in that cab. That is my cab. It was taken for my convenience. You and the gentleman who looks like the betting man have got to walk to the station, and a very good thing too. Solicitors don't walk nearly enough. They bolt. But they don't walk. I don't know any solicitor who takes sufficient exercise. As a rule they sit in stuffy offices all day long neglecting their business.

JACK   You can take the cab, Mr Gribsby.

GRIBSBY   Thank you, sir. (*Exit.*)

The Dictation Episode (Act Two) in the Licensing Copy

The following appears in the licensing copy (LC) after Cecily's speech instructing Algernon not to cough (p. 35 of the present edition). It is a slightly revised version of a passage in the MS draft and the Arents III typescript.

ALGERNON (*Speaking very rapidly.*)   Miss Cardew, ever since half past two this afternoon, when I first looked upon your wonderful and incomparable beauty, I have not merely been your abject slave and servant, but, soaring upon the pinions of a possibly monstrous ambition, I have dared to love you wildly, passionately, devotedly, hopelessly.

CECILY (*Laying down her pen.*)   Oh! Please say that all over again. You speak far too fast and too indistinctly. Kindly say it all over again.

ALGERNON   Ever since it was half past two this afternoon, when I first looked upon your wonderful and incomparable beauty—

CECILY   Yes, I have got that all right.

ALGERNON (*Stammering.*)   I—I—(CECILY *lays down her pen and looks reproachfully at him.*)
(*Desperately.*) I have not merely been your abject slave and servant, but, soaring on the pinions of a possibly monstrous ambition, I have dared to love you wildly, passionately, devotedly, hopelessly. (*Takes out his watch and looks at it.*)

CECILY (*After writing for some time looks up.*)   I have not taken down "hopelessly." It doesn't seem to make much sense, does it? (*A slight pause.*)

ALGERNON (*Starting back.*)   Cecily!

CECILY   Is that the beginning of an entirely new paragraph? Or should it be followed by a note of admiration?

ALGERNON (*Rapidly and romantically.*)   It is the beginning of an entirely new existence for me, and it shall be followed by such notes of admiration that my whole life shall be a subtle and sustained symphony of Love, Praise and Adoration combined.

CECILY   Oh, I don't think *that* makes any sense at all. The fact is that men should never dictate to women. They never know *how* to do it, and when they *do* do it, they always say something particularly foolish.

ALGERNON   I don't care whether what I say is foolish or not. All that I know is that I love you, Cecily! I love you! I can't live without you, Cecily! You know I love you. Will you marry me? Will you be my wife? (*Rushes over to her and puts his hand on hers.*)
     (*Enter* MERRIMAN.)

MERRIMAN   The dog-cart is waiting, sir.

The Conclusion of Act Two in the Licensing Copy

This extract begins on p. 46 of the present edition.

JACK   Yes, but you said yourself it was not hereditary, or anything of the kind.

ALGERNON   It usen't to be, I know—but I daresay it *is* now. Science is always making wonderful improvements in things.

JACK   May I ask, Algy, what on earth do you propose to do?

ALGERNON   Nothing. That is what I have been trying to do for the last ten minutes, and you have kept on doing everything in your power to distract my attention from my work.

JACK   Well, *I* shall go into the house and see Gwendolen. I feel quite sure she expects me.

ALGERNON   I know from her extremely cold manner that Cecily expects me, so *I* certainly shan't go into the house. When a man does exactly what a woman expects him to do, she doesn't think much of him. One should always do what a woman doesn't expect, just as one should always say what she doesn't understand. The result is invariably perfect sympathy on both sides.

JACK   Oh, that is nonsense. You are always talking nonsense.

ALGERNON   It is much cleverer to talk nonsense than to listen to it, my dear fellow, and a much rarer thing too, in spite of all the public may say.

JACK   I don't listen to you. I can't listen to you.

ALGERNON   Oh, that is merely false modesty. You know perfectly well you could listen to me if you tried. You always underrate yourself, an absurd thing to do nowadays when there are such a lot of conceited people about. Jack, you are eating the muffins again! I wish you wouldn't. There are only two left. (*Removes plate.*) I *told* you I was particularly fond of muffins.

JACK   But I hate tea-cake.

ALGERNON   Why on earth do you allow tea-cake to be served up for your guests, then? What ideas you have of hospitality!

JACK (*Irritably.*) Oh! that is not the point. We are not discussing tea-cake. (*Crosses.*) Algy! you are perfectly maddening. You can never stick to the point in any conversation.

ALGERNON (*Slowly.*)   No: it always hurts me.

JACK   Good heavens! What affectation! I *loathe* affectation!

ALGERNON   Well, my dear fellow, if you don't like affectation I really don't see what you *can* like. Besides, it isn't affectation. The point always *does* hurt me and I hate physical pain of any kind.

JACK (*Glares at* ALGERNON; *walks up and down stage. Finally comes up to table.*) Algy! I have already told you to go. I don't want you here. *Why don't* you go?

ALGERNON   I haven't quite finished my tea yet. (*Takes last muffin.*) (JACK *groans and sinks down into a chair and buries his face in his hands.*)

ACT-DROP

BACKGROUNDS

KARL BECKSON

London in the 1890s[†]

The ends of centuries have traditionally fascinated and terrified the imagination, for the sense of an ending and an irreversible but inexorable progression to the unknown (or, for Christians, the Last Judgment) have often conjured images of final decay and lingering death. In his diary for 1889, the London publisher Grant Richards recorded that the Reverend Michael Paget Baxter, the author of books of prophecy and editor of the *Christian Herald,* "holds forth that the world comes to an end in 1901 and that in 1896 144,000 devout Christians will be taken up to Heaven." No one can be certain whether such a number of the devout were in fact introduced to Paradise in 1896, but the Reverend Mr. Baxter was not entirely wrong in his other prediction, for Queen Victoria's world did come to an end in 1901, when she expired.

While the demise of a century may encourage such apocalyptic visions, ideological collapses, and exhausted psyches, the human imagination also has the capacity to create images of renewal (based on the perception of nature's rebirth). At the end of the nineteenth century, many intellectuals, having abandoned their religious faith but inspired by utopian dreams, envisioned a new age in the next century, convinced that the past—with its failures and disappointments—was a burden to be abandoned. In 1882, the positivist philosopher and advocate for social and political reform Frederic Harrison wrote: "We *are* on the threshold of a great time, even if our time is not great itself. In science, in religion, in social organisation, we all know what great things are in the air. . . . It is *not* the age of money-bags and cant, soot, hubbub, and ugliness. It is the age of great expectation and unwearied striving after better things." In his introduction to *The New Spirit* (1890), Havelock Ellis also looked forward to a future purged of previous errors: "Certainly old things are passing away; not the old ideals only, but even the regret they leave behind is dead, and we are shaping instinctively our new ideals. . . . The old cycles are for ever renewed, and it is no paradox that he who would advance can never cling too close to the past."

For many, such optimism was fueled by scientific discovery and technological innovation. Hundreds of new inventions, such as faster railroad locomotives, ocean-going steamships, photography, and electric lighting, as well as the rapid growth of such scientific disciplines as physics, astronomy, and chemistry, transformed the nineteenth-century view of the world so dramatically that, by the fin de siècle, Victorians referred to their age as "modern." In 1897, J. J. Thompson, of Cambridge University, discovered the electron (the discovery of the atom's nucleus was more than a decade away); by 1900, Gregor Mendel's work in genetics had been rediscovered, and, in the same year, Max Planck theorized that "quanta of energy were involved when light was being absorbed or emitted." In 1905, Einstein's "special theory of relativity" superseded Newton's laws of motion and gravitation as well as James Maxwell's electromagnetic theory of light, thereby making possible new concepts of time, space, and mass. In effect, Einstein established the principle that energy and mass were interconvertible, as indicated in the famous equation $E = mc^2$, the theoretical basis for later nuclear fission.

In *The Idea of Progress* (1920), J. B. Bury observed that, in the nineteenth century, "the achievements of physical science did more than anything else to convert the imaginations of men to the general doctrine of progress." At the same time, however, many expressed pessimism and doubt, particularly after the publication of Darwin's *Origin of Species* (1859), which followed a series of scientific discoveries and evolutionary theories that undermined orthodox belief in creationism, unsettled religious faith, and ultimately resulted in emotional crises for many Christians. Earlier in the century, the frightening specter of entropy arose from the second law of thermodynamics, which contends that heat from the sun's radiation becomes progressively unusable as it becomes dispersed in the universe (so-called "heat death"). In the 1850s, Sir William Thompson (Lord Kelvin), who was instrumental in formulating the principle, concluded that "the earth must have been, and within a finite period to come, the earth must again be, unfit for the habitation of man as at present constituted."

In his first science fiction novel, *The Time Machine* (1895), H. G. Wells depicts such a bleak future when the Time Traveller travels into the "fourth dimension" and reaches the year 802,701. The humans then living on the earth are the degenerate Eloi, whose gender is indeterminate. Indulging in such trivial pursuits as singing, dancing, and adorning themselves with flowers in their earthly paradise, they exist in a condition of apparent uselessness. However, the "ape-like" Morlocks live in the subterranean depths with the remnants of human technology and feed on the Eloi. Journeying further into the future, the traveler discovers no sign of humanity; instead, the earth is inhabited by giant crabs. Thirty million years later, he finds no traces of any significant life forms; he leaves when darkness

descends over the earth after an eclipse of the sun. The second law
of thermodynamics has achieved its ultimate triumph.[1]

A further cause of pessimism in the nineteenth century was the
social and psychological effect of the Industrial Revolution, which
enslaved millions of workers in gloomy "sweating" industries and
created cities of "dreadful night," such as Manchester, Sheffield, and
Birmingham. Moreover, the so-called "Great Depression" from the
early 1870s to the mid-1890s, resulting from poor harvests, declining arable land, and lower-priced imports, accelerated the migration
of almost three million farm workers to the crowded cities or to colonies abroad.[2] London's East End contained some of the worst
slums in England, where disease and despair flourished. Discour-
aged reformers sought desperate remedies. In his influential survey
In Darkest England and the Way Out (1890), William Booth, founder
and first general of the Salvation Army, rose to exalted rhetoric while
describing the degrading living conditions of the London poor: "Talk
about Dante's Hell, and all the horrors and cruelties of the torture-
chamber of the lost! The man who walks with open eyes and with
bleeding heart through the shambles of our civilisation needs no
such fantastic images of the poet to teach him horror." Such misery
also distressed the socialist and poet William Morris, who yearned
for the end of a moribund, corrupt society so that a genuine "barba-
rism" would return to the world to destroy its false "progress":

> I have [no] more faith than a grain of mustard seed in the future
> history of "civilization," which I *know* now is doomed to destruc-
> tion, and probably before very long: what a joy it is to think of!
> and how often it consoles me to think of barbarism once more
> flooding the world, and real feelings and passions, however
> rudimentary, taking the place of our wretched hypocrisies. . . .

During the final decades of the century, a widespread perception
that Britain and the empire were in a state of decline found expression in the periodicals, which published articles in profusion with

1. In 1904 at Cambridge University, Ernest Rutherford discovered, in such material as
   radium, the lasting power of radioactivity, which creates heat within the earth's rocks.
   He wrote that "the radioactive elements, which in their disintegration liberate enormous amounts of energy, thus increase the possible limit of the duration of life on this
   planet. . . ." Rutherford's finding challenged the second law of thermodynamics (quo-
   tation from Timothy Ferris, *Coming of Age in the Milky Way* [New York, 1988], 249).
2. The economist Alfred Marshall, testifying before the Precious Metals Commission in
   1887, asserted that the industrial depression had a greater impact on businessmen
   than on workers. The result was "a depression of prices, a depression of interest, and a
   depression of profits" without "any considerable depression in any other respect." Ger-
   trude Himmelfarb has recently written that, "among regularly employed workers, there
   were depressed seasons and years when unemployment rose and wages fell. . . . But
   these conditions, however grievous, did not add up, for the working classes as a whole,
   to a 'Great Depression'" (*Poverty and Compassion: The Moral Imagination of the Late
   Victorians* [New York, 1991], 70–71).

titles announcing the decline or decay of such phenomena as cricket, genius, war, classical quotations, romance, marriage, faith, bookselling, and even canine fidelity. There were also articles on the presumed degeneracy of the race and the startling increase in insanity and "suicidal mania." Writers pointed to the decline and fall of the Roman Empire as the analogy of the anticipated fate of the British Empire, though a writer in *Nineteenth Century* (August 1894) regarded such a view as a "dismal argument," for though the Romans were a "great nation" and "far ahead of their time," they were still "barbarians" compared to the modern British. The sensation of 1895, which appeared just before the even more sensational trials of Oscar Wilde, was the English translation of Max Nordau's *Degeneration*, which attacked the unorthodox works of such figures as Ibsen, Wagner, Wilde, Nietzsche, and Tolstoy as evidence of cultural decadence. Bernard Shaw argued that these artists were not suffering from degeneration but were indicative of the spirit of regeneration: "At every new wave of energy in art the same alarm has been raised, and . . . these alarms always had their public, like prophecies of the end of the world. . . ."

While many were deploring cultural degeneration and decay, others were hailing the new, which, like Ellis's New Spirit, was an indication of presumed liberation from the deadening hand of the past. As soon as late Victorian cultural developments appeared, they were habitually affixed with the "new" designation to elevate them to fashionable status and to ward off the pervasive pessimism of the age. Such were the New Drama, New Woman, New Journalism, New Imperialism, New Criticism, New Hedonism, and New Paganism, which appeared in William Sharp's one and only issue of the *Pagan Review* (August 1892), written under his various pseudonyms. As the critic H. D. Traill asserted in *The New Fiction and Other Essays* (1897): "Not to be 'new' is, in these days, to be nothing. . . ."

Cultural trends in the final decades of the century were thus moving in two simultaneously antithetical directions: declining Victorianism (the synthesis of moral, religious, artistic, political, and social thought that had produced the wealthiest and most powerful empire on earth) and rising Modernism (with its challenges by writers and artists to the cultural foundations of Philistine society, which habitually condemned daring innovations in the arts as "immoral" or "degenerate"). Such manifestations of Modernism were frequently described by both sympathetic and hostile critics as characteristic aspects of the fin de siècle. The term, adopted in Britain around 1890 to indicate the end of the century, had such associated meanings as "modern," "advanced," and "decadent." The French themselves had been using the term with increasing looseness: It served, for example, to describe both a shoemaker praised "for being a traditional cobbler rather than fin de siècle" and a blackmailer who lived off his wife's prostitution—"a fin de siècle husband." A verse at the time indicated its imprecision:

> Fin de siècle! Everywhere
> . . . It stands for all that you might care
> To name . . .

Some British writers employed it for its apocalyptic foreboding, as "advanced" writers delighted in uttering oracular premonitions while inspired by an exhausted century. In *The Picture of Dorian Gray* (1890/1891), Oscar Wilde may have been one of the first in England to make use of such implications. When a dinner guest ponders the current fashion that "all the married men live like bachelors, and all the bachelors like married men," the response is characteristic:

> *"Fin de siècle,"* murmured Lord Henry.
> *"Fin du globe,"* answered his hostess.
> "I wish it were *fin du globe*," said Dorian with a sigh. "Life is such a great disappointment."

In a letter to a Tory journalist in 1894, Wilde identified the fin de siècle with artistic achievement as opposed to cultural decadence: "All that is known by that term I particularly admire and love. It is the fine flower of our civilisation: the only thing that keeps the world from the commonplace, the coarse, the barbarous."

In John Davidson's comic novel, *A Full and True Account of the Wonderful Mission of Earl Lavender* (1895), a poem precedes the narrative involving Lavender's "mission" to spread the gospel of the "survival of the fittest" in a plot including sexual perversity (a Beardsley drawing for the frontispiece depicts a woman flagellating a figure of indeterminate gender):

> Though our thoughts turn ever Doomwards,
> Though our sun is well-night set,
> Though our Century lotters tombwards,
> We may laugh a little yet.

Later in the novel, a matronly Victorian woman evokes, in fractured French, her equivalent of fin de siècle to explain the chaos of modern life: "It's *fang-de-seeaycle* that does it, my dear, and education, and reading French."

The French were indeed the object of suspicion by the British, who regarded their neighbors across the Channel as potential invaders, either by sea or through a proposed tunnel connecting the two. Far worse to those who objected to subversive influences, however, was the invasion of French literature and critical attitudes, especially

Zola's Naturalistic novels, often called "decadent" by British critics,
as well as the tradition of an amoral *l'art pour l'art* and fin-de-siècle
Decadence, which impelled Tennyson to fulminate in verse against
the "troughs of Zolaism" and against those Aesthetes who had
objected to the moral teaching in the *Idylls of the King* (1869):

> Art for Art's sake! Hail, truest Lord of Hell!
> Hail Genius, Master of the Moral Will!
> "The filthiest all of paintings painted well
> Is mightier than the purest painted ill!"

To Tennyson, the doctrine of "art for art's sake" disregarded the
"ideal of an integrated culture." The poet and critic Richard Le Gallienne (father of the actress, Eva) also judged the invasion of French
Decadence as particularly grave. In the prefatory poem to his *English
Poems* (1892), he echoed the title of Tennyson's early poem "The Palace of Art" (1833) in expressing his own anxiety over the fin-de-
siècle separation of moral from aesthetic elements in art:

> Art was a palace once, things great and fair,
> And strong and holy, found a temple there:
> Now 'tis a lazar-house of leprous men.
> O shall we hear an English song again!

Such anxieties as Tennyson's and Le Gallienne's were widespread
at the end of the century, an indication that the earlier cultural synthesis of Victorianism was unraveling as such common beliefs and
assumptions concerning social relationships, the nature of reality,
and the nature of art were subjected to attack by such groups as the
New Women, the New Dramatists, the New Hedonists, the New
Naturalists, as well as the Aesthetes and Decadents.

For many decades, the 1890s have been casually disposed of as the
Yellow Nineties, suggestive of decay, principally because of the
famous periodical, the *Yellow Book* (1894–1897), and because of a
relatively small but articulate band of writers, Wilde included, who
proclaimed "art for art's sake." The decade has also been called the
"Decadent Nineties" or the "Naughty Nineties." But whatever those
terms may mean, the fin de siècle embraced such a wide variety of
literary and artistic modes of expression, including Impressionism,
Aestheticism, Decadence, Naturalism, and Symbolism, that reduc-
ing the late nineteenth century to one of them and branding it
"decadent" merely because it was anti-Establishment is to inflict
simplicity on complexity. The decade of the nineties was an extraordinary period of artistic activity and energy, many of the greatest
figures of the twentieth century, such as Shaw, Yeats, Conrad,
and Wells, in their apprenticeship years while older figures, such as

Whistler, Wilde, Morris, and Hardy had completed—or were in the process of completing—their major work.

Many moved freely from one mode of expression or group to another as inclination dictated. Wilde wrote an essay still widely read, "The Soul of Man under Socialism" (1891/1895), which fused Aestheticism and anarchist socialism in an attempt to locate beauty and freedom for the artist within a radically new economic and political system. Yeats's aesthetically conceived Celtic poems, such as "A Man Who Dreamed of Fairyland" (the title changed slightly in subsequent printings), were published in W. E. Henley's *National Observer,* a periodical devoted to activist, anti-Decadent causes. Henley nevertheless regarded Yeats the dreamer as one of his "young men." In the late 1880s, Yeats was also a member of Morris's circle at the Socialist League, a short-lived association that ended when the younger man discovered that Morris's literary "dream world . . . knew nothing of intellectual suffering." Shaw contributed to the first number of the *Savoy* (January 1896), the Symbolist/Decadent periodical that contained much of Beardsley's most daring literary and artistic work, an odd setting for a socialist who publicly expressed scorn for "art for art's sake."

This cultural history focuses on the legendary decade of the 1890s, more a symbol than a mere ten years of the calendar, for an entire age was simultaneously coming to an end as another was in the process of formation. London, also this history's principal focus, is here treated as the heart of the empire as well as the artistic and cultural heart of Britain. Between 1851 and 1901, the area of present-day Greater London had grown from 2.7 million people to 6.6 million, a progressive urbanization that concentrated artistic talent and cultural ferment more densely than in any other British city. As Malcolm Bradbury has shown, London became one of the major "cities of Modernism," closely associated in this international movement with Paris, Berlin, and Vienna. Writers and artists inevitably gravitated to London—as did Yeats, Wilde, and Shaw from Ireland and Henry James, Whistler, and Sargent from America, as well as countless others from provincial British cities. A *Yellow Book* contributor recalled that each was hoping that he might ride "on the crest of the wave that was sweeping away the Victorian tradition" with its undue restrictions in artistic expression based on an outdated conception of the world as one of stable, absolute values. As Modernism developed, the arts sought new forms of personal expression, the new aesthetic values replacing the formerly prescribed moral values of Victorian art.

Pater might have described London as "the focus where the greatest number of vital forces unite[d] in their purest energy." Down from Oxford, the young but "perpetually old" Max Beerbohm

luxuriated in such energy despite his dandiacal pose of feigned
indifference: "Around me seethed swirls, eddies, torrents, violent
cross-currents of human activity. What uproar! Surely I could have
no part in modern life." Henry James called London "the biggest
aggregation of human life—the most complete compendium of the
world." As a constant subject for verse in the nineties, the city
assumed the aura of Romantic artifice with its "iron lilies of the
Strand" in Richard Le Gallienne's "A Ballad of London": "Ah, London! London! Our delight, / Great flower that opens but at night. . . ."
The nights of London, when the city became a ghostly apparition in
the faint evening light as imagination transformed warehouses into
palaces, inspired Whistler's "nocturnes." And Arthur Symons envisioned a magical London in which two lovers, dancer and poet, are
entwined in each other's dreams, oblivious to the industrialism, poverty, and despair of the city:

> You the dancer and I the dreamer,
> Children together,
> Wandering lost in the night of London,
> In the miraculous April weather.

*   *   *

SHARON MARCUS

Victorian Theatrics: Response[†]

Victorian Theater: Three Axioms

If you know little about Victorian theater, and care still less, you
are in good company. Consider this statement, made in 1832:

> Acting had always appeared to me to be the very lowest of the
> arts. . . . It originates nothing: it lacks, therefore, the grand
> faculty which all other arts possess—creation. An actor is at
> best but the filler up of the outline designated by another. . . . A
> fine piece of acting is at best, in my opinion, a fine translation.
>   Art must be to a certain degree enduring. . . . To me [acting]
> seems no art, but merely a highly interesting and exciting
> amusement. (125)

† From *Victorian Studies* 54.2, Special Issue: Papers and Responses from the Ninth
Annual Conference of the North American Victorian Studies Association (Spring
2012): 438–50. Copyright © 2012, Indiana University Press. Reprinted with permission
of Indiana University Press. Notes are by the author.

The author of this pronouncement was neither a lofty sage nor an antitheatrical crusader, but a young actress, Fanny Kemble, whose family was the closest England had to thespian aristocracy. To be sure, the very reasons Kemble gave for denying acting the status of art would have led her to embrace dramatists capable of creating original, enduring works. Yet for most of the century Victorian plays and playwrights fared no better, precisely because they were considered subordinate to players. In 1866, for example, drama critic Henry Morley diagnosed the contemporary drama as "an ailing limb of the great body of our Literature" (8) and traced the cause of the disease to the public taste for plays that were "all leg and no brains" (6). The popularity of actors cutting capers and actresses flashing thighs resulted in "the too frequent perversion of the stage into an agent for the ruin of the written drama" (6–7).

With enemies like these in its past, it is not surprising that Victorian theater has so few friends in the present. The belief that drama is only aesthetically worthy if it approximates literature, and can become literary only by leaving theater's corporeality, popularity, and ephemerality behind, has few explicit adherents today. Nonetheless, an opposition between theatricality and dramatic literature shaped modernism (Puchner), modern literature departments (Jackson, *Professing*), and even performance studies programs (Carlson 196).[1] A persistent cleavage between art and entertainment helps to explain why theater has such a negligible place in Victorian literary studies today, despite (or even because of) theater's popularity for much of the nineteenth century. Like Kemble and Morley, most Victorianists prefer studying durable works by well-known authors to reconstructing the ephemeral work of acting, and have little interest in theater that elevated performers over authors (Stephens xiii) and does not lend itself to being read as literature. The work most often pressed into service as the representative Victorian play, Oscar Wilde's *The Importance of Being Earnest* (1895), is Victorian only on a technicality, produced six years before the monarch's death but well after the birth of the fin-de-siècle. The major Victorian playwrights—Thomas Holcroft, Douglas Jerrold, Dion Boucicault, Edward Bulwer-Lytton, Tom Taylor, Thomas Robertson, Charles Reade, W. S. Gilbert, Sydney Grundy, Arthur Jones, and Arthur Pinero—are mostly absent from histories of European drama, surveys of Victorian literature, and English department syllabi and orals lists.[2]

---

1. Parenthetical references throughout this essay for the most part serve bibliographic rather than citational purposes.
2. For a survey of Victorian literature that pays rare attention to drama, see Adams.

It is not exactly my contention here that we do the authors and texts of Victorian plays an injustice by neglecting them. Victorian playwrights rarely fancied themselves originators and creators of lasting works of art, and labored under conditions that vitiated the author function. Few playwrights developed individual styles; instead, most wrote to order for specific theaters and performers. Victorian actors often improvised dialogue, invented their own stage business, and claimed generic roles (butler, soubrette, fop) as "lines" whose distinctive points and costumes defined plays even more than the words penned by authors (Booth; Tolles; Wojcik 228–30). Indeed, until the 1890s, British playwrights had such weak property rights in their work and were so poorly paid that few took the time to write original works from scratch (Stephens; Tolles). For much of the nineteenth century, Kemble's point that acting was at best a fine translation applied even more literally to plays, which were often poor translations that adapted German and French hits to English tastes (Rowell; Marcus). As Henry James put it, with less hyperbole than one might think, "Nine-tenths of the plays performed upon [British soil] are French originals, subjected to the mysterious process of 'adaptation'; marred as French pieces and certainly not mended as English" (93; see also Tristan 175–76).

For these reasons, I come neither to praise Victorian plays nor to disinter them. This is not a manifesto for reading Victorian drama as literature; instead, it is a manifest, a list of reasons to take an interest in Victorian theater as performance, and of ways to study it that go beyond reading texts. Treated as literary texts, Victorian plays will neither instruct nor delight the English department professors and students who constitute the majority of those attending NAVSA and reading *Victorian Studies*. Reading plays is literally the last thing we should do to understand expressive cultural forms that achieved more on the stage than on the page (Booth, "Social" 8; Davies 269) in an era when, as actor-manager Henry Irving put it, theater was bigger than the playwright: "plays are made for the theatre and not the theatre for plays" (qtd. in Vardac 89). Weak authors made for bad literature but good theater, and some of the best methods for studying Victorian performance culture accordingly downplay the dramatic text.

Why, then, should literary critics study Victorian theater at all? The most familiar reason is that theatricality and performativity were central to Victorian literature. For the past several decades, scholars housed mostly in English departments have highlighted the importance of closet drama (Burroughs), improvisation (Esterhammer), and dramatic monologue to nineteenth-century poets, and analyzed how nineteenth-century novelists engaged with theatricality, performativity, melodrama, and spectacle (P. Brooks;

Marshall; Litvak; Auerbach; Hadley; Samuels; Allen). Simultaneously, scholars housed mostly in departments of drama, theater, and performance studies have expanded our understanding of expressive culture in nineteenth-century England (Booth; Altick; Meisel; Bratton; J. Davis; J. Davis and Emeljanow; T. Davis; Bailey; Newey; Williams; D. Brooks; Ziter).[3] A handful of scholars have done work that integrates both approaches (Hadley; Vlock; Voskuil; Kurnick), usually focusing on the novel as a form ineluctably entangled with theater. Most recently, for example, David Kurnick has argued that the era's greatest novelists longed for the theater and that rumors of the Victorian novel's interiority have been greatly exaggerated; even eminently literary techniques such as free indirect discourse embody a desire to incorporate theater's acoustic, collective, public state.

One of the many conceptual breakthroughs of the 2011 NAVSA papers I have chosen is that each illustrates how theater studies can generate fresh insights for literary criticism, social history, and cultural studies once we liberate it from novelistic frameworks that emphasize domesticity, individuality, *Bildung*, interiority, and narration. Kurnick radically and brilliantly suggests that we are already experiencing Victorian theater when we read Victorian novels, and that novels often tapped theater's potential energies more effectively than theater itself did. To make this claim, however, he must accept the standard historical account of theater's increasing domestication in the decades after 1840. The selected papers challenge the common view that over time, Victorian theater separated actors from audiences and private homes from public stages. Like Kurnick, Daniel Pollack-Pelzner suggests that theater defined the novel as much as the novel defined theater. Unlike Kurnick, Pollack-Pelzner makes theater the starting point for his argument, showing that stage burlesques of Hamlet's soliloquy were a site where the self-enclosed one could be invaded by the raucous many. A secure divide between adult and child is central to narratives of theater and private life taking an inward turn, but Marah Gubar shows that children on both sides of the curtain were as avid as adults to produce and consume actors as spectacles. Michael Meeuwis attests to the Victorian awareness and acceptance of theatrical emulation as crucial to social existence, alerting us to the many circuits connecting professional and amateur performances, public and private spaces.

All three papers also attest to what is perhaps the most compelling reason to study Victorian theater: like television a century later, it was a lingua franca (T. Davis 7). Even Matthew Arnold conceded,

---

3. For an astute historical analysis of why these inquiries have been pursued on different institutional tracks, see Jackson, *Professing*.

"The theatre is irresistible" (243). Almost everyone in London, from Queen Victoria to the London workers documented by Henry May-hew, attended theatrical performances, some as frequently as three times a week (Booth; Schoch), and theater thrived in the provinces and colonies as well as in the metropole. As Gubar shows, theater appealed to children and adults; as Pollack-Pelzner proves, it vaulted divides between high and low culture; as Meeuwis demonstrates, it linked the middle and upper classes; indeed, the importance of the-atricals in U.S. settlements like Hull House suggests that workers engaged in theatrical emulation as well (Jackson, *Lines*). The num-ber, profits, and types of theaters waxed and waned in the first half of the century, then steadily increased in the second, but across the Victorian period, in London alone, there were anywhere from a dozen to a hundred solvent venues, many seating up to three thou-sand people. In 1866, one manager estimated that 40,000 people attended London theaters and places of entertainment each night (Booth, "Social" 20); in 1865, London theaters had a yearly capacity of almost twelve million (T. Davis, "Sociable" 19). Given theater's popularity, our knowledge of canonical literature is incomplete if we ignore how performance boosted the domestic and global circulation of works by Dickens and sensation novelists, as well as *Jane Eyre* (1847) (Stoneman), *Far from the Madding Crowd* (1874), *Tess of the D'Urbervilles* (1891), and poems such as *Mazeppa* (1819) and *Enoch Arden* (1864).

The preceding papers document Victorian theater's influence and popularity and also explain its appeal: Victorians loved theater because they loved performers and performance. Novels and poetry ambivalent about theater people and theatricality were not neces-sarily representative of wider attitudes (Auerbach; Voskuil). The conjunction of an impoverished dramatic literature and a thriving theatrical culture is only an apparent paradox: Victorian plays are unrewarding to read precisely because they were designed to come alive when acted, heard, and seen. Actors reigned supreme in Vic-torian theater (Emeljanow 5–6, 161). Playbills gave lead actors higher billing than authors and described actors as "creating" roles; some of the period's most successful playwrights, such as Dion Boucicault, were also skilled performers (Walsh). Drama critic Max Beerbohm observed that stars such as Edmund Kean, Ellen Terry, Henry Irving, and Sarah Bernhardt represented the "signal triumph of histrionism over dramaturgy" (392). A writer himself, Beerbohm had mixed feelings about that triumph, but nonetheless understood that stars catered to the prevailing taste for theater over drama, and actors over authors.

The valorization of actors in Victorian theater was part of a larger aesthetic of spectacle that inhered less in playtexts than in stagecraft

(Booth, *Trades*). The young Henry James defined a play as "a production that gains from being presented to our senses" (178); plays written before novelistic stage directions became the norm do little to convey that sensory vitality in print. More than its Restoration predecessors and modernist followers, Victorian theater depended on technical innovations (Booth, *Spectacular*) that made possible a performance aesthetic that privileged "acrobatic virtuosity" (Moody 211), "corporeal expressivity" (216), and "intensity" (231).[4] That aesthetic later migrated to film, along with other key features of the theatergoing experience: convivial venues, star actors, luxurious costumes, rousing music, well-designed and rapidly changing illusionistic sets, elaborate and topical visual compositions, and special effects that included equestrian feats as well as the re-creation of fires, naval battles, and train wrecks (Bailey; Rowell 22–23; Mayer; Vardac; Meisel, *Realizations*; Booth, *Spectacular*; McConachie 13).

To understand Victorian theater's appeal thus requires that we, like Gubar, Meeuwis, and Pollack-Pelzner, leave the orbit of literature and instead study audiences, performances, and acting manuals, as well as theater architecture, lighting, stage design, costuming, and incidental music. Doing so can help us develop the theatrical equivalent of what art historian Michael Baxandall has called the "period eye": an understanding of the historically specific "cognitive styles" of perception that audiences brought to performances and that performances fostered in audiences, players, and critics (29–108 and passim; see also Bennett 1–2). Developing a period eye for Victorian theater is challenging because the elements that made theater exciting and artful—acting and stagecraft—are mostly absent from printed texts and not fully captured even by those silent films that convey something of nineteenth-century theater styles.

Victorian theater, once so exuberantly present, is now irrevocably absent. Reduced to print, Victorian performances become even more virtual and conjectural than novelistic worlds (Dames; Greiner), since nineteenth-century dramatists did not avail themselves of the techniques that prose writers can use to create vivacity (Scarry). Indeed, although theater is a more embodied medium than print, a Victorian novel is now more present to us than a Victorian play. To be sure, we can never read *Bleak House* (1852–53) as Victorians did, but where they read words, we too read words. However, since few of us believe that we can access Victorian novels and poems

---

4. Moody is writing, respectively, about pantomime, the clown Joseph Grimaldi, and actor Edmund Kean, but her phrases accurately capture descriptions of other genres, such as melodrama, and later performers, such as Irving and Bernhardt.

without mediation, we already have some practice meeting the epis-
temological demands of Victorian plays. Our main impediment is
not that Victorian entertainment no longer exists but that we lack
the knowledge and skills needed to imagine text as performance.

Rather than conclude, as is customary, by devoting a paragraph
to each of the papers I have chosen, I would like to let these exemplary articles speak for themselves and instead sum up with three
axioms about Victorian theater, derived from the selected papers
and from scholarship in theater studies. From these axioms, we can
extrapolate methods, questions, and sources specific to the study of
Victorian performance.

Axiom 1: Theater Is an Event

As Shakespeare scholars and performance theorists often remind
us, theater is an event involving live actors performing for live audiences, and cannot be warehoused as such (Carlson 205; T. Davis,
Economic 334). Print is therefore no substitute for the ephemeral,
multimedia theatrical event; in studying Victorian theater and even
individual plays, it is best to begin with actors, audiences, and performance spaces.[5] Was a given play a local affair, performed only a
few times, or, like Bulwer-Lytton's *Richelieu* (1839), in repertory for
most of the nineteenth century in both England and the United
States? At any given performance of a play, what else was on the
program? Even serious full-length dramas were usually accompa-
nied by one-act farces and musical interludes. How was a play cast
at different points in time? In what kinds of spaces was it performed,
and who regulated, staffed, managed, leased, owned, and fre-
quented them? What do we know about a given theater's décor and
ticket costs? At what hour did performances begin and end? Were
audience members allowed to eat, drink, or smoke? Did the theater
post a dress code, or sell spinoff products such as souvenir programs
and photographs of performers? What does all of this suggest about
the sociology of a play's audience, the status of its performers, and
the phenomenology of its performance?

This is a daunting series of questions, but many can be answered
by consulting the playbills, posters, and advertisements plentifully
represented in theater archives, increasingly available online (see,
for example, the Victoria and Albert's online East London Theater
archive and the University of Virginia's *Uncle Tom's Cabin* site). Theatrical albums and scrapbooks, compiled by enthusiastic playgoers,

5. It is also notable that despite the expansion of print culture during the nineteenth
   century, many Victorian plays were never published. For example, at most a third of
   Dion Boucicault's two hundred plays made it into print, despite Boucicault's immense
   success as a playwright (Stephens 118).

professional actors, and theater managers, also offer images of actors and productions, seating charts for theaters, clippings of articles about plays, performers, audiences, impresarios, and theaters, as well as materials that formed part of the theatrical event: ticket stubs, playbills, programs, and advertisements (Bush-Bailey; Johnson). Other essential sources include life writing by and about performers, playwrights, managers, and theatergoers (Corbett; Postelwait); parliamentary committee reports on the state of the theater (Hadley; Bratton; T. Davis, *Economics*; Schoch); court cases and police records pertaining to theaters and performances (Bratton); and the archives of the Lord Chamberlain in charge of licensing scripts for performance, who often speculated about staging decisions and audience response. Where available, sheet music and promptbooks supplement the descriptions and illustrations of stage business, blocking, sets, and costumes that can also be found in journalistic accounts of audiences, actors, and plays (Mayer).

Axiom 2: Know Your Theatrical Genres

As trained literary critics, we understand that to appreciate a novel or poem requires knowledge about its relationship to genre, but few of us are fluent in the many theatrical genres specific to the nineteenth century. If when diving directly into plays like Douglas Jerrold's *Rent Day* (1832) or Tom Robertson's *Society* (1865) we fail to grasp their literary historical significance and popular appeal, it is often because we know little about the key theatrical genres of the age: burlesque, revue, extravaganza, melodrama, pantomime, closet drama, nautical and equestrian drama, sensation drama, the well-made play, society play, drawing-room comedy, farce, and problem play. Luckily, we have scholarship that anatomizes these genres (Booth, *Prefaces* and "Social"; Tolles; Moody; Burroughs; Williams) and analyzes generic hybridizers such as Gilbert and Sullivan (Williams) and George Bernard Shaw (Meisel).

Gaining familiarity with Victorian dramatic genres can help us compare Victorian plays to one another instead of to earlier and later "masterpieces" by Shakespeare and Beckett with which they share few aesthetic goals. Identifying a play's genres can also help us better understand what it was like in performance, since most of the genres that flourished in the nineteenth century gave rise to approximate counterparts in the twentieth and twenty-first centuries. If you have seen a Meliès or Disney film, you have a sense of pantomime; if you have ever listened to a Weird Al song or enjoyed *Airplane!* (1980) or *The Naked Gun* (1988), you know from burlesque; when you watch *Saturday Night Live* or check out *The Ed Sullivan Show* on YouTube, you are tuning into a revue. Haymarket comedies begat Marx

Brothers movies; circus stunts, married to narrative stakes, begat
action-adventure films (Bratton 261); stage melodrama, as much as
print realism, gave rise to *The Wire* and *Downton Abbey*.

Axiom 3: Don't Just Read Plays; Perform Them

My first two axioms directed us to begin with materials other than
plays, but what happens when we turn to the dramatic texts themselves? Reading Victorian plays is challenging for those accustomed
to novels and poems. Indeed, you are most likely to be persuaded
that Victorian theater is worth studying if you have never actually
read any Victorian drama. If you have, you are probably muttering,
"But those plays are so bad!" Victorian drama doth make Arnoldians
of us all, thirsty for texts that better represent the best that has
been thought and said. But then, as good readers, we will notice
that Arnold wrote "thought and said," not "thought and written,"
and take this as a hint about how to approach Victorian plays,
which thrive as speech and wilt as writing. Such texts are best
thought of as blueprints or sketches to be translated, amplified,
extended, and brought to flickering, elusive life by trained minds
and bodies. The fault lies not in Victorian plays but in ourselves.
Although acting and reading are deeply related (Cole), it is not
enough to read plays in the ways we strive to read novels: silently,
immersively, alone. It is better, but still not sufficient, to read them
as we tend to read poetry, and as the Victorians often read poetry,
fiction, and drama: out loud, from memory, expressively, to others.
To really understand a play, however, we should gather friends, colleagues, and students and try to perform it. The difficulty we will
have in doing so with anything remotely resembling competence
will teach us more about Victorian performance in minutes than
we will learn from hours of reading.

Literary scholars will always revert to written playtexts because
print is for us the most accessible and familiar medium, but if we
insist on reading Victorian drama as literature, we will find Victorian plays woefully lacking. In the place of the restrictive definitions of art by Fanny Kemble and Henry Morley with which I
began, we might substitute Zadie Smith's "quick, useful definition
of an artist: someone with an expressive talent most of us do not
have." So certainly, read Victorian plays—but don't just read them;
read about them, peruse visual and verbal accounts of the people
who staged and watched them, read them aloud, try to block and
perform them, set them to music, imagine them with costumes and
lights and contraptions and scenery. Take a cue from the three
papers I have selected, which not only teach us about Victorian
theater but also show us how to study it. Emulate Meeuwis's

emulative amateurs, Gubar's unabashedly enthusiastic audience members, and (as best we can) Pollack-Pelzner's virtuoso delivery of passages from Gilbert's *Rosencrantz and Guildenstern* (1874), a performance that perfectly illustrated Pollack-Pelzner's analytical claims by eliciting a mid-paper round of applause from his NAVSA audience. Less skilled practitioners may fall short of his success at infusing reading and writing with acting, but even so, such experiments can encourage us to explore new forms of writing, and can teach us to take fun more seriously, to appreciate and to understand, inside and out, the distinctive skills, inventiveness, and intelligence that constituted the art of Victorian theater.

WORKS CITED

Adams, James Eli. *A History of Victorian Literature*. Chichester: Wiley-Blackwell, 2009.

Allen, Emily. *Theater Figures: The Production of the Nineteenth-Century British Novel*. Columbus: Ohio UP, 2003.

Altick, Richard. *The Shows of London*. Cambridge: Belknap P of Harvard UP, 1978.

Arnold, Matthew. "The French Play in London." *The Nineteenth Century* 6 (1879): 228–43.

Auerbach, Nina. *Private Theatricals: The Lives of the Victorians*. Cambridge: Harvard UP, 1990.

Bailey, Peter. *Popular Culture and Performance in the Victorian City*. Cambridge: Cambridge UP, 2003.

Bailey, Peter, ed. *Music Hall: The Business of Pleasure*. Open UP, 1986.

Baxandall, Michael. *Painting and Experience in Fifteenth-Century Italy: A Primer in the Social History of Pictorial Style*. New York: Oxford UP, 1988.

Beerbohm, Max. "Phèdre and Mascarille." *More Theatres*. New York: Taplinger, 1969.

Bennett, Susan. *Theatre Audiences: A Theory of Production and Reception*. London: Routledge, 1997.

Booth, Michael. *Prefaces to English Nineteenth-Century Theatre*. Manchester: Manchester UP, 1980.

———. *Victorian Spectacular Theatre 1850–1910*. Boston: Routledge, 1981.

———. "The Social and Literary Context." Booth et al. 1–57.

Booth, Michael, ed. *Victorian Theatrical Trades*. London: Society for Theatre Research, 1981.

Booth, Michael, et al. *The Revels History of Drama in English*. Vol. 6. London: Methuen, 1975.

Bratton, Jacky. "What Is a Play? Drama and the Victorian Circus." Davis and Holland 250–62.

Brooks, Daphne. *Bodies in Dissent: The Spectacular Performances of Race and Freedom, 1850–1910.* Durham: Duke UP, 2006.

Brooks, Peter. *The Melodramatic Imagination: Balzac, Henry James, Melodrama, and the Mode of Excess.* New Haven: Yale UP, 1976.

Burroughs, Catherine. *Closet Stages: Joanna Baillie and the Theater Theory of British Romantic Women Writers.* Philadelphia: U of Pennsylvania P, 1997.

Bush-Bailey, Gill. "Fitting the Bill: Acting out the Season of 1813/14 at the Sans Pareil." Davis and Holland 182–98.

Canning, Charlotte M., and Thomas Postlewait, eds. *Representing the Past: Essays in Performance Historiography.* Iowa City: U of Iowa P, 2010.

Carlson, Marvin. "Space and Theatre History." Canning and Postlewait 195–214.

Cole, David. *Acting as Reading: The Place of the Reading Process in the Actor's Work.* Ann Arbor: U of Michigan P, 1992.

Corbett, Mary Jean. "Performing Identities: Actresses and Autobiography." *The Cambridge Companion to Victorian and Edwardian Theatre.* Ed. Kerry Powell. Cambridge: Cambridge UP, 2004. 109–26.

Dames, Nicholas. "On Hegel, History, and Reading as if for Life: Response." *Victorian Studies* 53.3 (2011): 437–44.

Davies, Robertson. "Playwrights and Plays." Booth et al. 145–263.

Davis, Jim. "'Scandals to the Neighbourhood': Cleaning-up the East London Theatre." *New Theatre Quarterly* 6.21 (1990): 235–43.

Davis, Jim, and Victor Emeljanow. *Reflecting the Audience: London Theatregoing, 1840–1880.* Iowa City: U of Iowa P, 2001.

Davis, Tracy. *The Economics of the British Stage, 1800–1914.* Cambridge: Cambridge UP, 2000.

———. "The Sociable Playwright and Representative Citizen." Davis and Donkin 15–34.

Davis, Tracy, and Ellen Donkin, eds. *Women and Playwriting in Nineteenth-Century Britain.* Cambridge: Cambridge UP, 1999.

Davis, Tracy, and Peter Holland, eds. *The Performing Century: Nineteenth-Century Theatre's History.* Houndmills: Palgrave, 2007.

Emeljanow, Victor. *Victorian Popular Dramatists.* Boston: Twayne, 1987.

Esterhammer, Angela. *Romanticism and Improvisation, 1750–1850.* Cambridge: Cambridge UP, 2009.

Glavin, John. *After Dickens: Reading, Adaptation and Performance.* Cambridge: Cambridge UP, 1999.

Greiner, Rae. "Thinking of Me Thinking of You: Sympathy Versus Empathy in the Realist Novel." *Victorian Studies* 53.1 (2011): 417–26.

Hadley, Elaine. *Melodramatic Tactics: Theatricalized Dissent in the English Marketplace, 1800–1885.* Stanford: Stanford UP, 1995.

Jackson, Shannon. *Lines of Activity: Performance, Historiography, Hull-House Domesticity*. Ann Arbor: U of Michigan P, 2000.

———. *Professing Performance: Theatre in the Academy from Philology to Performativity*. Cambridge: Cambridge UP, 2004.

James, Henry. *The Scenic Art: Notes on Acting and the Drama: 1872–1901*. New Brunswick: Rutgers UP, 1948.

Johnson, Stephen Burge, ed. *A Tyranny of Documents: The Performing Arts Historian as Film Noir Detective; Essays Dedicated to Brooks McNamara*. New York: Theatre Library Association, 2011.

Kemble, Fanny. *Journal of a Young Actress*. New York: Columbia UP, 1990.

Kurnick, David. *Empty Houses: Theatrical Failure and the Novel*. Princeton: Princeton UP, 2012.

Litvak, Joseph. *Caught in the Act: Theatricality in the Nineteenth-Century English Novel*. Berkeley: U of California P, 1992.

McConachie, Bruce. "'The Theatre of the Mob': Apocalyptic Melodrama and Preindustrial Riots in Antebellum New York." McConachie and Friedman 17–46.

McConachie, Bruce, and Daniel Friedman, eds. *Theatre for Working-Class Audiences in the United States, 1830–1980*. Westport: Greenwood, 1985.

Marcus, Sharon. "The Theater of Comparative Literature." *A Companion to Comparative Literature*. Ed. Ali Behdad and Dominic Thomas. Chichester: Wiley-Blackwell, 2011. 136–54.

Marshall, David. *The Figure of Theater: Shaftesbury, Defoe, Adam Smith, and George Eliot*. New York: Columbia UP, 1986.

Mayer, David, ed. *Henry Irving and* The Bells: *Irving's Personal Script of the Play*. Manchester: Manchester UP, 1980.

Meisel, Martin. *Realizations: Narrative, Pictorial, and Theatrical Arts in Nineteenth-Century England*. Princeton: Princeton UP, 1983.

———. *Shaw and the Nineteenth-Century Theater*. Princeton: Princeton UP, 1963.

Moody, Jane. *Illegitimate Theatre in London, 1770–1840*. Cambridge: Cambridge UP, 2000.

Morley, Henry. *Journal of a London Playgoer*. London, 1866. *Google Book Search*. 29 Feb. 2012.

Newey, Katherine. *Women's Theatre Writing in Victorian Britain*. Houndmills: Palgrave, 2005.

Postlewait, Thomas. "Autobiography and Theatre History." *Interpreting the Theatrical Past: Essays in the Historiography of Performance*. Ed. Thomas Postlewait and Bruce A. McConachie. Iowa City: U of Iowa P, 1989. 248–72.

Puchner, Martin. *Stage Fright: Modernism, Anti-Theatricality, and Drama*. Baltimore: Johns Hopkins UP, 2002.

Rowell, George. *The Victorian Theatre 1792–1914: A Survey.* Cambridge: Cambridge UP, 1978.

Samuels, Maurice. *The Spectacular Past: Popular History and the Novel in Nineteenth-Century France.* Ithaca: Cornell UP, 2004.

Scarry, Elaine. *Dreaming by the Book.* Princeton: Princeton UP, 2001.

Schoch, Richard. "Shakespeare and the Music Hall." Davis and Holland 236–49.

Smith, Zadie. "The Zen of Eminem." *Vibe* (2005): N. pag. *Book Rags.* Web. 29 Feb. 2012.

Stephens, John Russell. *The Profession of the Playwright: British Theatre 1800–1900.* Cambridge: Cambridge UP, 1992.

Stoneman, Patsy. Jane Eyre *on Stage, 1848–1898.* Aldershot: Ashgate, 2007.

Tolles, Winton. *Tom Taylor and the Victorian Drama.* New York: AMS, 1966.

Tristan, Flora. *Flora Tristan's London Journal.* Trans. Dennis Palmer and Giselle Pincetl. London: George Prior, 1980.

Vardac, Nicholas A. *Stage to Screen: Theatrical Origins of Early Film: David Garrick to D. W. Griffith.* 1949. New York: Da Capo, 1987.

Vlock, Deborah. *Dickens, Novel Reading, and the Victorian Popular Theatre.* Cambridge: Cambridge UP, 1998.

Voskuil, Lynn M. *Acting Naturally: Victorian Theatricality and Authenticity.* Charlottesville: U of Virginia P, 2004.

Walsh, Townsend. *The Career of Dion Boucicault.* New York: Dunlap Society, 1915.

Williams, Carolyn. *Gilbert and Sullivan: Gender, Genre, Parody.* New York: Columbia UP, 2011.

Wojcik, Pam. "Typecasting." *Criticism* 45.2 (2003): 223–49.

Ziter, Edward. *The Orient on the Victorian Stage.* Cambridge: Cambridge UP, 2003.

MICHAEL PATRICK GILLESPIE

The Branding of Oscar Wilde†

> "There is only one thing in life worse than being talked about and that is not being talked about."—*The Picture of Dorian Gray*

Many readers would readily assent to the proposition that Oscar Wilde took on the role of a performance artist a century before the term came into vogue, citing numerous accounts in letters,

---

† *Études Anglaises* 69. 1 (Jan.–March 2016): 23–35. Reprinted with permission of the author.

memoirs, and biographies illustrating how he masterfully captured public attention through what he said and what he did. Nonetheless, too often readers and critics treat such behavior as eccentricities that give a flourish to accounts of his life, without seeing the significance of such behavior as part of the creative milieu from which his works emerged. That takes a reductive approach to Wilde's character and assumes that he had a simple performative relation with society, embodied in *bons mots* like the one that serves as an epigraph for this essay and the self-dramatizing moments cited by Richard Ellmann and others.[1]

In fact, Wilde went beyond presenting a startling, amusing persona. While he had no aversion to outlandish behaviour, the patterns it followed suggest that he carefully choreographed each word and gesture, precisely calculated its impact, and showed a remarkable dexterity for maximizing the benefits that accrued from each. The words of Lord Henry to Dorian Gray, late in the novel, apply equally to Wilde: "Life has been your art" (*Dorian Gray*, 179). I intend to pursue the implications of that point from our contemporary perspective on celebrity and branding.

The concept of a brand has a long affiliation with product identification, initially serving as a way of identifying the source or maker of a particular product and distinguishing it from similar items produced by others. The more precisely applied use of the term began to evolve in the 19th century. As industrialization moved manufacturing from cottage industries to factories, brand took on a singular importance, attesting to the qualities of a particular product no matter where or by whom it was sold. In short order, these brand names developed psychological associations as well. By the 20th century, when competing mass-produced products—from cigarettes to automobiles—had little material difference and companies sought to attract customers through emotional associations, branding became even more important.[2]

Let me cite one example of the power of branding. From 1954–1999 the Philip Morris Tobacco Company ran an advertising

1. That perception, like all generalizations, requires some qualification. Regenia Gagnier's ground-breaking work presents insights into the commodified context surrounding Wilde's writing. It is an important starting point for anyone making the connection between Wilde's creativity and the material influences of his world. Rachel Bowlby's work on the development of consumer society in Britain, France, and the United States in the late 19th century anticipates Gagnier's efforts and for those interested in the topic nicely complements her work.
2. Branding itself, while existing within broad parameters that find general acceptance, remains an extremely mutable concept, open to and welcoming almost any modifications that the specific brander introduces. The most successful brands both fall within this easily identified category and work diligently to distinguish themselves. Brands that do not do both, like creative works with similar limitations, quickly slip into banality. My definition of branding remains self-consciously general to avoid the constrictions of over-specificity.

campaign for its Marlboro cigarettes. The ads featured a series of models dressed as cowboys, emphasizing manly traits and trying to associate them with the sort of person who chose to smoke Marlboro cigarettes. Neither the models nor most of those who purchased the cigarettes worked on ranches, but the impression of manliness created by the branding associated with that image was enough to generate significant sales.

Within the last few decades, the concept of branding has moved beyond associations with products. People have begun to use the term "brand," as a noun and verb, to summarize the characteristics linked in the communal mind with an individual (the first use of the term seems to have been in 1997 in a journal article written by Tom Peters). This involves more than the simple imposition of label. One's brand has a far more dynamic quality as the signifier of a consistent and unique public persona. The brand, in this contemporary sense, creates in those who perceive it material and psychological expectations, and it imposes on the branded individuals the obligation to cultivate, enhance, and even protect the brand that they have created. As the brand grows in renown, the distinction between it and the individual behind it becomes increasingly difficult for the public, and often for the branded person, to discern. Furthermore, with the growing success of the brand comes its increasing control over the individual's public actions. Examples of this are embarrassingly abundant.

Though only recently named as such, branding is by no means a twenty-first or even a 20th century phenomenon. It stands firmly fixed in the cult of popularity which goes back as far as the first social groups, but it has become increasingly prominent as the reach of mass communication has grown. The printing press greatly enhanced accessibility, allowing the broadsides and pamphlets of the 17th century to grow into the newspapers and journals of the eighteenth. By the 19th century daily and weekly publications numbered in hundreds in the British Isles (see Curran). One of the many consequences of this burgeoning was that personal branding became an important element in the popular culture in 19th-century England, and its practitioners stretched from Beau Brummel to Max Beerbohm (see Moers). In Wilde's time, a number of established writers, painters and actors followed similar paths towards defining themselves in the public eye. In addition to the extravagances of Beerbohm, Wilde had direct competition from James Abbott McNeill Whistler and later Aubrey Beardsley. Women like Lillie Langtry and Sarah Bernhardt demonstrated equal inclination for display. However, Wilde showed an ability to distinguish himself from all through a deeper understanding of the process and a firmer commitment to carrying it through. From the time he arrived in Oxford, he cultivated the persona of a pure brand, someone famous for being famous.

"Soon I shall [. . .] be known simply as 'The Wilde' or 'The Oscar'" (Holland 4).

I propose taking the concept of branding as seriously as did Wilde to examine further a thesis that I introduced several years ago, noting how the both/and qualities of Wilde's public persona shaped his writing (Gillespie 1–16). In my reading, this duality intensified society's sense of Wilde's identity through oscillating perspectives: someone whose sexuality exuded homoerotic and heteroerotic sensibilities. Someone whose nationality asserted both Englishness and Irishness. Someone at the centre of Society and someone always clearly marked as marginal. These are the dandy-like qualities that set Wilde apart (Gillespie 115–132), but it was his sophisticated understanding of the impact of duality that allowed him to extend their impact to shape the way readers and audiences interpreted his work. The dandy-like qualities of his life pervaded his writing, and the pluralistic perspectives that they generated enabled a range of often contradictory readings to coexist within his works. The most graphic illustration of this approach comes from a negative example. Once his 1895 prison conviction erased in the public mind the possibility of both/and qualities informing Wilde's nature, his written work became equally unambiguous and far less engaging (Gillespie 155–173).

In this sense, the power of Wilde's writing came directly out of the care he took in cultivating his brand. Over the next few pages, I will focus most of my attention on how this came about. I will look at the period before Wilde came to true literary prominence, exploring the self-conscious campaign to capture the public imagination that he began in his undergraduate days. I will trace its growth through the publication of the novel-length version of *The Picture of Dorian Gray* in 1891 and touch on how it continued with *The Importance of Being Earnest*. I will conclude with how his trial and conviction in 1895 effaced the both/and qualities of his brand and how Wilde lost the power to engage the public imagination in the complex way that he had previously enjoyed.

Early evidence of Wilde's disposition for branding remains scarce, so it can be difficult to pinpoint its inception. Only one letter from his time at Portora Royal School survives (along with a piece, not in Wilde's hand and signed by himself and five others, protesting against a school punishment) and that demonstrates little more than the precociousness one would expect from the future writer (*Complete Letters*, 3–5). No letters from his time at Trinity College seem to have been preserved, so it is not until after he took up residence at Oxford that evidence appears of Wilde's concerted effort to set himself apart from the university's other gifted, eccentric,

self-absorbed students. (Information on Wilde's early life is anec-
dotal, and the reliability of many stories is difficult to ascertain. In
this essay I have tried to rely on primary sources, like Wilde's correspondence.) For example, several sources at Oxford, catalogued
in the Ellmann biography, reported that Wilde fretted over his ability to live up to his blue china (Ellmann 45). It remains unclear
whether that originated with Oscar Wilde or whether he simply
embraced the remark as his own. For the purpose of this essay that
question stands as a distinction without a difference. The blue china
witticism sums up for Wilde, and for us, the persona, the brand, that
he wished to project to the world.

That anecdote is only one of many that highlight Wilde's efforts—
through his dress, his language, and his actions—to underscore his
creative uniqueness and to suggest for others the paradigm for the
behavior they might expect from him. Wilde's challenge was to distinguish his form of eccentricity from all the others flourishing in
Oxford's academic hothouse which so readily nourished self-
absorption and self-aggrandizement. In a tight-knit world of self-
promoters, Wilde worked tirelessly to set himself apart. Richard
Ellmann sums up the evolution saying "And so Wilde created himself at Oxford" (Ellmann 98). Despite the phrase's lack of precision,
it does capture Wilde's determination to refine his public persona.[3]

From his first days at the university, Wilde's correspondence shows
a flair for a flamboyant view of his environment, as in this passage
from a 28 June 1876 letter to Reginald Harding: "My dear Kitten,
Many thanks for your delightful letters; they were quite a pleasant
relaxation to us to get your letters every morning at breakfast. (This
is sarcasm.) [. . .] Bouncer's people stayed up till Monday [. . .] I like
Mrs. Bouncer immensely and the eldest Miss B. is very charming
indeed" (*Complete Letters*, 17). He was equally adept at taking serious subjects lightly but without triviality. In an early March 1877
letter to William Ward, he alludes to a possible conversion to Cathol-
icism. In an interesting balance, Wilde glosses, with simultaneous
flamboyance and keen sense of its public implications, the spiritual
impact of such a decision:

> I have got rather keen on Masonry lately and believe in it
> awfully—in fact would be awfully sorry to have to give it up in
> case I secede from the Protestant Heresy [. . .] altogether am
> caught in the fowler's snare, in the wiles of the Scarlet Woman
> [. . .]. If I *could hope* that the Church would wake in me some

---

3. Ellmann's biography shows less discrimination than one would expect, making liberal
use of questionable sources like Frank Harris's life of Wilde. The prefatory matter to
the 1930 American edition of Harris's biography (xi–xlvi) shows the difficulty of judg-
ing the accuracy of many of his statements.

earnestness and purity I would go over *as a luxury* [. . .] [but] to go over to Rome would be to sacrifice and give up my two great gods "Money and Ambition". (*Complete Letters*, 38–39)

Wilde's efforts were not lost on his classmates, and a letter written by George Macmillan to his father, one of the founders of the Macmillan publishing house, gives a keen description of Wilde's already well-formed public persona: "He is aesthetic to the last degree, passionately fond of secondary colours, low tones, Morris papers, and capable of talking a good deal of nonsense thereupon, but for all that a very sensible, well-informed and charming man" (*Complete Letters*, 44). Wilde, however, aspired to more than a reputation as a campus character. A 14 May 1877 letter written to William Gladstone, then head of the Liberal Party, shows Wilde is already honing the ability to cultivate influential people:

> Sir, Your noble and impassioned protests, both written and spoken, against the massacres of the Christians in Bulgaria have so roused my heart that I venture to send you a sonnet which I have written on the subject.
>
> I am little more than a boy, and have no literary interest in London, but perhaps if *you* saw any good stuff in the lines I send you, some editor [. . .] might publish them. (*Complete Letters*, 46)

A final Oxford letter, again to William Ward and written around 24 July 1878, balances sardonic temperament with genuine pride over his achievements as he sums up public reaction to his winning the Newdigate Prize for Poetry and gaining a First in Greats: "It is too delightful altogether this display of fireworks at the end of my career [. . .]. The dons are 'astonied' beyond words—the Bad Boy doing so well in the end" (*Complete Letters*, 70). These informal letters to school friends have a more relaxed air than would his later public performances, but Wilde is already honing the art of self-publicizing.

In London, the town's sheer size in contrast to that of parochial Oxford made gaining recognition of any sort a greater challenge. Wilde, however, proved remarkably adaptable. The letters show him quickly making contact with academics, writers, painters, publishers and people of the theatre. He became both an outspoken advocate of art for art's sake, offered in language less cerebral than what he had learned from his tutor Walter Pater, and a daring exemplar of extravagant behavior. He immediately understood how important it was not simply to be noticed but to be known. Early on Wilde paid court to actress Ellen Terry (*Complete Letters*, 81), writing a poem to her by way of introduction. He invited opera singer and actress

Genevieve Ward to tea, promising the company of Lillie Langtry and Lady Lonsdale (*Complete Letters*, 90–91). He became an intimate of Lillie Langtry's, and, according to the editors of the *Complete Letters*, "[b]esides acting as her amanuensis, Wilde also advised and instructed her on other matters" (*Complete Letters*, 91, n4). Ellmann, for example, repeats Ada Leverson's account of Wilde throwing an armful of lilies at the feet of Sarah Bernhardt when she arrived in Folkestone. He goes on to say "Bernhardt was charmed. She soon inscribed her signature on the white panelling of Thames House as one of Wilde's guests, and one night she offered to show how high up the wall her foot could kick" (Ellmann 117). The letters enumerate Wilde's methodical efforts to cultivate a range of celebrities. The fact that they were usually women suggests a keen sense of whose opinion facilitated access to Society, an important prerequisite for any unknown seeking to establish a brand. As Lady Bracknell would later tell Algernon, "Never speak disrespectfully of Society, Algernon. Only people who can't get into it do that" (*The Importance of Being Earnest*, 9 [51]).

These efforts, and connections already established from his time at Oxford, made Wilde a London celebrity in short order. As his grandson Merlin Holland notes, though at the time "still only the author of a few poems and a review or two," Wilde was already being caricatured in various London journals (Holland 56). Holland reprints a number of them that appeared from 1880–1881 in various magazines (Holland 56–59). Like the most interesting celebrities, Wilde combined flamboyance and wit to capture attention, but he always knew the limits of extravagant behavior and stopped well short of provoking ostracism, at least at that stage in his career.

When Wilde lectured in America in 1882, he demonstrated his keen sense of how to build the brand he had chosen. The tour was arranged by Colonel W. F. Morse, the American representative of Richard D'Oyly Carte, the producer of Gilbert and Sullivan's *Patience*, a comic opera lampooning aesthetics with several characters who had traits caricaturing Wilde's behavior (*Complete Letters*, 123). Richard Ellmann notes that D'Oyly Carte expected the opera and the lecture tour would spur interest in one another, increasing the profits to be gained from both (Ellmann 151). The fact that D'Oyly Carte saw Wilde's excursion as a means of promoting *Patience* underscores the strength that Wilde's brand had already attained. For his part, Wilde was not content to rest on this achievement. Rather, he spent his time in the United States assiduously enhancing his celebrity. Arriving on 2 January 1882, he was asked by a Customs officer what he had to declare, and he famously responded "nothing but my genius" (Lewis and Smith 35). The remark shows he came prepared to capture attention and excite comment, but

Wilde also proved quick to adapt his approach to American marketing strategies. "The public was fond of buying pictures of notables and of filing them in albums" (Lewis and Smith 39). In consequence, while he was in New York City, Wilde had a series of photographs taken, posing extravagantly in a seal-skin hat, a fur-lined coat, and knee breeches. (For selected reproductions, see Holland 64–92.)

Wilde used two lectures as the staple of his tour: "The Decorative Arts" and "The House Beautiful." On any specific night, he chose the talk he felt best suited to his audience. His presentations were primarily performances rather than expositions. The intent was to entertain rather than to illuminate, and to that end the Wilde brand was an important factor in creating audience expectations and response. Not only did he hone his brand during the tour, cultivating American writers and intellectuals—Oliver Wendell Holmes, Walt Whitman, Charles Eliot Norton, Julian Hawthorne, Louisa May Alcott—and professionals in publishing—like J. M. Stoddart, who later published the novella version of "The Picture of Dorian Gray," and William Henry Hurlbert—but he accumulated anecdotes, like his dinner with Colorado silver miners deep inside a mine in Leadville (Lewis and Smith 317–318), that would serve him well later.[4] On March 27, for example, he described his reception in San Francisco to his friend Norman Forbes-Robertson:

> There were 4000 people waiting at the "depot" to see me, open carriage, four horses, an audience at my lecture of the most cultivated people in 'Frisco, charming folks [. . .] I am really appreciated by the cultured class. The railway have offered me a special train and private car to go down to Los Angeles, a sort of Naples here, and I am fêted and entertained to my heart's content. (*Complete Letters*, 158–159)

Three weeks later he told Forbes-Robertson of being in St. Joseph, Missouri, a week after Jesse James was killed: "Outside my window, about a quarter of a mile to the west there stands a little yellow house with a green paling, and a crowd of people pulling it all down. It is the house of the great train robber and murderer, Jesse James, who was shot by his pal last week, and the people are relic-hunters" (*Complete Letters*, 164).

Shortly after returning home, Wilde undertook a tour of the United Kingdom that allowed him to expand the brand by recounting, and no doubt embellishing, his experiences abroad. Despite the

4. Until recently the Lewis and Smith study was the primary reference for Wilde in North America. It is as much a cultural history as an account of Wilde's tour. Roy Morris's recent book is less expansive, more focused, and relies more on secondary sources. The Hofer and Scharnhorst volume, collecting interviews given by Wilde to American newspapers, offers a first-hand view of his tour.

triumphs he announced—"civilizing the provinces by my remarkable lectures" (*Complete Letters*, 225)—he continued to cultivate a sense of his brand, through a mixture of elaborate compliments and deft self-aggrandizing, among those in England whom he saw as useful to its enhancement. In late January 1884, he wrote to Lillie Langtry, complimenting her for having "invaded America a second time and carried off new victories" (*Complete Letters*, 224). Not wishing to miss an opportunity, he went on to bring attention to his successes by using hyperbole seemingly to deflate them: "I am hard at work lecturing and getting quite rich" (*Complete Letters*, 224).

In London he continued to build the brand, even with yet relatively little artistic production, using his impending marriage as another vehicle for notoriety. *The World* of 26 December 1883 reported that "Mr Whistler's last Sunday breakfast of the year was given in honor of two happy couples, Lord Garmoyle and his fairy queen, and Oscar and the lady he has chosen to be *chatelaine* of the House Beautiful" (*Complete Letters*, 225 n2). Wilde's association with notables and his lecture tour had now demonstrably earned him the distinction that he prophesied as an Oxford undergraduate of being recognized solely by his first name.

His public exchanges with Whistler, generally deft on Wilde's part and always edgy and at times vicious on Whistler's, enhanced his reputation and distinguished him from his would-be competitor. In a letter written a month or so into his American tour, Wilde announced his success to Whistler, and in a sentence that used flippancy to mask dismissiveness, contrasts his success with the latter's ineffectualness: "My Dear Jimmy, They are 'considering me *seriously*'. Isn't it dreadful? What would you do if it happened to you?" (*Complete Letters*, 139). When Whistler attempted to move from creator to critic in his 20 February 1885 "Ten O'Clock" lecture on art, Wilde sent subtle but pointed warnings about brand infringement. The day following the talk, Wilde wrote a sardonic review in the *Pall Mall Gazette*, and then about three days later, sent Whistler the following note:

> Dear Butterfly, By the aid of a biographical dictionary I discovered that there were once two painters, called Benjamin West and Paul Delaroche, who recklessly took to lecturing on Art.
>
> As of their works nothing at all remains, I conclude that they explained themselves away. Be warned in time, James; and remain, as I do, incomprehensible: to be great is to be misunderstood. (*Complete Letters*, 250)

Whistler sought to protect his public standing, and that moved him to engage Wilde time and again. The difference in tone in their correspondences underscores the difference between brand and reputation. Whistler's self-absorption led to a vigorous assertion of his renown but made his witticisms less palatable to the general audience that Wilde cultivated so assiduously (see, for example, *Complete Letters*, 147). In the end, Wilde showed himself more than able to relegate Whistler to the role of an also-ran as evidenced from a passage from a letter in the journal *Truth* on 9 January 1890: "the only thoroughly original ideas I have ever heard [Whistler] express have had reference to his own superiority over painters greater than himself" (*Complete Letters*, 420).

By the time of the controversy over the publication in the July 1890 issue of *Lippincott's Magazine* of the novella version of "The Picture of Dorian Gray," Wilde's brand was well established. He had moved from the task of developing a trademark into the role of protecting it. The novella was well received in America, but a firestorm of criticism broke out in British papers. The opening of an anonymous review appearing in the 24 June 1890 issue of the *St. James's Gazette*, entitled "A Study in Puppydom," offers a good example of the contumely the story aroused, and parenthetically, a thumbnail sketch of the evolution of the Wilde brand:

> Time was (it was in the '70's) when we talked about Mr Oscar Wilde; time came (it came in the '80's) when he tried to write poetry and, more adventurous, we tried to read it; time is when we had forgotten him, or only remember him as the late editor of *The Woman's World*—a part for which he was singularly unfitted, if we are to judge him by the work which he has been allowed to publish in *Lippincott's Magazine* and which Messrs Ward, Lock & Co. have not been ashamed to circulate in Great Britain. Not being curious in ordure, and not wishing to offend the nostrils of decent persons, we do not propose to analyse "The Picture of Dorian Gray": that would be to advertise the developments of an esoteric prurience. Whether the Treasury or the Vigilance Society will think it worth while to prosecute Mr Oscar Wilde or Messrs Ward, Lock & Co., we do not know; but on the whole we hope they will not. (Reprinted in *Dorian Gray*, 352)

Wilde had inspired criticism throughout his time in London, from caricatures in *Punch* and other magazines to burlesques in theatrical productions like *Patience*. He was generally good-natured in defending himself from public attacks. In this case, however, the reviews went beyond criticism of the writing. By implying in both his character and his art, they attacked the brand. In response, Wilde engaged in epistolary debates with several editors of prominent English journals, not necessarily out of ethical outrage but from a desire to protect the brand. One finds a number of letters to the *St James's Gazette* (*Complete Letters*, 428–432), the *Daily Chronicle* (*Complete Letters*, 435–436), *Punch* (*Complete Letters*, 442) and the *Scot's Observer* (*Complete Letters*, 438–439, 440–442, 446–449). (See also *Dorian Gray*, 357–73.) The rhetorical argument of this correspondence proves to be particularly interesting in terms of this essay. Wilde began with an airy dismissal of the idea of morality as a factor in a work of art. As the criticisms persisted, his tone shifted. It became more defensive and devoted a great deal of attention to denials of any immorality in his writing. The back and forth with journal editors died out after a few months, but Wilde made sure that he had the last word and that he reconfigured the debate to reinforce the concept he wished for his brand. In a Preface that he wrote for the Ward, Lock novel-length version of *The Picture of Dorian Gray*, which appeared a year after the novella, he returned to his original theme that art is without morality:

> Those who find ugly meanings in beautiful things are corrupt without being charming.
>
> There is no such thing as a moral or an immoral book. Books are well written, or badly written.
>
> All art is quite useless. (*Dorian Gray*, 3–4)

Although the novel met with none of the criticism given the novella, its Preface sums up Wilde's keen sense of what he needed to do to keep his assiduously cultivated public persona safe. He did not want to become embroiled in the same kind of public debate that punctuated the previous summer. Clear-cut distinctions between moral and immoral did the brand no good, and it was important to maintain in his writing the same "both/and" quality that he projected in his life.

What in fact was the Wilde brand by this point? He was seen as an arbiter of taste, pushing what was accepted to the extreme without making it intolerable to his public. He was someone whose wit could shock and amuse without going so far as to offend. He was a marvel of hyperbole without slipping into heavy-handed falsehood. He was interesting because he seemed almost, but never quite, dangerous. The lawsuit against Queensberry changed all that, removing ambiguity and destroying the brand. To a large degree, Wilde's branding had been successful because of his deft use of ambiguity. He did not simply call attention to himself. He presented a range of possible perspectives open to multiple interpretations. From the blue-china-worshipping persona he projected at Oxford to the green-carnation-wearing dandy of the first night's performance of *The Importance of Being Earnest*, Wilde's presence provoked response without prescribing the terms of one's reaction. He did this because he perfectly controlled the dynamics of the environment in which he operated. As shown in the trial transcripts, edited and published by H. Montgomery Hyde in his *The Three Trials of Oscar Wilde*, this changed when he submitted himself to the tightly-defined protocol of the British judicial system.

At his first trial at the Old Bailey, under examination by his attorney, Sir Edward Clarke, Wilde succeeded in sustaining the brand that he had so carefully cultivated (Hyde 116–120). However, as soon as he came under cross-examination by Edward Carson, judicial intolerance for ambiguity began to exert an effect. Initially Carson made Wilde admit relative trifles and seemingly innocent lies—that, for example, Wilde had dropped two years when he gave his age at the beginning of his testimony (Hyde 120). Carson went on to a sharper and more focused interrogation attacking Wilde's character, questioning him, for example, about a homosexual story, "The Priest and the Acolyte," written by Jack Bloxam. In the process, Carson set a trap that forced Wilde to respond under conditions that undercut the advantage Wilde usually gained when he invoked the hyperbole and ambiguity at the heart of his brand. When Carson denounced Bloxam's story as "blasphemous," Wilde simply said "it violated every artistic canon of beauty." Carson then pressed the issue, drawing on the Preface to *The Picture of Dorian Gray*, and demanding to know if Wilde felt "that there is no such thing as an immoral book." When Wilde assented to that view, Carson continued to build a case for the blasphemous quality of the story (Hyde 120–123, 140–164). Throughout the exchanges, Wilde maintained an insouciant air, and at times he was able to exercise his wit at Carson's expense. At one point, Wilde expressed his preference for champagne, despite his doctor's orders not to drink it. "Never mind your doctor's orders," said Carson. "I never do," responded Wilde (Hyde 144). In the end, however, it was not enough to bring about success in the suit against Queensberry or to forestall the criminal prosecution that followed.

The pattern established in the civil suit continued in the two subsequent criminal trials. Wilde maintained in his testimony the brand that he had so carefully cultivated throughout his public life. Time and again, however, Carson used blunt unambiguous language to build a damning legal case against Wilde that challenged the acceptability of that brand through a relentless application of conventional 19th-century moral values. Carson culminated this assault by engineering a series of questions that led Wilde to say that he would not kiss a sixteen-year-old servant because he thought the boy ugly (Hyde 150). Ultimately, the studied frivolousness with which Wilde met Carson's interrogation could not overcome the relentless linearity of a cross-examination that ignored form, denigrated the brand, and focused only on a single issue. It would travesty the

102   MICHAEL PATRICK GILLESPIE

serious injustice perpetrated by the trials to suggest that Wilde's
brand brought about his conviction. However, it is fair to say that
his conviction revealed the limits of a brand's power to affect public perception.

The real impact of the brand on his art becomes clear at his trials
and afterwards. At the Old Bailey branding had him trapped. His
testimonies reflected the wit, grace, and calculated outrageousness
that he had cultivated for three decades. However, the legal system
showed no interest in a "both/and" approach to life, and his own
brand loyalty did not permit modification.[5] Wilde's conviction
destroyed his brand, and in its absence we become aware of the
extent to which the success of Wilde's public performances shaped
his art and its reception. Wilde's late work—*The Ballad of Reading
Gaol* and *De Profundis*—is not nearly as artistically successful and
certainly nowhere near as ambiguous as what preceded it. In both,
a linearity prevails and the trust in one's audience that ambiguity
conveys is absent. Robbed of his brand, Wilde produced art much
less engaging for it and he had lost the ability to leave us, like the
Oxford dons of his school days, "astonied."

REFERENCES

Bowlby, Rachel. *Just Looking: Consumer Culture in Dreiser, Gissing,
and Zola.* New York: Routledge, 1985.
Cohen, Ed. *Talk on the Wilde Side: toward a Genealogy of Discourse
on Male Sexualities.* New York: Routledge, 1992.
Cohen, Phillip K. *The Moral Vision of Oscar Wilde.* Rutherford, N.J.:
Fairleigh Dickinson University Press, 1978.
Croft-Cooke, Rupert. *The Unrecorded Life of Oscar Wilde.* New York:
David McKay Company, Inc., 1972.
Curran, George. *Newspaper History. Seventeenth Century to the Pre-
sent.* London: Constable, 1978.
Ellmann, Richard. *Oscar Wilde* [1987]. New York: Alfred A. Knopf,
1988.
Forbes Magazine. Online: www.forbes.com/profile/kim-kardashian/
(last accessed 9 Feb. 2021)
Gagnier, Regenia. *Idylls of the Marketplace: Oscar Wilde and the Vic-
torian Public.* Stanford: Stanford University Press, 1999.
Gillespie, Michael Patrick. *Oscar Wilde and the Aesthetics of Chaos.*
Gainesville: University Press of Florida, 1996.

5. A discussion of Wilde's "brand" after the trials would require a separate essay, looking
at how the original brand suffered in his final years and how different groups of readers have recuperated and reconfigured it, from those who see the brand as embodying a gay writer (Ed Cohen) to those who see it as embodying a writer who is gay
(Phillip Cohen). This is just one example underscoring the mutability of branding mentioned in note 2.

Harris, Frank. *Oscar Wilde: His Life and Confessions*. Garden City, New York: Garden City Publishing Co., 1930.

Hofer, Matthew & Gary Scharnhorst, eds. *Oscar Wilde in America: the Interviews*. Urbana and Chicago: University of Illinois Press, 2010.

Holland, Merlin, ed. *Oscar Wilde: a Life in Letters*. New York: Carroll and Graf, 2003.

Hyde, H. Mongomery, ed. *The Three Trials of Oscar Wilde*. New York: University Books, 1956.

Lewis, Lloyd and Henry Justin Smith. *Oscar Wilde Discovers America*. New York: Harcourt, Brace and Company, 1936.

Moers, Ellen. *The Dandy from Brummel to Beerbohm*. New York: Viking Press, 1960.

Morris, Jr., Roy. *Declaring His Genius: Oscar Wilde in North America*. Cambridge, Massachusetts and London: The Belknap Press of Harvard University Press, 2013.

Pearce, Matt. *The Los Angeles Times*, online version. 27 January 2014: http://www.latimes.com/nation/nationnow/la-na-nn-marlboro -men-20140127-story.html (last accessed 9 Feb. 2021)

Peters, Tom. "The Brand Called You." *Fast Company*. August/September 1997. http://www.fastcompany.com/28905/brand-called -you (last accessed 9 Feb. 2021)

Wilde, Oscar. *The Complete Letters*. Ed. Merlin Holland and Rupert Hart-Davis. New York: Henry Holt and Company, 2000.

———. *The Importance of Being Earnest* [1895]. A Norton Critical Edition. Ed. Michael Patrick Gillespie. New York: W. W. Norton & Company, 2005.

———. *The Picture of Dorian Gray* [1890–91]. A Norton Critical Edition. Ed. Michael Patrick Gillespie. New York: W. W. Norton & Company, 2020.

CRITICISM

Early Reviews and Reactions

WILLIAM ARCHER

On *The Importance of Being Earnest*†

The dramatic critic is not only a philosopher, moralist, æsthetician, and stylist, but also a labourer working for his hire. In this last capacity he cares nothing for the classifications of Aristotle, Polonius, or any other theorist, but instinctively makes a fourfold division of the works which come within his ken. These are his categories: (1) Plays which are good to see. (2) Plays which are good to write about. (3) Plays which are both. (4) Plays which are neither. Class 4 is naturally the largest; Class 3 the smallest; and Classes 1 and 2 balance each other pretty evenly. Mr. Oscar Wilde's new comedy, *The Importance of Being Earnest*, belongs indubitably to the first class. It is delightful to see, it sends wave after wave of laughter curling and foaming round the theatre; but as a text for criticism it is barren and delusive. It is like a mirage-oasis in the desert, grateful and comforting to the weary eye—but when you come close up to it, behold! it is intangible, it eludes your grasp. What can a poor critic do with a play which raises no principle, whether of art or morals, creates its own canons and conventions, and is nothing but an absolutely wilful expression of an irrepressibly witty personality? Mr. Pater, I think (or is it some one else?), has an essay on the tendency of all art to verge towards, and merge in, the absolute art—music. He might have found an example in *The Importance of Being Earnest*, which imitates nothing, represents nothing, means nothing, is nothing, except a sort of *rondo capriccioso*, in which the artist's fingers run with crisp irresponsibility up and down the keyboard of life. Why attempt to analyse and class such a play? Its theme, in other hands, would have made a capital farce; but 'farce' is far too gross and commonplace a word to apply to such an iridescent filament of fantasy. Incidents of the same nature as Algy Moncrieffe's [*sic*] 'Bunburying' and John Worthing's invention and subsequent suppression of his scapegrace brother Ernest have done duty in many

† Signed review in the *World* (20 Feb. 1895).

107

a French vaudeville and English adaptation; but Mr. Wilde's
humour transmutes them into something entirely new and individual. Amid so much that is negative, however, criticism may find one
positive remark to make. Behind all Mr. Wilde's whim and even
perversity, there lurks a very genuine science, or perhaps I should
rather say instinct, of the theatre. In all his plays, and certainly not
least in this one, the story is excellently told and illustrated with
abundance of scenic detail. Monsieur Sarcey himself (if Mr. Wilde
will forgive my saying so) would 'chortle in his joy' over John Worthing's entrance in deep mourning (even down to his cane) to announce
the death of his brother Ernest, when we know that Ernest in the
flesh—a false but undeniable Ernest—is at that moment in the
house making love to Cecily. The audience does not instantly
awaken to the meaning of his inky suit, but even as he marches
solemnly down the stage, and before a word is spoken, you can feel
the idea kindling from row to row, until a 'sudden glory' of laughter
fills the theatre. It is only the born playwright who can imagine and
work up to such an effect. Not that the play is a masterpiece of construction. It seemed to me that the author's invention languished a
little after the middle of the second act, and that towards the close
of that act there were even one or two brief patches of something
almost like tediousness. But I have often noticed that the more successful the play, the more a first-night audience is apt to be troubled
by inequalities of workmanship, of which subsequent audiences are
barely conscious. The most happily-inspired scenes, coming to us
with the gloss of novelty upon them, give us such keen pleasure,
that passages which are only reasonably amusing are apt to seem,
by contrast, positively dull. Later audiences, missing the shock of
surprise which gave to the master-scenes their keenest zest, are
also spared our sense of disappointment in the flatter passages, and
enjoy the play more evenly all through. I myself, on seeing a play a
second time, have often been greatly entertained by scenes which
had gone near to boring me on the first night. When I see Mr. Wilde's
play again, I shall no doubt relish the last half of the second act
more than I did on Thursday evening; and even then I differed
from some of my colleagues who found the third act tedious.
Mr. Wilde is least fortunate where he drops into Mr. Gilbert's
Place-of-Truth mannerism, as he is apt to do in the characters of
Gwendolen and Cecily. Strange what a fascination this trick seems
to possess for the comic playwright! Mr. Pinero, Mr. Shaw, and
now Mr. Wilde, have all dabbled in it, never to their advantage. * * *

HAMILTON FYFE

On *The Importance of Being Earnest*†

Oscar Wilde may be said to have at last, and by a single stroke, put his enemies under his feet. Their name is legion, but the most inveterate of them may be defied to go to St. James's Theatre and keep a straight face through the performance of *The Importance of Being Earnest*. It is a pure farce of Gilbertian parentage, but loaded with drolleries, epigrams, impertinences, and bubbling comicalities that only an Irishman could have ingrafted on that respectable Saxon stock. Since *Charley's Aunt* was first brought from the provinces to London I have not heard such unrestrained, incessant laughter from all parts of the theatre, and those laughed the loudest whose approved mission it is to read Oscar long lectures in the press on his dramatic and ethical shortcomings. The thing is as slight in structure and as devoid of purpose as a paper balloon, but it is extraordinarily funny, and the universal assumption is that it will remain on the boards here for an indefinitely extended period.

GEORGE BERNARD SHAW

On *The Importance of Being Earnest*‡

It is somewhat surprising to find Mr Oscar Wilde, who does not usually model himself on Mr Henry Arthur Jones, giving his latest play a five-chambered title like *The Case of Rebellious Susan*. So I suggest with some confidence that *The Importance of Being Earnest* dates from a period long anterior to Susan. However it may have been retouched immediately before its production, it must certainly have been written before *Lady Windermere's Fan*. I do not suppose it to be Mr Wilde's first play: he is too susceptible to fine art to have begun otherwise than with a strenuous imitation of a great dramatic poem, Greek or Shakespearian; but it was perhaps the first which he designed for practical commercial use at the West End theatres. The evidence of this is abundant. The play has a plot—a gross anachronism; there is a scene between the two girls in the second act quite in the literary style of Mr Gilbert, and almost inhuman enough to have been conceived by him; the humour is adulterated by stock mechanical fun to an extent that absolutely scandalizes one in a play

† Notice signed "H.F." (Hamilton Fyfe) in the *New York Times* (Feb. 17, 1895): 1.
‡ Review signed "G.B.S." in *Saturday Review* (Feb. 23, 1895): lxxix, 249–50. Note is by the editor of this Norton Critical Edition.

with such an author's name to it; and the punning title and several of the more farcical passages recall the epoch of the late H. J. Byron. The whole has been varnished, and here and there veneered, by the author of *A Woman of No Importance*; but the general effect is that of a farcical comedy dating from the seventies, unplayed during that period because it was too clever and too decent, and brought up to date as far as possible by Mr Wilde in his now completely formed style. Such is the impression left by the play on me. But I find other critics, equally entitled to respect, declaring that *The Importance of Being Earnest* is a strained effort of Mr Wilde's at ultra-modernity, and that it could never have been written but for the opening up of entirely new paths in drama last year by *Arms and the Man*.[1] At which I confess to a chuckle.

I cannot say that I greatly cared for *The Importance of Being Earnest*. It amused me, of course; but unless comedy touches me as well as amuses me, it leaves me with a sense of having wasted my evening. I go to the theatre to be moved to laughter, not to be tickled or bustled into it; and that is why, though I laugh as much as anybody at a farcical comedy, I am out of spirits before the end of the second act, and out of temper before the end of the third, my miserable mechanical laughter intensifying these symptoms at every outburst. If the public ever becomes intelligent enough to know when it is really enjoying itself and when it is not, there will be an end of farcical comedy. Now in *The Importance of Being Earnest* there is plenty of this rib-tickling: for instance, the lies, the deceptions, the cross purposes, the sham mourning, the christening of the two grown-up men, the muffin eating, and so forth. These could only have been raised from the farcical plane by making them occur to characters who had, like Don Quixote, convinced us of their reality and obtained some hold on our sympathy. But that unfortunate moment of Gilbertism breaks our belief in the humanity of the play. Thus we are thrown back on the force and daintiness of its wit, brought home by an exquisitely grave, natural, and unconscious execution on the part of the actors. * * * On the whole I must decline to accept *The Importance of Being Earnest* as a day less than ten years old; and I am altogether unable to perceive any uncommon excellence in its presentations.

1. A play by Shaw first performed on April 21, 1894.

H. G. WELLS

On *The Importance of Being Earnest*[†]

It is, we were told last night, 'much harder to listen to nonsense than
to talk it'; but not if it is good nonsense. And very good nonsense,
excellent fooling, is this new play of Mr. Oscar Wilde's. It is, indeed,
as new a new comedy as we have had this year. Most of the others,
after the fashion of Mr. John Worthing, J.P., last night, have been
simply the old comedies posing as their own imaginary youngest
brothers. More humorous dealing with theatrical conventions it
would be difficult to imagine. To the dramatic critic especially who
leads a dismal life, it came with a flavor of rare holiday. As for the
serious people who populate this city, and to whom it is addressed,
how they will take it is another matter. Last night, at any rate, it was
a success, and our familiar first-night audience—whose cough, by-
the-bye, is much quieter—received it with delight. . . .

. . . It is all very funny, and Mr. Oscar Wilde has decorated a
humour that is Gilbertian with innumerable spangles of that wit that
is all his own. Of the pure and simple truth, for instance, he remarks
that 'Truth is never pure and rarely simple'; and the reply, 'Yes, flowers are as common in the country as people are in London,' is particularly pretty from the artless country girl to the town-bred
Gwendolen. . . .

How Serious People—the majority of the population, according
to Carlyle—how Serious People will take this Trivial Comedy written for their learning remains to be seen. No doubt seriously. One
last night thought that the bag incident was a 'little far-fetched'.
Moreover, he could not see how the bag and the baby got to Victoria
Station (L.B. and S.C.R. station) while the manuscript and perambulator turned up 'at the summit of Primrose Hill'. Why the summit? Such difficulties, he said, rob a play of 'convincingness'. That
is one serious person disposed of, at any rate.

On the last production of a play by Mr. Oscar Wilde we said it
was fairly bad, and anticipated success. This time we must congrat-
ulate him unreservedly on a delightful revival of theatrical satire.
Absit omen. But we could pray for the play's success, else we fear it
may prove the last struggle of its author against the growing seriousness of his dramatic style.

† Unsigned review in the *Pall Mall Gazette* (Feb. 15, 1895): 4.

Essays in Criticism

E. H. MIKHAIL

The Four-Act Version of *The Importance of Being Earnest*[†]

It has been known to a few of the many readers and playgoers who have delighted in *The Importance of Being Earnest* that Oscar Wilde originally wrote this comedy in four acts. In the form in which the play was first produced, it consisted of three acts, and it has been played in that form ever since. The original version contained a whole scene, with one fresh character, besides a good deal of additional dialogue, all of which Wilde cut out in revising the script. George Alexander, the manager of the St. James's Theatre and the producer of the play, did not like the idea of another character who appeared only in one particular scene. So, to oblige him, the author condensed Acts II and III to form a single act, and dropped the scene[1] with the extra character, whose name was Gribsby. That the most drastic part of the curtailment, the actual compression of the four acts in three, was done shortly before the comedy was presented is clear from the fact that the counterfoil of the license to perform, issued by the office of the Lord Chamberlain which is dated 30 January 1895, states that the play is in four acts, although the actual copy deposited is in three.[2]

Wilde's early biographers do not seem to have known of the four-act version of his play; at least they do not mention it. Nor does there seem to be any comment on the four-act text in the collected editions of Wilde's works. The author himself alludes to his play in more

---

† From *Modern Drama* 11 (1968): 263–66. Reprinted by permission of University of Toronto Press (https://utpjournals.press). doi:10.1353/mdr.1968.0047. Notes are by the author.

1. The scene was performed for the first time in the B.B.C. Home Service on 27 October 1954 and reproduced in *The Listener*, 4 November 1954. It was performed on the stage by the Wanstead Players in January 1955.
2. This information has been supplied by Mr. C. D. Heriot, of the Lord Chamberlain's Office. See *The Importance of Being Earnest; A Trivial Comedy for Serious People. In Four Acts as Originally Written by Oscar Wilde*, ed. by Sarah Augusta Dickson (New York, 1956).

than a dozen letters, of which five were written in 1894–1895 when he was working on it, and soon after it was first produced, and the rest in 1898–1899 at the time of its publication. In none of these letters is anything said of the important changes made in the text of the play. St. John Hankin, however, in an article for *The Fortnightly Review* in 1908,[3] mentions that the four acts had been "boiled down" into three, apparently being the first to note the fact in print. He was not aware that the original version had survived, as he expresses a wish that it might some day be found and published, saying, "If the deleted act is half as delightful as the three that survive, every playgoer will long to read it." The play is mentioned in Hesketh Pearson's *The Life of Oscar Wilde* (1946) as a four-act comedy shortened to three at George Alexander's insistence, a fact divulged to Pearson by Alexander himself. James Agate, alluding to the German translation in an essay for *The Masque* (1947), declared that "The fun in the act that Wilde deleted is better than any living playwright can do."[4] Either Robert Ross, Wilde's friend and the executor of his estate, or someone acting for him submitted a four-act typescript in 1903 to the German translator (Herman Frieherr von Teschenberg; published at Leipzig in 1903 and entitled *Ernst Sein!*). At that date Wilde's works were still ostracized in England. This publication seems to have attracted little attention beyond bibliographical listings until long afterwards a copy of the German translation came into the hands of James Agate who searched for the original English text, but could not find it.

What had happened to the manuscript is curious. It consisted of four quarto-size note-books. Somehow they got separated. In 1909, Wilde's literary executor, Robert Ross, presented a number of Wilde manuscripts to the British Museum, but only the fourth of the notebooks was amongst them. The whereabouts of the other three, which included the missing scene, remained a mystery for many years. Apparently they had been borrowed by a friend of Wilde's named Arthur Clifton, who was also a business associate of Ross, and they were never returned. They came to light on the death of Clifton's widow, being discovered among her effects in an old trunk. They were sold by public auction in London in 1950. Their eventual purchaser was an American collector, Mr. George Arents, and they are now in the Arents Collection in the New York Public Library. From these sources a coherent version of an early draft was assembled and published in 1956.[5]

3. St. John Hankin, "The Collected Plays of Oscar Wilde," *The Fortnightly Review*, LXXXIX (May 1908), 791–802.
4. James Agate, "Oscar Wilde and the Theatre," *The Masque*, No. 3 (1947).
5. Montgomery H. Hyde, "*The Importance of Being Earnest*; The Lost Scene from Oscar Wilde's Play," *The Listener* (4 November 1954), 753; Vyvyan Holland, "Explanatory

The difference between the three-act play and the four-act version is aptly summed up in the following words:

> In the original four-act play, Act I takes place in Algernon Moncrieff's rooms in London; Act II in the garden of the Manor House, Woolton; and Acts III and IV in the sitting-room of the Manor House. In the shortened three-act version, as it is always performed, Act I remains substantially unchanged, the action taking place, as before, in Algernon Moncrieff's rooms. Act II is a combination and condensation of Acts II and III of the four-act play, the whole of the action taking place in the garden. Act III is Act IV of the four-act play, though there are considerable alterations in the dialogue, necessitated by the revisions in the earlier acts; the action remains in the sitting-room of the Manor House. The three-act version is at least twenty per cent shorter than the four-act version; in the process of shortening about six hundred words were deleted from the end of the original Act II alone.
>
> In the three-act version, again, two of the characters in the original play were cut out: Mr. Gribsby, of the firm of Gribsby, solicitors, and Moulton, the gardener of the Manor House. The exclusion of Moulton did not affect the play, as he appeared only once and then he had only four lines to speak. But the removal of Gribsby seems to be a pity. He was an amusing character who only appeared in a short scene in the second act; but his disappearance made a great deal of alteration necessary in the subsequent dialogue, as in the four-act version frequent references were made to the object of his visit, which was to serve a writ on the mythical Mr. Ernest Worthing. These references had, of course, to be modified or deleted. In the original version, also, Lady Bracknell was called Lady Brancaster, and Algernon Moncrieff was called Montford.[6]

Dr. Sarah A. Dickson, the editor of the New York four-act edition, maintains that this is the best edition and one Wilde would have preferred:

Foreword" to *The Original Four-Act Version of "The Importance of Being Earnest"* (London, 1957); Sarah Augusta Dickson, "Introduction" to *The Importance of Being Earnest; A Trivial Comedy for Serious People. In Four Acts As Originally Written by Oscar Wilde* (New York, 1956); Theodore Bolton, "The Importance of Being Earnest," *Papers of the Bibliographical Society of America*, L (1956), 205–208; "Wilde's Comedy in Its First Version," *The Times Literary Supplement* (1 March 1957), 136; "The Importance of Publishing 'Earnest'," *Bulletin of the New York Public Library*, LX (July 1956), 368–372; William W. Appleton, "Making A Masterpiece: *The Importance of Being Earnest*," *The Saturday Review* (12 May 1956), 21; and *Oscar Wilde: The Importance of Being Earnest*, ed. by Vincent F. Hopper and Gerald B. Lahey (Great Neck, N.Y., 1959), p. 50.
6. Vyvyan Holland, "Explanatory Foreword" to *The Original Four-Act Version of "The Importance of Being Earnest"* (London, 1957), pp. vi–vii.

It is difficult to keep from believing that, if Oscar Wilde had known that the four-act version of *The Importance of Being Earnest* was still available . . . he would have preferred to publish his comedy as he had originally conceived it. By printing the entire text of the comedy as Wilde wrote it . . . we believe we are fulfilling what would have been the wishes of the author.[7]

Actually, the examination of the text shows that the New York four-act edition is not a preferable or even an alternative version at all, but merely an early draft. The organisation of the plot is looser and the arrest of Jack for debt diffuses the action. Many of the best lines are missing; the dialogue is less polished than in the regular edition; certain witticisms are even repeated from act to act, showing that Wilde had not finally decided where they should go. The theatrical qualities of the four-act version are of course untested, but the play as it has been known to the English-speaking theater since 1895 is surely a better play to read. The shortening of the comedy, mainly by the compression of Acts II and III, and with the regrettable omission of a rather amusing solicitor called Gribsby who comes to arrest Algernon for debt, are accomplished with skill and effectiveness. In the course of his cutting Wilde deprived us, it is true, of some amusing moments, such as that in the last scene when Miss Prism, leafing through a volume in search of the name of Jack's father, the General, remarks: "To me . . . you have given two copies of the Price Lists of the Civil Service. I do not find generals marked anywhere. There either seems to be no demand or no supply." Despite the interesting additional material in the four-act version, the three-act version is superior in artistic neatness and verbal economy, the action moves more smoothly and the wit crackles a little more sharply, and the play is a little less elaborately mannered in style. However, in reading the text of the four-act version, there is the satisfaction gained from an examination of the manuscripts presented therein. One could follow the dramatist as he worked, almost incessantly, on what he considered his best play, which was not "dashed off" at the seashore as some writers believe,[8] but was Wilde's chief concern and care from the summer of 1894 to the end of January 1895, when he deposited his shortened version at the Lord Chamberlain's Office.

---

7. Sarah Augusta Dickson, *op. cit.*, p. xxvii.
8. Montgomery H. Hyde, *"The Importance of Being Earnest*; The 'Lost' Scene from Oscar Wilde's Play," *The Listener* (4 November 1954), 753. Francis Winwar writes in *Oscar Wilde and the Yellow Nineties* (p. 258) that "it was dashed off in about a fortnight." Robert Harborough Sherard says in *The Real Oscar Wilde* (p. 363) that the play "was turned out in about a fortnight."

BURKHARD NIEDERHOFF

Parody, Paradox and Play in *The Importance of Being Earnest*†

1. Introduction

The Importance of Being Earnest is an accomplished parody of the conventions of comedy. It also contains numerous examples of Oscar Wilde's most characteristic stylistic device: the paradox. The present essay deals with the connection between these two features of the play.[1] In my view, the massive presence of both parody and paradox in Wilde's masterpiece is not coincidental; they are linked by a number of significant similarities. I will analyse these similarities and show that, in *The Importance of Being Earnest*, parody and paradox enter into a connection that is essential to the unique achievement of this play.

2. Parody

The most obvious example of parody in Wilde's play is the anagnorisis that removes the obstacles standing in the way to wedded bliss for Jack and Gwendolen. The first of these obstacles is a lack of respectable relatives on Jack's part. As a foundling who was discovered in a handbag at the cloakroom of Victoria railway station, he does not find favour with Gwendolen's mother, the formidable Lady Bracknell. She adamantly refuses to accept a son-in-law "whose origin [is] a Terminus." The second obstacle is Gwendolen's infatuation with the name "Ernest," the alias under which Jack has courted her. When she discovers that her lover's real name is Jack, she regards this as an "insuperable barrier" between them. Both difficulties are removed when the true identity of the foundling is revealed. It turns out that Jack has been christened "Ernest" and that he is Lady Bracknell's nephew. Thus he bears the name that Gwendolen insists on, and he has also acquired respectable relatives—even Lady Bracknell would find it hard to raise convincing objections against herself.

The anagnorisis comes about through a visible sign, a time-honoured method first discussed in Aristotle's *Poetics*. The most

---

† *Connotations* 13.1–2 (2003–04): 32–55. Reprinted by permission of *Connotations: Society for Critical Debate*. Notes are by the author.

1. To the best of my knowledge, this connection has not been systematically explored. In "Raymond Chandler: Burlesque, Parody, Paradox," Winifred Crombie analyses the links between clauses in Chandler's prose; she touches upon paradox only in the rather remote sense of inter-clausal connections of an illogical kind. She also claims that Chandler parodies the genre of detective fiction, but fails to establish a connection between parody and paradox.

famous example of this method, also mentioned by Aristotle,[2] is the scar which Odysseus owes to his courageous fight with a boar and which reveals his identity to his nurse Eurycleia when he returns to Ithaca after an absence of twenty years. In *The Importance of Being Earnest*, the sign that proves Jack's identity is the handbag in which he was found. His former nurse, Miss Prism, explains how the baby ended up in the bag:

> MISS PRISM.   [. . .] On the morning of the day you mention, a day that is for ever branded on my memory, I prepared as usual to take the baby out in its perambulator. I had also with me a somewhat old, but capacious hand-bag in which I had intended to place the manuscript of a work of fiction that I had written during my few unoccupied hours. In a moment of mental abstraction, for which I can never forgive myself, I deposited the manuscript in the bassinette and placed the baby in the hand-bag.
>
> JACK.   (*who had been listening attentively*) But where did you deposit the hand-bag?
>
> MISS PRISM.   Do not ask me, Mr Worthing.
>
> JACK.   Miss Prism, this is a matter of no small importance to me. I insist on knowing where you deposited the hand-bag that contained that infant.
>
> MISS PRISM.   I left it in the cloak-room of one of the larger railway stations in London.
>
> JACK.   What railway station?
>
> MISS PRISM.   (*quite crushed*) Victoria. The Brighton line. (*Sinks into a chair*) [. . .]
>
> *Enter Jack with a hand-bag of black leather in his hand*
>
> JACK.   (*rushing over to Miss Prism*) Is this the hand-bag, Miss Prism? Examine it carefully before you speak. The happiness of more than one life depends on your answer.
>
> MISS PRISM.   (*calmly*) It seems to be mine. Yes, here is the injury it received through the upsetting of a Gower Street omnibus in younger and happier days. Here is the stain on the lining caused by the explosion of a temperance beverage, an incident that occurred at Leamington. And here, on the lock, are my initials. I had forgotten that in an extravagant mood I had had them placed there. The bag is undoubtedly mine. I am delighted to have it so unexpectedly restored to me. It has been a great inconvenience being without it all these years.

2. See *Poetics* 1454b.

Even in comedy, anagnorises that bring about family reunions tend to be tearful events, or at least highly emotional ones,[3] but the emphasis placed on Miss Prism's battered old bag undercuts any such sentiments. It introduces the comic incongruity between debased or trivial content and dignified form that figures prominently in most definitions of parody.[4] To Miss Prism, the scene is not about the restoration of a lost child but about the recovery of a handbag. The sign whose function it is to identify the hero usurps the status of the hero. Instead of identifying Jack by means of the bag, Miss Prism identifies the bag by means of the "injury" that it received from a Gower Street omnibus—an injury that would appear to be a parodic allusion to the famous scar which shows Eurycleia whose feet she is washing (in both cases, two decades or more have passed when the hero re-encounters his nurse).

Parodies have a metaliterary tendency. By both imitating and distorting a text or a genre, they lay bare its conventions, pulling the audience out of the represented world and making it aware of the means and methods of representation. This is especially true of the anagnorisis of *The Importance of Being Earnest*. Wilde makes no attempt to hide the fact that he is using a literary convention. On the contrary, by offering an extremely ingenious and improbable solution to Jack's problems he highlights the contrived and artificial character of the convention. A metaliterary note is also struck by the curious replacement of a baby with a manuscript, of a child with a brainchild. While the manuscript obviously stands for literature, the baby represents life in its most pristine and natural form. When Miss Prism puts the former in the place of the latter, literature prevails over life. Perhaps we may even detect an allegory of parody in Miss Prism's mistake. After all, there are two contents and two containers: a baby who belongs in a pram, and a manuscript which belongs in a bag. Exchanging the baby and the manuscript brings about the very incongruity of form and content which is typical of parody. Be that as it may, the metaliterary quality of the anagnorisis is also suggested by the comments of the participants, who talk as if they knew that they are characters in a play. When Jack rushes off to search for the handbag, Lady Bracknell states that "strange coincidences are not supposed to occur" and Gwendolen adds, "This suspense is terrible. I hope it will last"—a

---

3. A particularly lachrymose example is the anagnorisis in Richard Steele's *The Conscious Lovers* (5.3), in which the merchant Sealand is reunited with his long-lost daughter Indiana.
4. See, for instance, Abrams 26, and Genette 19.

paradoxical wish that combines the point of view of a character with that of a spectator.[5]

The way to the true anagnorisis is paved with a number of ludicrously false ones. After Miss Prism's assumption that the scene is about handbags rather than about human beings, Jack makes a discovery that is no less ridiculous:

> JACK.   (*in a pathetic voice*) Miss Prism, more is restored to you than this hand-bag. I was the baby you placed in it.
> MISS PRISM.   (*amazed*) You?
> JACK.   (*embracing her*) Yes—mother!
> MISS PRISM.   (*recoiling in indignant astonishment*) Mr Worthing! I am unmarried!
> JACK.   Unmarried! I do not deny that is a serious blow. But after all, who has the right to cast a stone against one who has suffered? Cannot repentance wipe out an act of folly? Why should there be one law for men, and another for women? Mother, I forgive you. (*Tries to embrace her again*)
> MISS PRISM.   (*still more indignant*) Mr Worthing, there is some error. (*Pointing to Lady Bracknell*) There is the lady who can tell you who you really are.

Just as in the exchange about the handbag, moods and attitudes are singularly mismatched. Jack feels all the emotions appropriate to an anagnorisis scene. He is so full of joy and gratitude that he is moved to forgive his mother for straying from the path of virtue. But Miss Prism, who has maintained a rigid respectability throughout the play, is highly offended by Jack's assumption that she has given birth to an illegitimate child. To her, his generous words of forgiveness come as a gross insult. It should be added that the exchange between Jack and Miss Prism amounts to an exercise in self-parody on Wilde's part. It makes fun of the fallen woman, a subject that he deals with in a serious manner in *Lady Windermere's Fan* and *A Woman of No Importance*. Jack's speech is a comic echo of the message of these earlier plays, including an almost verbatim repetition of Hester's complaint about the double standard in *A Woman of No Importance*.[6]

The scene in which Jack proposes to Gwendolen provides us with another interesting example of Wildean parody:

---

5. There is an additional metadramatic comment in the original four-act version, which Wilde cut at the behest of the director, George Alexander. After Jack has left the scene to search for the handbag, Lady Bracknell says, rather like an Aristotelian drama critic, "I sincerely hope nothing improbable is going to happen. The improbable is always in bad, or at any rate, questionable taste." See *The Original Four-Act Version of* The Importance of Being Earnest 105.

6. This parodic self-echo is also pointed out by Meier 190 and Gregor 512–13.

JACK.   Gwendolen, I must get christened at once—I mean we must get married at once. There is no time to be lost.

GWENDOLEN.   Married, Mr Worthing?

JACK.   (*astounded*) Well . . . surely. You know that I love you, and you led me to believe, Miss Fairfax, that you were not absolutely indifferent to me.

GWENDOLEN.   I adore you. But you haven't proposed to me yet. Nothing has been said at all about marriage. The subject has not even been touched on.

JACK.   Well . . . may I propose to you now?

GWENDOLEN.   I think it would be an admirable opportunity. And to spare you any possible disappointment, Mr Worthing, I think it only fair to tell you quite frankly beforehand that I am fully determined to accept you.

JACK.   Gwendolen!

GWENDOLEN.   Yes, Mr Worthing, what have you got to say to me?

JACK.   You know what I have got to say to you.

GWENDOLEN.   Yes, but you don't say it.

JACK.   Gwendolen, will you marry me? (*Goes on his knees*)

GWENDOLEN.   Of course I will, darling. How long you have been about it! I am afraid you have had very little experience in how to propose.

JACK.   My own one, I have never loved anyone in the world but you.

GWENDOLEN.   Yes, but men often propose for practice. I know my brother Gerald does. All my girl-friends tell me so. What wonderfully blue eyes you have, Ernest! They are quite, quite blue. I hope you will always look at me just like that, especially when there are other people present.

Even more than in the anagnorisis scene, in which she and her mother make comments with metadramatic overtones, Gwendolen thinks of the occasion in terms of a script and of a part that has to be played and to be practiced. In this case, the parodic incongruity does not result from a clash between a high, dignified form and a low, ignoble content, but from the contrast between Gwendolen's formal and artificial script and Jack's more flexible and spontaneous one. He talks extempore, assuming that there is no need to utter what has already been implied. Gwendolen, however, does not tolerate any deviation from her script; she makes her suitor play his part and say all his lines. Paradoxically, her very insistence on following the script brings about a major deviation from it. In a proposal conducted along traditional lines, it is the man who plays the active part, while the woman reacts to his demands. In the case of Jack and Gwendolen, these roles are exchanged. Not only is Gwendolen in charge of the conversation, she even assumes that ultimate privilege of the male sex, the praise of the beloved's eyes.[7]

A final parodic feature of the proposal and other exchanges between Jack and Gwendolen becomes evident if one compares them with similar scenes from the second courtship plot. I have already mentioned the way in which *The Importance of Being Earnest* parodies Wilde's treatment of the fallen woman in his previous works. In addition, the play offers something like a parody of itself, with later scenes or speeches providing comic repetitions of earlier ones. Jack's proposal to Gwendolen is replayed by Algernon and Cecily, with minor variations on the same themes. Cecily also confesses her fascination with the name "Ernest"; she also admires her lover's beauty—not his eyes, but his curls—and she also thinks of the proposal in terms of a script. In her case, this script is not merely a metaphorical or mental one; the story of her courtship by Algernon has literally been written down in her diary. The parodic effect of this has been pointed out by Neil Sammells, who makes a number of perceptive comments on Wildean parody in an essay on Tom Stoppard's *Travesties*:

> The structure of Wilde's play is that of a travesty: Jack's proposal to Gwendolen is played again, and travestied, by Algy and Cecily; Lady Bracknell's interrogation of Jack in Act One reappears in a different form in her haranguing of Miss Prism. Similarly, individual scenes are themselves structured by travesty with one voice restating and confounding the other. (383)

Sammells does not explain what he means by the latter kind of travesty based on "one voice restating and confounding the other" in a single scene, but the following exchange between Gwendolen and Cecily might qualify as an example. It is the quarrel that follows their mistaken discovery that they are both engaged to the same man:

> CECILY. (*rather shy and confidingly*) Dearest Gwendolen, there is no reason why I should make a secret of it to you. Our little county newspaper is sure to chronicle the fact next week. Mr Ernest Worthing and I are engaged to be married.

---

7. Female dominance is not limited to the proposal scene or the relationship between Gwendolen and Jack; it characterizes all of the heterosexual relationships in the play, and some others elsewhere in Wilde's oeuvre. In *The Picture of Dorian Gray*, for instance, Lord Henry gossips about a forward American heiress who "has made up her mind to propose" to Lord Dartmoor. On female dominance in *The Importance of Being Earnest*, see Kohl, *Das literarische Werk* 176–77, Parker 176–77, and Raby 63.

GWENDOLEN. (*quite politely, rising*) My darling Cecily, I think there must be some slight error. Mr Ernest Worthing is engaged to me. The announcement will appear in the *Morning Post* on Saturday at the latest.

CECILY. (*very politely, rising*) I am afraid you must be under some misconception. Ernest proposed to me exactly ten minutes ago. (*Shows diary*)

GWENDOLEN. (*examines diary through her lorgnette carefully*) It is very curious, for he asked me to be his wife yesterday afternoon at 5.30. If you would care to verify the incident, pray do so. (*Produces diary of her own*) I never travel without my diary. One should always have something sensational to read in the train. I am so sorry, dear Cecily, if it is any disappointment to you, but I am afraid *I* have the prior claim.

CECILY. It would distress me more than I can tell you, dear Gwendolen, if it caused you any mental or physical anguish, but I feel bound to point out that since Ernest proposed to you he clearly has changed his mind.

GWENDOLEN. (*meditatively*) If the poor fellow has been entrapped into any foolish promise I shall consider it my duty to rescue him at once, and with a firm hand.

CECILY. (*thoughtfully and sadly*) Whatever unfortunate entanglement my dear boy may have got into, I will never reproach him with it after we are married.

Gwendolen and Cecily imitate each other to an extraordinary degree. They perform the same actions (showing a diary to their rival), strike the same attitudes ("*meditatively*" and "*thoughtfully*"), and say exactly the same things, a fact that is only highlighted by their elaborate efforts at finding synonyms: "some slight error"—"some misconception"; "I am so sorry"—"It would distress me"; "the poor fellow"—"my dear boy"; "entrapped"—"entanglement"; etc. The parodic effect is brought about in a rather unusual manner in this dialogue. It would be misleading to say that the speeches uttered by one woman are exaggerated, distorted or debased versions of the speeches delivered by the other. Instead, the parodic effect results from the closeness of the imitation. Gwendolen and Cecily violate the assumption that human beings should be individuals, not Bergsonian parrots who repeat somebody else's words and actions. If there is an element of parodic debasing, it consists in this reduction of a human being to a puppet. At any rate, the repetitions across or within the scenes from the two courtship plots are similar to the more obvious examples of parody, such as the anagnorisis, in that they strongly emphasize the artificiality of the characters' words and actions; instead of being spontaneous and unpredictable, these are governed by prior scripts and models.

Before we move on to paradox, a final word needs to be said about the mode of parody in *The Importance of Being Earnest*. Parodies can be satiric; witness Henry Fielding's *Shamela*, which ridicules both the literary form and the social values of Samuel Richardson's *Pamela*. Richard Foster interprets *The Importance of Being Earnest* along these lines. He argues that "[b]y exposing and burlesquing the vacuities of a moribund literature Wilde satirizes, too, the society that sustains and produces it" (23). According to this view, the girls' romantic scripts, which they have imbibed from novels and plays and which they impose on their lovers, are bound up with hollow social values, and the parody of the literary conventions becomes a satiric attack on these values. In my view, however, the play's parody is ludic rather than satiric.[8] The parodic scenes discussed in this essay offer a lot of comic incongruity, but the laughter evoked by this incongruity is not directed at a particular target. It is not satiric laughter that attacks one set of values in the name of another. As Andreas Höfele argues, the play lacks a precondition of effective satire: a standpoint (191). In the proposal scenes, for instance, we laugh at the young women's infatuation with an artificial social ritual, but we also admire the energy and the inventiveness that they show in shaping this ritual. And we laugh at their lovers just as much as at the young women. It would be simplistic to argue that the proposal scenes ridicule formality and etiquette in order to endorse a more natural and spontaneous way of interacting with other human beings.

To clarify what I mean by ludic parody, it might be helpful to borrow a distinction from Wayne Booth's *Rhetoric of Irony*, a borrowing that seems to me justified because of the proximity of irony and parody. Both of these rhetorical strategies entail the assumption of

---

8. I borrow the term *ludic* from Gerard Genette's typology of parody and its related modes. One of Genette's distinctions concerns the attitude that a text may take towards the text(s) that it transforms or imitates. There are three basic modes: first, a satirical or polemical mode in which the source text is ridiculed; second, a ludic mode which creates comic tension between the two texts but no ridicule or derision at the expense of the source; third, a serious mode that translates a text into another genre or cultural context without any comic distortion (33–37). An example of the first mode is Henry Fielding's *Shamela*, of the second (as I would like to claim), *The Importance of Being Earnest*, of the third, Thomas Mann's *Doktor Faustus*. In his important article on parody and comedy, Ian Donaldson makes a distinction which is similar to the distinction between the first two of Genette's modes: "[M]uch of our delight in watching a comedy comes from our recognition of the presence of time-honoured situations, complications, and resolutions, which are introduced in a spirit not so much of ridicule or burlesque as of playful affection. The kind of comic parody which I want to explore [. . .] is not the open and sustained parody of the better-known burlesque and rehearsal plays, but a parody altogether more genial and gentle, devoid of major satirical intent, playing wryly but nonetheless delightfully with the conventions of the comic form" (45). * * *

a voice that is not one's own; in irony, this voice is usually an invented one that is created by the ironist him- or herself; in parody, it is borrowed from a prior text. Booth distinguishes between stable and unstable irony. Faced with stable irony, the audience notices that the speaker cannot possibly mean what he or she says, and it infers what is meant instead (usually the opposite of what has been said). Faced with unstable irony, the audience notices that the speaker cannot possibly mean what he or she says, but it is incapable of taking the second step, of concluding what is really meant; the speaker does not commit him- or herself to any particular meaning. If we apply this distinction to our topic, stable irony becomes the equivalent of satiric parody, while unstable irony becomes the equivalent of ludic parody. With satiric parody, the audience realizes that the parodist ridicules the parodied text and its values, and it infers what a more natural text and a saner set of values would look like. With ludic parody, the audience notices that there is some sort of comic incongruity (in other words, that there is parody), but finds itself incapable of taking the second step, of inferring a set of values and a text that could replace the parodied text and its values. The experience of watching or reading *The Importance of Being Earnest* is of the latter sort.

3. *Paradox in Wilde*

I have given a fairly extensive analysis of parody in *The Importance of Being Earnest* as this topic has not been discussed by many critics. The topic of paradox in this play and in Wilde's writings generally has received more attention;[9] thus it need not detain us very long. However, before moving on to the connection between parody and paradox we should consider a distinction between two types of paradox that is relevant to Wilde's use of this device. The first type links opposite terms in a contradictory manner, as in "less is more." Paradoxes of this sort are infrequent in Wilde. He prefers a second type, which consists in stating the opposite of a received opinion; in other words, this second type of paradox contradicts not itself but common sense.[1] An example is provided by Gwendolen. As the analysis of the proposal scene has shown, she has little respect for traditional gender roles. This also becomes evident in the following speech: "Outside the family circle, papa, I am glad to say, is entirely unknown. I think that is quite as it should be. The home seems to me to be the proper sphere for the man." There is nothing self-contradictory about this speech; what it contradicts is the Victorian

---

9. See, for instance, Catsiapis, Hess-Lüttich, Nassaar and Zeender.
1. On the differences between these two types of paradox and on their ultimate similarity, see Niederhoff 49–52.

view that a wife should be the angel in the house, while her husband goes abroad to fight the battles of the world. A further example of the anti-commonsensical paradox comes from "The Decay of Lying," an essay that is in the tradition of the paradoxical encomium, a genre that praises what is normally dispraised.[2] Wilde's praise of lying attacks a number of received ideas, in particular the nineteenth-century doctrine of realism. Whereas the realists argue that it is the task of art to imitate life, Wilde claims that the exact opposite is valid: "Life imitates Art far more than Art imitates Life."

Furthermore, it should be kept in mind that a mere contradiction, of whatever kind, does not amount to a paradox. With both types of paradox, the element of contradiction has to be complemented by the possibility of sense. On the one hand, a paradox startles us with a violation of logic or common sense; on the other hand, it allows and challenges us to make sense of it, to endow absurdity with meaning. If this possibility of sense did not exist, we would not be dealing with a paradox but with mere error and inconsistency.

4. The Connection between Parody and Paradox

Para means 'beside,' *ode* means 'song,' and *doxa* means 'opinion.' Literally, a parody is something that positions itself 'beside a song' (or, more generally, beside a text), whereas a paradox positions itself 'beside an opinion.' This etymological consideration suggests a first link. The text or opinion that parody or paradox responds to must be generally known. There is no point in positioning oneself beside something which no one is familiar with; if a parody or a paradox [is] to be recognized as such, the audience must be acquainted with the text or the opinion they are based on.

The preposition *para*, which is present in both terms, refers to the procedure that parody or paradox appl[ies] to a text or to an opinion. If we stick to the principal meaning of *para*, this procedure places parody 'beside' a familiar text, and paradox 'beside' a received opinion. In the case of paradox, 'beside' does not designate the concept with sufficient precision. The meaning has to be shifted to 'against' or 'contrary to.' For a paradox is not merely incongruous with a received opinion; it maintains the exact opposite. In the case of parody, the meaning of *para* cannot be narrowed down in a similar fashion. The preposition has a greater range of meaning as the techniques of parody are various: it can exaggerate the stylistic features of the parodied text, debase its content, or invert one of its

---

2. On this genre, see Henry Knight Miller and Niederhoff 50–52, where further studies of the genre are listed.

elements, turning it into its opposite. In other words, a parody can place itself 'beside,' 'below,' or 'against' a text. Thus there is a partial overlap in the procedures of parody and paradox: inversion, or the change to the opposite, which amounts to the principal procedure of the latter, is at least one of the techniques of the former.

The main difference between the two terms is that between *ode* and *doxa*. A parody responds to a song or, more generally, a text, while a paradox responds to a received opinion. However, this difference is minimised if a received opinion is routinely expressed in a particular text, if text and opinion are so closely connected that a response to one entails a response to the other. A connection of this kind exists, for example, in proverbs and idioms, in which a commonsensical notion is coupled with a fixed expression. Interestingly, Wilde has a predilection for taking such an expression and replacing one of its words with its opposite.[3] What results is both a parody and a paradox. An example is provided by the following speech from *The Importance of Being Earnest*, in which Algernon anticipates the tedium of a dinner at Lady Bracknell's:

> She will place me next Mary Farquhar, who always flirts with her own husband across the dinner-table. That is not very pleasant. Indeed, it is not even decent . . . and that sort of thing is enormously on the increase. The amount of women in London who flirt with their own husbands is perfectly scandalous. It looks so bad. It is simply washing one's clean linen in public.

Algernon parodies the idiom *to wash one's dirty linen in public* by performing a minimal formal change; he replaces the adjective *dirty* with its antonym *clean*. The resulting inversion of the idiom's meaning also produces a paradox. While common sense maintains that one should not publicise one's affairs and adulteries, Algernon thinks the same about marital happiness and harmony. He considers it "perfectly scandalous" for a couple to flaunt the lack of scandal in their marriage.

A second example of the combination of parody and paradox from *The Importance of Being Earnest* is slightly more complex. The received opinion that is targeted here is the notion that a person's social rank is reflected not merely in birth and possessions but also in his or her manners. The 'text' that expresses this opinion is not a fixed string of words but, more loosely, a convention in the characterization of masters and servants in comedy. In this genre, the masters drink, preferably wine or champagne, whereas the servants eat,

---

3. For further examples of this technique, see Donaldson 45 and Ogala 228–29.

usually fairly rich food.[4] Wilde brings about an exchange of these roles in the first scene of his play:

> ALGERNON.   [H]ave you got the cucumber sandwiches cut for Lady Bracknell?
>
> LANE.   Yes, sir. (*Hands them on a salver*)
>
> ALGERNON.   (*Inspects them, takes two, and sits down on the sofa*) Oh! . . . by the way, Lane, I see from your book that on Thursday night, when Lord Shoreham and Mr Worthing were dining with me, eight bottles of champagne are entered as having been consumed.
>
> LANE.   Yes, sir; eight bottles and a pint.
>
> ALGERNON.   Why is it that at a bachelor's establishment the servants invariably drink the champagne? I ask merely for information.
>
> LANE.   I attribute it to the superior quality of the wine, sir. I have often observed that in married households the champagne is rarely of a first-rate brand.
>
> ALGERNON.   Good heavens! Is marriage so demoralizing as that?
>
> LANE.   I believe it *is* a very pleasant state, sir. I have had very little experience of it myself up to the present. I have only been married once. That was in consequence of a misunderstanding between myself and a young person.
>
> ALGERNON.   (*languidly*) I don't know that I am much interested in your family life, Lane.
>
> LANE.   No, sir; it is not a very interesting subject. I never think of it myself.
>
> ALGERNON.   Very natural, I am sure. That will do, Lane, thank you.
>
> LANE.   Thank you, sir. *Lane goes out*
>
> ALGERNON.   Lane's views on marriage seem somewhat lax. Really, if the lower orders don't set us a good example, what on earth is the use of them? They seem, as a class, to have absolutely no sense of moral responsibility.

---

4. Some examples of servants who like to eat: Sosia in the various versions of *Amphitryon*; Dromio of Ephesus, who advises the man whom he believes to be his master, "Methinks your maw, like mine, should be your clock, / And strike you home without a messenger" (*The Comedy of Errors* 1.2.66–67); Jeremy, who, in the opening scene of William Congreve's *Love for Love*, prefers real food to the nourishment of the mind. The link between masters and wine is shown by Congreve's Mellefont who is praised as "the very Essence of Wit, and Spirit of Wine" (*The Double-Dealer* 1.1.34–35), or by Sheridan's Charles and Careless who see it as "the great Degeneracy of the Age" that some of their fellows do not drink, that "they give into all the Substantial Luxuries of the Table—and abstain from nothing but wine and wit" (*The School for Scandal* 3.3.1–5). Another case in point is the debate about the respective merits of wine and women, a debate frequently conducted by young gentlemen in comedy (e.g. by Merryman and Cunningham in Charles Sedley's *Bellamira*); the debate is never about food and women.

Wilde parodies the convention by inverting it. The servant drinks champagne, while the master eats voraciously.[5] By the time Lady Bracknell arrives, Algernon has devoured all of the cucumber sandwiches, and in a later scene he will make short work of the muffins served at Jack's country residence. The dialogue between Algernon and Lane nicely illustrates the closeness between parody and paradox in the play, as it culminates in a paradox which is also based on an inversion of the roles of master and servant. Whereas Victorian common sense regards it as a task of the middle and upper classes to set a good example to those lower down the social scale, Jack expects Lane to act as a role model for him: "Really, if the lower orders don't set us a good example, what on earth is the use of them?" One might retort that Lane is still useful to Algernon in serving the cucumber sandwiches, but such mundane considerations are foreign to Algernon, who shares his author's penchant for sweeping generalisation.

My final and most important argument for the connection between parody and paradox hinges on the concept of play. This concept has already been touched upon in the second section of this essay, where the mode of parody in *The Importance of Being Earnest* has been described as ludic. This ludic mode should not be confused with recreational drollery. It is not a temporary relaxation from (and thus subordinate to) seriousness. It is rather motivated by a fundamental uncertainty, by a skepticism that finds it difficult to take anything seriously. It is this mode of skeptical play which also characterizes Wilde's paradoxes—at least if we follow the author's own suggestions. Wilde offers us a theory of paradox in which the concept of play figures prominently. This theory is to be found in the first chapters of *The Picture of Dorian Gray*, and it is mainly associated with Lord Henry, Dorian's aristocratic mentor (and tempter). The following passage describes Lord Henry enchanting a dinner-table audience with his paradoxical rhetoric:

> "Nowadays most people die of a sort of creeping common sense, and discover when it is too late that the only things one never regrets are one's mistakes."
>
> A laugh ran round the table.
>
> He played with the idea, and grew wilful; tossed it into the air and transformed it; let it escape and recaptured it; made it iridescent with fancy, and winged it with paradox. The praise of folly, as he went on, soared into a philosophy, and Philosophy herself became young, and catching the mad music of Pleasure, wearing, one might fancy, her wine-stained robe and

5. This inversion of roles is missed by James M. Ware in his article on Algernon's appetite; Ware relates this appetite to the hedonism of the rakes in Restoration comedy.

wreath of ivy, danced like a Bacchante over the hills of life, and mocked the slow Silenus for being sober. [. . .] It was an extraordinary improvisation.

Lord Henry's rhetoric is essentially paradoxical. He starts out by disparaging common sense, the antagonist of paradox, and continues with the paradox that "the only thing one never regrets are one's mistakes." In his poetic description of Lord Henry's talk, the narrator mentions the term explicitly ("winged it with paradox"), and he also weaves the title of the most famous paradoxical encomium of world literature, Erasmus's *Praise of Folly*, into this description.[6] The terms used to characterize Lord Henry's paradoxical rhetoric emphasize its ludic quality. It is play and improvisation; instead of weighing and pondering his ideas, Lord Henry throws them into the air and juggles them. This intellectual play is slightly mad and inebriated, but it is also far from mere drollery and facetiousness. For all its folly, it maintains the rank of a philosophy.

Lord Henry's interlocutors frequently claim that he does not mean what he says, or they ask him whether his paradoxes are to be taken seriously. He carefully avoids giving a straight answer to this question. If he answers in the affirmative, the ludic quality of the paradoxes will be eliminated. If he answers in the negative, the play will be at least diminished, framed and diminished by a context of seriousness. Lord Henry prefers a more radical kind of play, a play which includes seriousness at least as a *possibility*, which leaves its audience in the dark as to whether, and to what degree, it should be taken seriously. Here is how Lord Henry responds to Basil Hallward's charge that he lacks sincerity:

> "I don't agree with a single word that you have said, and, what is more, Harry, I feel sure you don't either."
> [. . .] "How English you are, Basil! That is the second time you have made that observation. If one puts forward an idea to a true Englishman—always a rash thing to do—he never dreams of considering whether the idea is right or wrong. The only thing he considers of any importance is whether one believes it

6. This allusion may be more than a passing reference; it may indicate an influence of Erasmus on Wilde or at least a profound affinity between them. *The Praise of Folly* evinces some very close similarities to Wilde's writings and to *The Importance of Being Earnest* in particular. First, it draws on the literary traditions of both parody and the paradoxical encomium, as C. A. Patrides points out in an article on Erasmus and Thomas More (39). Second, the preface asserts that "[n]othing is more puerile, certainly, than to treat serious matters triflingly; but nothing is more graceful than to handle light subjects in such a way that you seem to have been anything but trifling" (3). This seems fairly close to the subtitle of Wilde's play, *A Trivial Comedy for Serious People*. Third, *The Praise of Folly* is also informed by a spirit of sceptical play, by the eschewal of a fixed position. As Patrides writes, "Erasmus's mercurial protagonist is wont to disavow a number of specifically Erasmian tenets, admit as many others, and—more often than not—disavow and admit them at once" (40).

oneself. Now, the value of an idea has nothing whatsoever to do with the sincerity of the man who expresses it. Indeed, the probabilities are that the more insincere the man is, the more purely intellectual will the idea be, as in that case it will not be coloured by either his wants, his desires, or his prejudices."

Again, Lord Henry carefully avoids stating how serious he is about the claims he has made. Instead, he launches a surprising but not unpersuasive attack on the merits of seriousness and sincerity, thus giving a defence of the cognitive value of intellectual play.

In the following passage, we see two listeners responding to a paradox uttered by Lord Henry at his aunt's dinner table:

"I can stand brute force, but brute reason is quite unbearable. There is something unfair about its use. It is hitting below the intellect."

"I do not understand you," said Sir Thomas, growing rather red.

"I do, Lord Henry," murmured Mr Erskine, with a smile.

"Paradoxes are all very well in their way . . ." rejoined the Baronet.

"Was that a paradox?" asked Mr Erskine. "I did not think so. Perhaps it was. Well, the way of paradoxes is the way of truth."

The first response comes from Sir Thomas, the advocate of common sense. At first he finds Lord Henry's remark so absurd that he fails to understand it; then he grudgingly concedes that it might qualify as a paradox. But the manner in which he phrases this admission— "paradoxes are all very well *in their way*"—indicates that he considers them an aberration from the path of reason and virtue. To him, paradox is a frivolous and inferior mode of speech that should not be admitted into postprandial conversation, let alone into serious intellectual debate. The second response comes from Mr Erskine, introduced by the narrator as a "gentleman of considerable charm and culture." Mr Erskine does not find Lord Henry's remark absurd. He does not even regard it as a paradox, so convincing does it appear to him. Then he admits, like Sir Thomas but from a very different point of view, that it might be considered a paradox, but he hastens to add that paradoxes lead towards truth. Mr Erskine picks up the image of the way introduced by Sir Thomas, an image that implies movement, and his own response is significantly dynamic, characterized by a to and fro. Lord Henry's paradox has set Mr Erskine's mind in motion. This is, on the listener's part, the same intellectual motion that also characterizes the rhetorical play of paradox on the speaker's part, a kind of play that embraces seriousness as one possibility among others.[7]

---

7. The present explanation of the ludic quality of Wilde's paradoxes consists in a commentary on some passages from *The Picture of Dorian Gray*. Elsewhere I have given a

I would like to make a final stab at defining the ludic mode discussed here by looking at the pun on which the comedy ends. As it plays with a word that refers to the opposite of play, it has an obvious bearing on the present discussion:

> LADY BRACKNELL. My nephew, you seem to be displaying signs of triviality.
>
> JACK.   On the contrary, Aunt Augusta, I've now realized for the first time in my life the vital Importance of Being Earnest.

The form of the final sentence conveys the exact opposite of its content. The ludic manner in which it states the vital importance of being earnest amounts to an assertion of the vital importance of not being earnest. Because of this combination of opposites, it amounts to a kind of paradox and provides another example of the link between paradox and play that I have discussed with respect to Lord Henry's rhetoric. In playing with the word "Earnest," the final pun repeats what the entire play has done with the name "Ernest" and the concept of seriousness. Throughout the comedy, Ernest is only played: it is a fiction invented by Jack, a role used by him and Algernon, a fantasy embellished by Gwendolen and Cecily. When the final twist of the plot reveals that Jack's name is Ernest after all, it does so in the same spirit of parodic play that we have seen at work in the earlier stages of the anagnorisis, such as the recovery of a long-lost handbag. "Earnest" may be the final word of the comedy, but only according to the letter; according to the spirit, the final word is play.

5. *Why Is* The Importance of Being Earnest *Wilde's Masterpiece?*

The Importance of Being Earnest is generally considered Wilde's supreme achievement. Some critics have justified this view by arguing that in his earlier plays, and in *Dorian Gray*, the sophisticated rhetoric of such characters as Lord Henry, Mrs Erlynne or Lord Illingworth is at odds with other elements of the work, whereas in *The Importance of Being Earnest* this rhetoric is part of a coherent whole.[8] Erika Meier describes the artistic discrepancy in the early

---

more technical analysis of the ludic paradox, which distinguishes it from the comico-satirical paradox on the one hand, and the serious paradox on the other. This distinction is based on the relative weight of the opposites linked in a paradox, on the relative weight of the two principles which are at work in a paradox (contradiction and sense), and on the attitude taken by the speaker; see Niederhoff 60–76.

8. Ian Gregor claims that Wilde found a fitting dramatic environment for the dandy only in his final play but not in the earlier ones, a claim that is echoed in Raby 34. Norbert Kohl takes a similar view of the earlier plays: "Der grelle Kontrast zwischen Pathos und Paradoxon, zwischen der unvermittelten sprachlichen Melodramatik rührseliger

plays as a clash between witty dialogue and melodramatic plot. Only in his final play does Wilde succeed in fusing action and dialogue:

> The surprising events find their counterpart in the unexpect-edness of the epigrams; the plot, with its final ironic twist, is complemented by the innumerable paradoxical sayings; and the parallel development of the action (the romance of Gwendolen and Jack on the one hand and of Cecily and Algernon on the other hand) corresponds to the formal and often symmetrical dialogue. In his last play Wilde indeed succeeded in fusing the drama of language (as created in his earlier works) and the drama of action. (195)[9]

I find myself in basic agreement with Meier's claims. In fact, the present essay provides an explanation of how "the plot [. . .] is complemented by the innumerable paradoxical sayings." It is because the treatment of the plot is parodic, and because of the links between parody and paradox pointed out above, that The Importance of Being Earnest is all of a piece. In the earlier plays and in Dorian Gray, the plot is treated in a serious or even melodramatic fashion; these works lack the coherence between parody and paradox that characterizes Wilde's last play.

The incompatibility between playful paradoxes and a serious plot in the earlier works is illustrated by the ending of Dorian Gray. In this novel, the protagonist and his portrait change places in the first chapters. The man remains pure and beautiful like a work of art, whereas the picture turns more and more hideous with every evil act that Dorian commits. When he finally attempts to destroy the portrait, wishing to eliminate the visual record of his sins, he brings about his own death. Portrait and protagonist change places again; the former regains its original beauty, while the latter turns into an ugly and withered corpse. Thus the ending of the novel depicts a punishment of sin; it underlines the allegorical and cautionary character of the plot, whose orthodox morality and seriousness are a far cry from the exuberant and playful skepticism of Lord Henry's paradoxes.

The incompatibility between the plot and the paradoxes of Dorian Gray is not merely a matter of mode and atmosphere; there are even

---

Heroinen und dem artifiziellen Idiom der Dandys resultiert in Disharmonien, die der ästhetischen Homogenität der Stücke nicht eben zuträglich sind" (Leben und Werk 189). [The glorious contrast between pathos and paradox, between the unmediated sparse melodrama of melodious heroines and the artificial idiom of the Dandy results in disharmonies which are not exactly conducive to the aesthetic homogeneity of the pieces.]

9. See also Dariusz Pestka, who argues that in the early plays "the plot is not comic at all, and only verbal wit and a few amusing characters counterbalance the serious problems; whereas in the latter [The Importance of Being Earnest] the plot contributes to the playful mood and reinforces other comic devices" (191).

more specific contradictions between them. At one point, Lord Henry states:

> The mutilation of the savage has its tragic survival in the self-denial that mars our lives. We are punished for our refusals. Every impulse that we strive to strangle broods in the mind, and poisons us. The body sins once, and has done with its sin, for action is a mode of purification. [. . .] The only way to get rid of a temptation is to yield to it.

Whereas common sense maintains that we keep morally pure by resisting temptation and avoiding sin, Lord Henry claims that the opposite is true. Self-denial poisons; sinning purifies. The plot, however, does not follow this paradoxical logic. Every temptation that Dorian yields to leaves its mark on the portrait; every sin that he commits adds another blemish. It is only in Lord Henry's speech that action is a mode of purification; in the plot of the novel, it remains a mode of defilement. The plot also clashes with the paradoxes of "The Decay of Lying" mentioned in the third section of this essay. Admittedly, there is a temporary period in which these paradoxes seem to govern the plot. After the man and the portrait have changed places, life does imitate art in that Dorian is and remains as beautiful as the picture of his younger self. But in the portrait the traditional principles of mimesis and morality are upheld; art imitates life and teaches an ethical lesson in that every sin committed by Dorian is mirrored in the painting. It is the logic of the portrait that prevails in the end. Dorian's self-fashioning fails; the beautiful lie that his life is built on collapses, while the ugly truth is revealed. To sum up, the ending of *Dorian Gray* is at odds with the paradoxical rhetoric in this novel and in "The Decay of Lying," and this discrepancy remains unresolved.

The ending of *The Importance of Being Earnest* is comparable to the ending of *Dorian Gray* in that it also concerns the identity of the protagonist and his relationship with a kind of *doppelgänger* that enables him to lead a double life. In the novel, the *doppelgänger* is the miraculously changing image that inhabits the picture painted by Basil Hallward. This image allows Dorian to lead a life of sin because it bears the marks of this life, thus making it possible for him to appear spotless and innocent in the eyes of the world. The ending of the novel shows the tragic folly of this double life; the *doppelgänger* is annihilated when the picture returns to its former status as an ordinary portrait that is no longer subject to miraculous change. The *doppelgänger* of the play is "Ernest," the role that Jack has invented for the time he spends in London; this *doppelgänger* is surprisingly confirmed by the ending. It is revealed that Jack has indeed been christened "Ernest"; he has invented the truth, as it were. Of course, this confirmation is given in the same spirit of parodic play that characterizes the entire anagnorisis up to the final pun; the *doppelgänger* is confirmed precisely because he, too, is a manifestation of playing. Thus the ending does not amount to a lapse into seriousness; it is informed by the ludic mode that also inspires the paradoxical rhetoric of the play. The ending is also in tune with the very paradoxes of "The Decay of Lying"[1] that are negated by the ending of *Dorian Gray*. In *The Importance of Being Earnest*, life imitates art in that "Ernest," the creative lie, turns out to be true. The role is the ultimate reality; the truest poetry is the most feigning.

WORKS CITED

Abrams, Meyer Howard. *A Glossary of Literary Terms*. 7th ed. Boston: Heinle & Heinle, 1999.

Aristotle. *Poetics: Classical Literary Criticism*. Eds. D. A. Russell and M. Winterbottom. The World's Classics. Oxford: OUP, 1989. 51–90.

Booth, Wayne C. *A Rhetoric of Irony*. Chicago: U of Chicago P, 1974.

Catsiapis, Hélène. "Ironie et paradoxes dans les comédies d'Oscar Wilde: une interprétation." *Thalia: Studies in Literary Humor* 1 (1978): 35–53.

Congreve, William. *The Complete Plays*. Ed. Herbert Davis. Chicago: U of Chicago P, 1967.

Crombie, Winifred. "Raymond Chandler: Burlesque, Parody, Paradox." *Language and Style: An International Journal* 16 (1983): 151–68.

Donaldson, Ian. "'The Ledger of the Lost-and-Stolen Office': Parody in Dramatic Comedy." *Southern Review: Literary and Interdisciplinary Essays* 13 (1980): 41–52.

Erasmus, Desiderius. *The Praise of Folly*. Ed. Hoyt Hopewell Hudson. New York: Random House, 1970.

Foster, Richard. "Wilde as Parodist: A Second Look at *The Importance of Being Earnest*." *College English* 18 (1956–57): 18–23.

Genette, Gérard. *Palimpsestes: La littérature au second degré*. Paris: Seuil, 1982.

Gregor, Ian. "Comedy and Oscar Wilde." *Sewanee Review* 74 (1966): 501–21.

Hess-Lüttich, Ernest W. B. "Die Strategie der Paradoxie: Zur Logik der Konversation im Dandyismus am Beispiel Oscar Wildes." *Semiotics of Drama and Theatre: New Perspectives in the Theory of Drama and Theatre*. Eds. Herta Schmid and Aloysius van Kesteren. Amsterdam: Benjamins, 1984. 197–234.

---

1. A link between this essay and the play is also established by E. B. Partridge in his article, "The Importance of Not Being Earnest."

Höfele, Andreas. *Parodie und literarischer Wandel: Studien zur Funktion einer Schreibweise in der englischen Literatur des ausgehenden 19. Jahrhunderts*. Heidelberg: Winter, 1986.

Kohl, Norbert. *Oscar Wilde: Leben und Werk*. Frankfurt a. M.: Insel, 2000.

——. *Oscar Wilde: Das literarische Werk zwischen Provokation und Anpassung*. Heidelberg: Winter, 1980.

Meier, Erika, *Realism and Reality: The Function of the Stage Directions in the New Drama from Thomas William Robertson to George Bernard Shaw*. Bern: Francke, 1967.

Miller, Henry Knight. "The Paradoxical Encomium with Special Reference to Its Vogue in England, 1600–1800." *Modern Philology* 53 (1955): 145–78.

Nassaar, Christopher S. "On Originality and Influence: Oscar Wilde's Technique." *Journal of the Eighteen Nineties Society* 24 (1997): 37–47.

Niederhoff, Burkhard. *"The Rule of Contrary": Das Paradox in der englischen Komödie der Restaurationszeit und des frühen 18. Jahrhunderts*. Trier: Wissenschaftlicher Verlag Trier, 2001.

Ogala, Aatos. *Aestheticism and Oscar Wilde*. 2 vols. Helsinki: n. p., 1955.

Parker, David. "Oscar Wilde's Great Farce." *Wilde: Comedies: A Casebook*. Ed. William Tydeman. London: Macmillan, 1982. 166–79.

Partridge, E. B. "The Importance of Not Being Earnest." *Bucknell Review* 9 (1960): 143–58.

Patrides, C. A. "Erasmus and More: Dialogues with Reality." *Kenyon Review* 8 (1986): 34–48.

Pestka, Dariusz. "A Typology of Oscar Wilde's Comic Devices." *Studia Anglica Posnaniensia: An International Review of English Studies* 22 (1989): 175–93.

Raby, Peter. *The Importance of Being Earnest: A Reader's Companion*. New York: Twayne, 1995.

Sammells, Neil. "Earning Liberties: *Travesties* and *The Importance of Being Earnest*." *Modern Drama* 29 (1986): 376–87.

Shakespeare, William. *The Complete Works*. Ed. Stanley Wells et al. Oxford: Clarendon P, 1986.

Sheridan, Richard Brinsley. *Sheridan's Plays*. Ed. Cecil Price. Oxford: OUP, 1975.

Ware, James M. "Algernon's Appetite: Oscar Wilde's Hero as Restoration Dandy." *English Literature in Transition* 13 (1970): 17–26.

Wilde, Oscar. *The Importance of Being Earnest and Other Plays*. Ed. Peter Raby. Oxford World's Classics. Oxford: OUP, 1995.

——. *The Major Works*. Ed. Isobel Murray. Oxford World's Classics. Oxford: OUP, 2000.

———. *The Original Four-Act Version of* The Importance of Being Earnest: A Trivial Comedy for Serious People. Ed. Vyvyan Holland. London: Methuen, 1957.
Zeender, Marie-Noelle. "Oscar Wilde: Le jeu du paradoxe." *Cycnos* 10 (1993): 53–61.

CHRISTOPHER S. NASSAAR

Some Remarks on "Parody, Paradox and Play in *The Importance of Being Earnest*"†

Niederhoff's article is interesting and reaches a significant conclusion, but it does challenge critical debate. I shall follow its own divisions in my response to it.

(1) Parody

The essay begins by stating that the "most obvious example of parody in Wilde's play is the anagnorisis that removes the obstacles standing in the way to wedded bliss for Jack and Gwendolen." [117]. Perhaps, but to my mind the double identity of Jack and Algernon as a parody of Dorian Gray is even more obvious.

Niederhoff then moves on to discuss the scar which Odysseus received during his fight with a boar and which ultimately reveals his identity to his nurse Eurycleia, and ties it to the handbag that reveals Jack's identity in *The Importance of Being Earnest*: "Instead of identifying Jack by means of the bag, Miss Prism identifies the bag by means of the 'injury' that it received from a Gower Street omnibus—an injury that would appear to be a parodic allusion to the famous scar which shows Eurycleia whose feet she is washing." [119] To connect the two events without further and more cogent proof than just the scar and the injury does not seem convincing to me, nor does the following statement in the next paragraph: "While the manuscript [—] stands for literature, the baby represents life in its most pristine and natural form." Prism's manuscript does *not* stand for literature in general, nor is the baby—as far as I can see— presented as a symbol of anything.

Niederhoff then goes on to discuss *The Importance of Being Earnest* as a parody of literary conventions, and here he is quite good. One should caution, though, that Wilde's target in the play is Victorianism as a whole, and that the parody of literary conventions is

† *Connotations* 14.1–3 (2004/05): 173–76. Reprinted by permission of *Connotations: Society for Critical Debate*. Page numbers in square brackets refer to this Norton Critical Edition.

part of this larger frame. There is also a good deal of self-parody in *Earnest*. Niederhoff rightly argues that Jack's exchange with Miss Prism, in which Jack mistakenly assumes that she is his mother, is a parody of the fallen woman as seriously presented in *Lady Windermere's Fan* and *A Woman of No Importance*. I would add that the entire double-identity situation of Jack and Algernon reduces to nonsense the sinister double life of Dorian Gray, that Dr. Chasuble—especially in his repressed sexuality—is a parody of Jokanaan, that Algernon's engagement makes fun of the theme of determinism prominent in some of Wilde's earlier works, that Gwendolen and Cecily constitute a split personality, that Jack's misadventures as a baby parody not only the Victorian convention of the abused child but also Wilde's serious use of this convention in some of his earlier works, and so on. The result is that *Earnest* is at one level a self-parody, in which Wilde reduces not only Victorianism but his own earlier works to the level of nonsense.

The author ends by making a useful distinction between satiric parody and ludic parody. In the former, the author satirizes society while presenting a saner set of values. In the latter, however, there is no standpoint, no set of values to replace those that are being satirized. Niederhoff argues convincingly that Wilde's play is an excellent example of ludic parody.

He also makes a very valuable point during his argument which can easily be developed into a separate essay. "In addition," he writes, "the play offers something like a parody of itself, with later scenes or speeches providing comic repetitions of earlier ones." This is an idea well worth exploring, especially since Wilde parodies his earlier works so heavily in *Earnest*.

(2) *Paradox*

This section is short, and perhaps rightly so, as paradox in *Earnest* has been discussed by many critics. The author points out that a paradox startles us by violating logic or common sense, but also challenges us to make sense of it.

(3) *The Connection between Parody and Paradox*

The Importance of Being Earnest is full of both parody and paradox, but what is the connection between them? While paradox maintains the exact opposite of received opinion, Niederhoff states, parody can exaggerate, debase or invert. When it inverts, parody overlaps with paradox, as for instance when Wilde takes an expression and replaces one of its words with its opposite.

His main point, though, comes later: "My final and most important argument for the connection between parody and paradox

hinges on the concept of play. [. . .] Wilde offers us a theory of paradox in which the concept of play figures prominently." Here Niederhoff is excellent. He connects Wilde with Lord Henry's rhetoric,
presenting them both as jugglers of ideas, but complex jugglers
whose play includes seriousness as a *possibility*. This is a correct and
valuable description of Wilde's method, for he leaves us constantly
guessing if he is serious, and if yes, to what extent. He is forever playing not only with ideas but with the very concept of earnestness.

(4) *Why Is* The Importance of Being Earnest *Wilde's Masterpiece?*

According to Niederhoff, who echoes other critics here, the reason
for *Earnest's* great success is the fusion of form and content. In his
other works, Wilde's wit clashed with a sober content, but not so in
Earnest. This is undoubtedly true. In creating his never-never land
of wit and nonsense, Wilde captured a mood, a state of mind, that
no one before or after him has been able to capture so perfectly. As
we enter this fabulous children's world for adults, form and content
blend perfectly. One can even argue that Wilde's experimentation
with literary forms was, at least in part, a lifelong search for the right
form to house his matchless wit. In his last play, he finally found it.

CLIFTON SNIDER

Synchronicity and the Trickster in *The Importance of Being Earnest*†

The idea that Wilde wrote to subvert received ideas—the *zeitgeist*
or spirit of the age—is not new. Jack Zipes asserts, for example,
Wilde's 'purpose' in writing his fairy tales was 'subversion': 'He clearly
wanted to subvert the messages conveyed by [Hans] Andersen's tales,
but more important his poetical style recalled the rhythms and language of the Bible in order to counter the stringent Christian code'
(p 114). In Wilde's masterpiece, *The Importance of Being Earnest*,
Christianity is certainly one of the prevailing ideas Wilde subverts,
but I contend that the entire play is a subversion of prevailing scientific ideas about how the universe works, the Newtonian notion that
the universe is governed by immutable laws of cause and effect. As
Allan Combs and Mark Holland maintain, 'the mechanistic mythos
of the Newtonian cosmos—presents itself in awesome and austere

---

† From *The Wildean: Journal of the Oscar Wilde Society* 27 (2005): 55–63. Reprinted
with permission of the author. Clifton Snider is a poet, novelist, and scholar. Notes are
by the author. Page numbers in square brackets refer to this Norton Critical Edition.

beauty, but at the same time robs us of a sense of wonder about the small events of everyday life. Improbable coincidences are diminished to the trivial' (p xxix). Perhaps Wilde had something like this idea in mind when he subtitled his play, 'A Trivial Comedy for Serious People.' In any event, the subtitle, like the play itself, is an elegant joke.

Wilde, of course, was not the first Victorian writer to make havoc with a rigid world view. Before him, and certainly influencing him, came Lewis Carroll, Edward Lear, and W. S. Gilbert. As the editors of *The Oxford Anthology of English Literature* put it, the world of *Earnest* is 'the world of nonsense' (Trilling and Bloom p 1130). And, as I have shown in my study of the work of Lear, the world of nonsense is the world of the Trickster archetype (Snider, 'Victorian Trickster'). Furthermore, 'Of all mythological characters,' as Combs and Holland write, 'it is the Trickster who is most associated with chance and synchronicity . . .' (p xxxix). Synchronicity, a word coined by C. G. Jung, refers to '*meaningful coincidence[s]*' that have an 'a causal connection,' yet are 'numinous' (Jung, 'Synchronicity' p 426; emphasis Jung's). One method of making sense of the nonsense of Wilde's great play is to examine the subversive ways Wilde uses, consciously or not, synchronicity and the Trickster to create a pleasing psychic wholeness at the play's conclusion.

The Importance of Being Earnest is most obviously a comic critique of late Victorian values. Some sixty years ago, Eric Bentley wrote that the play 'is about *earnestness*, that is, Victorian solemnity, that kind of false seriousness which means priggishness, hypocrisy, and lack of irony' (p 111; emphasis Bentley's).[1] As a work of art, Wilde's last play has been recognized from its first performance on 14 February 1895 as a masterpiece of comedy,[2] one of the supreme examples in English of the genre, and consequently it has been interpreted from a variety of critical points of view. Although Richard Aldington, writing about the same time as Bentley, claimed the play 'is a comedy-farce without a moral, and it is a masterpiece' (p 40), Katharine Worth does see a moral in her Freudian/existential/New

---

1. Writing shortly after Bentley, Edouard Roditi takes an opposing approach: 'In spite of the polished brilliance of its paradoxical dialogue and the sure pace of its surprising action, *The Importance of Being Earnest* . . . never transcends, as a work of art, the incomplete or the trivial. Its tone is that of satire, but of a satire which, for lack of a moral point of view, has lost its sting . . .' (p 94). To the contrary, Wilde's contemporary achievement (or 'trick') was to draw to the theatre the very people he satirized and make them laugh at themselves, as it were, at their own moral shortcomings. I agree with Isobel Murray that *Earnest* provides 'a version of life with great similarities to London Society, but with a few 'Through The Looking-Glass' qualities' (p xix). Subsequent criticism has shown Roditi's assessment of Wilde's masterpiece as wrong-headed, to say the least.

2. Richard Ellmann writes: 'Everyone liked the play except Shaw, who thought it all froth and no pith. Thank God for froth. *The New York Times*, not given to praising Wilde, announced next day, 'Oscar Wilde may be said to have at last, and by a single stroke, put his enemies under his feet" (pp 430–31).

Critical analysis. In *Earnest,* she writes, 'the pleasure principle at last enjoys complete triumph' (p 153; this triumph is an aspect of the Trickster archetype). Worth continues: 'As well as being an existential farce, *The Importance of Being Earnest* is . . . [Wilde's] supreme demolition of late nineteenth-century social and moral attitudes, the triumphal conclusion to his career as revolutionary moralist' (p 155).

Various deconstructionists and Lacanians have dismantled the play, and perhaps the foremost queer critic, Eve Kosofsky Sedgwick, tackles the play in a piece called, 'Tales of the Avunculate: Queer Tutelage in *The Importance of Being Earnest.*' After covering the deconstructionist and Lacanian territory as explored by Christopher Craft, Joel Fineman, and Jonathan Dollimore, Sedgwick, in one of her more lucid pronouncements, declares:

> As we have seen, the indispensable—but, I am arguing insufficient—deconstructive reading of *Earnest* always seems, like the play's hero, to have its origin in a terminus. It doesn't pass Go; it doesn't collect $200; it heads straight for the end-of-the-third-act anagnorisis (recognition or de-forgetting) of the Name of the Father. (p 195)

Instead of the Name of the Father, Sedgwick would have us consider the aunts and uncles (the 'avunculate' of her title). Leaving aside the fact that her discussion of the 'family' as an issue in current politics (and in Wilde's play) is already dated***, Sedgwick's article, while providing certainly a legitimate approach to the play, alas vacillates between diction that is clear and semi-colloquial (such as the allusion to Monopoly above) and hyper-academic diction that violates the spirit of Wilde's comedy (besides 'anagnorisis,' for which she feels she must provide a definition, consider 'avunculosuppressive' (p 199) or '*Uncle* is very different [from '*Aunt*'], *not* a persona or type but a relation, relying on a pederastic/pedagogical model of male filiation to which also . . . the modern rationalized inversion and 'homo-' models answer only incompletely and very distortingly' (p 197).

Personally, until I noticed the predominance of the Trickster in *The Importance of Being Earnest,* I found myself agreeing with Peter Raby: 'The play's success and originality do not make it easier to discuss' (p 120). The comic social satire is obvious; so are the many examples of Wilde's masterful use of language, from paradox and parallelism to litotes and understatement. As for the homosexual subtext, it is not easy to uncover any more than a traditional Jungian discussion of archetypes is easy. Yes, we have the Great Mother archetype, embodied by Lady Bracknell, but to uncover Jung's concept of Individuation is more difficult. However, I believe I have found a way (not *the* way) to unravel the nonsense of the play, at least so that the nonsense itself is meaningful.

One of the problems of an archetypal interpretation of *Earnest* which is at the same time informed by contemporary queer criticism is that the play is so much of its time and place (if you consider time to include the previous hundred or more years and the following more than a hundred years). I tend to agree with Camille Paglia: 'Lord Henry [of *The Picture of Dorian Gray*], with the four young lovers of *The Importance of Being Earnest*, belongs to a category of sexual personae that I call the androgyne of manners, one of the most western of types' (531). Lady Bracknell is also 'an androgyne, a 'Gorgon' with (in the original script) a 'masculine mind'" (535). A western type is not in itself an archetype; an androgyne is. Androgyny ought to imply psychic wholeness, what Jung calls the Self, yet despite the allusion to a character from Greek myth, among these specific characters we have at best shallow images of traditional archetypes, a wholeness only latent until the play concludes. They are indeed universal beneath the surface, but a more insightful method of viewing them is to explore how the Jungian concept of synchronicity and the archetypal Trickster work in the play to bring about a kind of wholeness at the play's end.

'Synchronicity,' Jung says, 'tells us something about the nature of . . . the *psychoid* factor, i.e., the unconscious archetype (not its conscious representation!)' (Letter to Michael Fordham p 508; emphasis Jung's). Moreover, as Combs and Holland note, 'Synchronicity itself implies wholeness and, therefore, meaningful relationships between causally unconnected events' (p xxxi). As well, Jungian therapist and author Robert H. Hopcke maintains that synchronistic 'events' have four aspects:

> First, such events are *acausally* connected, rather than connected through a chain of cause and effect that an individual can discern as intentional and deliberate on her or his own part. Second, such events always occur with an accompaniment of *deep emotional experience* . . . Third, the content of the synchronistic experience, what the event actually is, is always *symbolic* in nature, and almost always, I have found, related specifically to the fourth aspect of the synchronistic event, namely, that such coincidences occur at points of *important transitions* in our life. A synchronistic event very often becomes a turning point in the stories of our lives. (p 23; emphasis Hopcke's)

Jung's comment, cited above, that synchronistic events are 'numinous' is what Hopcke means by '*deep emotional experience*.'[3]

---

3. Hopcke says, 'Numinosity is that experience we have when we feel that we are undeniably, irresistibly, and unforgettably in the presence of the Divine, our experience of something which transcends our human limitations' (p 30).

Archetypes (universal ideas, themes, patterns, characters, etc., that reside in and whose images stem from the collective unconscious), Jung maintained, are 'the sources of synchronicity' (Combs and Holland p 57). The archetype most closely related to synchronicity is the Trickster, and the Trickster Combs and Holland see as the best example of this relationship is Hermes.[4] Among many other attributes, Hermes 'symbolizes the penetration of boundaries—boundaries between villages, boundaries between people, boundaries between consciousness and unconsciousness' (pp 61–62). These boundaries are analogous to the transitions Hopcke refers to, and they are keys to the appearances of the Trickster in Wilde's *Earnest*.

Two important boundaries in the play are those between Algernon and Cecily and Jack/Ernest and Gwendolen. One of the most amusing scenes in the play is that in which Cecily reveals to Algernon, just after they've met, that they have been engaged 'for the last three months' [35]. One might say that the Trickster, Hermes, 'who personifies the imagination' (Combs and Holland p 88), has been the catalyst for the synchronistic event taking place here: the actual appearance of the man Cecily has imagined as her fiancé and who, subsequently, becomes in fact her fiancé. In a less dramatic fashion, Gwendolen too has imagined before meeting him her engagement to Jack, who she believes is really named Ernest. She tells him: 'The moment Algernon first mentioned to me that he had a friend called Ernest, I knew I was destined to love you' [15]. Although logic suggests that the meetings of the two couples are not accidental (and therefore not synchronistic), their mutual attraction is both intentional *and* acausal, one of the play's paradoxes. In a Newtonian cosmos, one can not force love. In a Looking-Glass world, love flowers for the most superficial reasons even before the lovers meet. We have here a pair of, to use Jung's words about synchronicity in another context, 'parallel events,' which are 'utter nonsense . . . looked at from the causal point of view' (*C. G. Jung Speaking* p 314). The world Wilde has created is a world of nonsense. Synchronicity gives meaning to the nonsense of these crazy, child-like characters to whom love and marriage depend on the name of the men and the physical attributes of the women. Their comical meetings

---

4. Combs and Holland point out that 'the Trickster is often connected with storytelling, and in the case of Hermes with writing' (pp 112–113). Among Wilde's possessions was 'a large plaster cast of the Hermes of Olympia' (Ellmann p 258), and he surely was aware of the myth. He would not, however, have been aware of Jung's ideas about synchronicity and the Trickster, nor would such a knowledge have been necessary for him to have employed these concepts in his play. Although Jung coined the term, synchronicity has existed as long as the human psyche has existed, as has the Trickster, whose pre-human genesis among animals is hinted at by the Native American stories of the coyote, raven, and so forth. The archetypes are primal; they derive from our pre-human, animal ancestors.

and engagements are as numinous they can be in their Looking-Glass world.

The most obvious cluster of synchronistic events comes in the final act with the appearances of Miss Prism (the dark side of the Great Mother archetype, for unlike Lady Bracknell she has not only committed a serious crime but also moralizes in a way foreign to the aristocratic Aunt Augusta), Lady Bracknell, and the famous handbag. That Miss Prism, of all people, should be the tutor of Cecily, ward of the grown-up baby Prism had abandoned, is in itself a synchronistic event. The discovery of her identity and of the handbag that solves the mystery of Jack/Ernest's identity coming at the same time is, of course, a brilliant theatrical device. Lady Bracknell tells Dr. Chasuble, 'in families of high position [such] strange coincidences are not supposed to occur' [56]. But of course they do occur, and collectively they make a splendid example of synchronicity. Together, these events symbolize the wholeness of Jack/Ernest's life story (as well as the life stories of the other lovers, including those of Miss Prism and Dr. Chasuble). Coupled with the confirmation of his real given name, these events confirm and give meaning to his personal myth.

The trickster myths of native North America, as recounted by Paul Radin, fit Wilde's play as much as the myth of Hermes does (in fact, being an archetypal trickster, Hermes is not unlike native North American tricksters himself):

> The overwhelming majority of all so-called trickster myths in North America . . . have a hero who is always wandering, who is always hungry, who is not guided by normal conceptions of good or evil, who is either playing tricks on people or having them played on him and who is highly sexed. Almost everywhere he has some divine traits. (p 155)

Both Algernon and Jack use their fictitious friend or brother, Bunbury and Ernest, to wander from the city to the country and vice versa. Algernon, for instance, declares he has 'Bunburyed all over Shropshire on two separate occasions' [11]. And, of course, he, among the several tricksters in the play, is the one with the unquenchable appetite.

None of the major characters is governed by conventional morality. Indeed, part of the humour—the play, as it were—of *Earnest* is the inversion of conventional morality. 'Divorces are made in Heaven,' says Algy [8]. Both he and Jack are ready to be christened, not on grounds of faith but on their perceived need to change their names to Ernest. One of the chief reasons Cecily is enamoured with Algernon/Ernest is that she thinks he is leading an evil life: 'I hope you have not been leading a double life,' she says to him, 'pretending to be wicked and being really good all the time. That would be hypocrisy' [27–28]. And Lady Bracknell, who views christening as a 'luxury' [58], also views Cecily as a suitable bride for Algernon only after she learns how much money Cecily has.

As for the sexual aspect of the trickster, this is a vital subtext of the play. More so than he does in *The Picture of Dorian Gray* or *Salomé*, Wilde keeps sex implicit in *Earnest*. His characters are too child-like for readers or audiences to imagine them actually having sex. And it should be said that the child-like playfulness of the Trickster is part of the action, appealing to the reader/viewer's inner child. Such play, Jung found, is necessary for wholeness and psychic healing (see Rosen pp 128–132). For queer critics the most obvious example of the embedded sexuality is Bunbury, a play on various dimensions of homosexuality in Britain, including sodomy, male bordellos, and Wilde's own sexual practices (see Craft p 28 and Fineman p 89). Craft asserts that

> serious Bunburyism releases a polytropic sexuality so mobile, so evanescent in speed and turn, that it traverses, Ariel-like, a fugitive path through oral, genital, and anal ports until it expends itself in and as the displacements of language. It was Wilde's extraordinary gift to return this vertigo of substitution and repetition to his audience. (p 29)

If Craft's assertions seem too broad, one should recall the unrestrained sexuality of the Trickster, whose 'unbridled sexuality' is one of his chief traits (Radin p 167). Remember that one of Hermes's functions is that of boundary marker, and 'boundary marking,' according to Jungian analyst Eugene Monick, 'is itself a phallic expression' (p 78), to which the ancient Grecian herms attest.[5] Bunburyism allows Algy to cross boundaries and thus free himself to pursue his pleasures, just as Jack's invention of a brother does for him. Bunburyism is, then, tricking *par excellence*.

By necessity Wilde had to dress his characters up as heterosexuals; hence a great deal of the sexual comedy at least seems heterosexual. Surely the humour of Gwendolen's comment to Jack about her being 'quite perfect' depends on its sexual connotations:

JACK: You're quite perfect, Miss Fairfax.
GWENDOLEN: Oh! I hope I am not that. It would leave no room
            for developments, and I intend to develop in *many direc-*
            tions. [13]

5. Rafael López-Pedraza suggests that 'this god, Hermes, "Lord of the Roads" as he came to be known . . . marks our psychological roads and boundaries; he marks the borderlines of our psychological frontiers and marks the territory where, in our psyche, the foreign, the alien, begins' (p 14).

During her mock tea table battle with Cecily, Gwendolen declares: 'I never travel without my diary. One should always have something sensational to read in the train' [40]. Of this passage, Paglia writes: 'The life recorded by her diary is, says Gwendolen, 'sensational,' a source of public scandal and eroticized fascination. To find one's life sensational is to be aroused by oneself' (p 540). Again the Trickster is at play, for few if any in Wilde's initial audience would have recognized the erotic humour here.

Lady Bracknell, whose knowledge of the world befits her role as matriarch of the play, responds to Jack's revelation of the place the handbag in which he was found was located thus:

> As for the particular locality in which the hand-bag was found, a cloak-room at a railway station might serve to conceal a social indiscretion—has probably, indeed, been used for that purpose before now. . . . [19–20]

Clearly for 'social' we can read 'sexual' here and, more specifically, 'heterosexual,' albeit homosexual indiscretions are surely hinted at as well. Miss Prism, perhaps the chief moralizer and hypocrite of the play, ironically responds 'bitterly' to Jack's admission that his brother Ernest was unmarried: 'People who live entirely for pleasure usually are' [31]. The bitterness of her reply is no doubt due to the fact that she, an unmarried woman, has been not able to live for pleasure. That the pleasure is at least in part of a sexual nature we can take for granted.

The Importance of Being Earnest has been performed by all-male casts, a kind of conscious 'trick' on the audience, who would be well aware of the casting. Paglia declares: 'The play's hieratic purity could best be appreciated if all the women's roles were taken by female impersonators' (p 535). I maintain another purpose would be served, and that is to reinforce the shape-changing aspect of the Trickster. Will Roscoe discusses this aspect of the Scandinavian trickster, Loki, who, among other shapes, changes himself into a woman in several stories (p 184). While having female impersonators play the women's roles would reinforce Paglia's thesis about the androgynous nature of the characters, it would also bring to the surface the homosexual subtext of the play and the corresponding Trickster role. In fact, dual identity is a Trickster theme throughout the play, with Jack/Ernest, Algernon/Bunbury, and even with Gribsby/Parker in the excised 'Gribsby Episode' [61]. The idea is played with in Act I when Jack and Algernon argue about the identity of Cecily.

One more aspect of the Trickster needs to be mentioned: his 'divine' aspect (Radin p 155). The 'divine' nature of *The Importance of Being Earnest* derives from its numinous quality, the satisfaction the characters, along with the reader/audience, receive when, at the play's conclusion, three couples are united. If they are, in Lady Bracknell's words, 'displaying signs of triviality,' the signs are psychologically meaningful. For the moment at least, each couple forms a psychic whole, a fulfilment of their personal myths, wrought by synchronicity and the Trickster archetype. Indeed, the entire play can be viewed as a performance of the Trickster, the masterwork of the last great Victorian Trickster himself.

WORKS CITED

Aldington, Richard, and Stanley Weintraub, eds. *The Portable Oscar Wilde*. Revised Ed. New York: Penguin, 1981.

Bentley, Eric. '*The Importance of Being Earnest*.' from *The Playwright as Thinker* (New York: Reznal & Hitchcock, 1946).

Combs, Allan, and Mark Holland. *Synchronicity: Through the Eyes of Science, Myth, and the Trickster*. New York: Marlowe, 1996.

Craft, Christopher. 'Alias Bunbury: Desire and Termination in *The Importance of Being Earnest*.' *Representations* 31 (1990): pp 19–46.

Dollimore, Jonathan. 'Different Desires: Subjectivity and Transgression in Wilde and Gide.' *Genders* 2 (1988): pp. 24–41.

Ellmann, Richard. *Oscar Wilde*. New York: Knopf, 1987.

Fineman, Joel. 'The Significance of Literature: *The Importance of Being Earnest*.' *October* 15 (1980): pp 79–90.

Hopcke, Robert H. *There Are No Accidents: Synchronicity and the Stories of Our Lives*. New York: Riverhead, 1997.

Jung, C. G. *C. G. Jung Speaking: Interviews and Encounters*. Ed. William McGuire and R. F. C. Hull. Princeton UP, 1977.

——— Letter to Michael Fordham. *The Symbolic Life: Miscellaneous Writings* Trans. R. F. C. Hull. Princeton: Princeton UP, 1967. Vol. 18 of *The Collected Works of C. G. Jung*. Ed. H. Read, M. Fordham, and Gerhard Adler (*CW*). pp 508–509.

——— 'Synchronicity: An Acausal Connecting Principle.' *The Structure and Dynamics of the Psyche*. 2nd ed. Trans. R. F. C. Hull. Princeton: Princeton UP, 1967. Vol. 8 of *CW*. pp 417–519.

López-Pedraza, Rafael. *Hermes and His Children. 1977*. Einsiedein, Switzerland: Daiman Verlag, 1989.

Monick, Eugene. *Phallos: Sacred Image of the Masculine*. Toronto: Inner City, 1987.

Murray, Isobel. *Introduction. Plays, Prose Writings, and Poems. By Oscar Wilde*. London: Dent, 1975, pp vi–xx.

Oscar Wilde: A Collection of Critical Essays. Ed. Richard Ellmann. Englewood Cliffs, NJ: Prentice-Hall, 1969. pp 111–115.

Paglia, Camille. *Sexual Personae: Art and Decadence from Nefertiti to Emily Dickinson. 1990*. New York: Vintage, 1991.

Raby, Peter. *Oscar Wilde*. Cambridge: Cambridge UP, 1988.

Radin, Paul. *The Trickster: A Study in American Indian Mythology.*
New York: Schocken, 1956.

Roditi, Edouard. *Oscar Wilde.* New York: New Directions, 1947.

Roscoe, Will. *Queer Spirits: A Gay Man's Myth Book.* Boston: Beacon, 1995.

Rosen, David. *The Tao of Jung: The Way of Integrity.* New York: Penguin, 1996.

Sedgwick, Eve Kosofsky. 'Tales of the Avunculate: Queer Tutelage in *The Importance of Being Earnest.*' *Professions of Desire: Lesbian & Gay Studies in Literature.* Ed. G. E. Haggerty and Bonnie Zimmerman. New York: MLA, 1995. pp 191–209.

Snider, Clifton. 'Victorian Trickster: A Jungian Consideration of *Edward Lear's Nonsense Verse.*' *Psychological Perspectives.* No. 24 (Spring-Summer 1991): pp 90–110. For a revised version of this article, see www.csulb.edu/~csuider/edward.lear.html.

Trilling, Lionel, and Harold Bloom, eds. 'Victorian Prose and Poetry.' *The Oxford Anthology of English Literature.* Vol. II. Ed. Frank Kermode and John Hollander. New York: Oxford UP, 1973.

Wilde, Oscar. *The Importance of Being Earnest. The Plays of Oscar Wilde.* New York: Vintage, 1988. pp 345–432.

Worth, Katharine. *Oscar Wilde.* New York: Grove, 1983.

Zipes, Jack. *Fairy Tales and the Art of Subversion: The Classical Genre for Children and the Process of Civilization.* New York: Methuen, 1983.

BRIGITTE BASTIAT

The Importance of Being Earnest (1895) by Oscar Wilde: Conformity and Resistance in Victorian Society[†]

The Importance of Being Earnest (1895) by Oscar Wilde is a popular play that is still widely performed in English-language theatres and also in many different languages.

When first performed, the play was mostly considered as a light comedy and classified as entertainment for Victorian society. However, the writing of the play relies on a creativity and richness that combine different styles. Oscar Wilde was gay in a society stifled by social conventions and governed by very tough laws on homosexuality. Nevertheless, some critics have argued that the

† *Cahiers victoriens et édouardiens* 72 (Oct. 2010): 53–63. Reprinted with permission of the publisher. Unless otherwise indicated, notes are by the author. The original bibliography has been omitted. Page numbers in square brackets refer to this Norton Critical Edition.

playwright dared include homosexual connotations in the text. However, I would argue that more generally, despite very little room for manœuvre, he managed brilliantly to challenge the social norms, sexual stereotypes and gender representations of his time while pleasing aristocratic London socialites.

How does Oscar Wilde implement strategies to create tensions and confusion between the norms imposed by social, moral and aesthetic orders? In an article published in *The Guardian* in July 2007 Terry Eagleton wrote: "Wilde, typically perverse, challenged and conformed at the same time."[1] In this essay I will show that conformity and resistance are present simultaneously at each stage of the play.

In an article published in 2008 in *Études irlandaises,* Pascal Aquien argues that 19th century French bourgeois drama exerted a powerful influence on Wilde's dramatic works. He often used this convenient formal frame to structure his society comedies. By importing a popular and successful French form he could thus conceal his attack on official order and discourse while making English audiences laugh at their own values and beliefs.[2] He also draws on the popular forms of melodrama and farce. In so doing Wilde keeps the appearances of a genre the audience is familiar with but subverts it with great subtlety. Because he can't afford to shock his audience too much and needs success for financial reasons his attack is not frontal. However, he manages to combine commercial success with conservative audiences whilst mocking the very conventions that these audiences are supposed to live by. It is cleverly done so that the audience may ignore the subversive politics in the play if it chooses to. As the Canadian media theorist Marshall McLuhan said in the 1960's "the medium is the message" and Wilde uses the form to speak of the content. The choice of genre seems to say "beware of appearances," which is one of the themes of the play. It has all the elements of a comedy of manners: the title delivered as a punchline to the proceedings, the marriage problem, the foundling child, the idea of the double life, the highly-formalised style of language, the fast-moving verbal exchanges and a lot of entrances and exits. The play thus looks like a comedy of manners but it is something else. What is it then? It can be argued that by refusing a specific genre Oscar Wilde produces a discourse on theatrical art. He rejects the naturalist style and the traditional forms of drama of his time. So, is it a modernist experimental drama? Is Wilde "a pre-Ionesco challenger and re-interpreter of language," as Pascal Aquien said?[3] The genre is uncertain and resists characterisation. Wilde was influenced

1. Terry Eagleton, "Only Pinter remains," www.guardian.co.uk, 7/7/07.
2. Pascal Aquien, "Sardoodledum Revisited, or a Few Trivial Remarks about Oscar Wilde's *An Ideal Husband* (1895)," *Études irlandaises,* no 33-2., automne 2008, pp. 9–19.
3. Pascal Aquien, *op. cit.*

by Walter Pater, the co-founder of the aesthetic movement in art, literature and criticism for whom all art forms are self-sufficient. Therefore, it may be argued that *The Importance of Being Earnest* exists for its own sake and, as Algernon, one of the characters in the play would put it, "it is perfectly phrased"[4] [21], and that is enough to justify its existence.

Wilde uses absurd and exaggerated situations, nonsensical language, paradoxical humour and puns. In fact, he invents a new genre, difficult to imitate, combining farce, comedy of manners, social satire and, I would add, "gender parody." Judith Butler defines "gender parody" as follows: "Gender parody reveals that the original identity after which identity fashions itself is an imitation without an origin."[5] For her the origin is a myth and there is a "fluidity of identities." In the play Jack and Algernon are not Ernest, but they can become Ernest through baptism. If they take the name of Ernest without even undergoing a physical and psychological transformation they will fit Gwendolen's and Cecily's tastes. They will also imitate a model with no origin since Ernest never existed in the first place. Wilde also plays with the illusions created by appearances and mocks the expressive model of gender and the notion of true gender identity. For example, Cecily's outside appearance is "feminine" but her attitude may be considered as "masculine" since she "has got a capital appetite" and "goes on long walks"[6] [22]—in Victorian times women were not supposed to have body functions or practise sport. Jack and Algernon are men, but they are effeminate dandies. Algernon spends money extravagantly on clothes and is greedy, qualities often associated with women. Here, and throughout the play, Oscar Wilde asks the following question: is biology always the framework which constrains socialisation practices, making it impossible for culture to minimise, rather than eliminate, the effects of natural biological differences between men and women? The tension between the body as real and the body as discursive remains a key axis of the debate within gender studies. For example, for R. W. Connell in socialisation theories, "the underlying image is of an invariant biological base,"[7] whereas for Judith Butler "the body is not a 'being' but a variable boundary, a surface whose permeability is politically regulated, a signifying practice within a cultural field or gender hierarchy and compulsory heterosexuality."[8] By citing the example of drag (in which a person performs a gender that does not match his/

4. Oscar Wilde, *The Importance of Being Earnest*, version bilingue (traduction de Gérard Hardin), Pocket, 2004, p. 62
5. Colin Counsell and Laurie Wolf (eds), *Performance Analysis*, Routledge, Londres, 2001, p. 75.
6. Oscar Wilde, *op. cit.*, p. 64.
7. R. W. Connell, *Gender and Power*, Polity, Cambridge, 1987, p. 50.
8. Judith Butler, *Gender Trouble*, Routledge, Londres, 1999 (2e édition), p. 177.

her sex) she wants to show that bodies are not "beings" but are the effects of discourses. Maybe the 2005 production at the Abbey Theatre, showing the actor Alan Stanford first dressed as Oscar Wilde transforming himself into Lady Bracknell—Lady Bracknell being a perfect figure to be played by a man—was trying to take this notion on board. It could be argued, though, that this production only emphasized the superficial and camp side of the play, hardly touching the idea of what J. Butler calls "the illusion of an interior and organizing gender core."[9] If used, gender performativity must "trouble gender." In other words, it must arouse curiosity and stir traditional feelings and ideas about gender. It is indeed an attractive and challenging notion, although Judith Butler has admitted herself that performativity does not always allow the degree of "free play" with gender that some other queer theorists have suggested.[1]

The play is subtitled "A trivial comedy for serious people." If it is trivial it thus means that it has no important message to convey. However, Paul Watzlawick, the communication theorist, said that "one cannot not communicate," therefore although there seems to be no message in the play, the message might be precisely that, that there is no message, Oscar Wilde tells us that our world is absurd and that it is pointless to try to find any meaning to it. Life is simply like a bubble of champagne: it makes one's head light and makes one talk nonsense and act silly, just like the play's characters. However, it may not necessarily be better to know about the absurdity of the world because as Lady Bracknell puts it "Ignorance is like a delicate exotic fruit; touch it and the bloom is gone!"[2] [17] In fact, Oscar Wilde seems to say that nothing really seems to matter in life.

Nevertheless, Wilde chose to tackle serious subjects such as marriage, hereditary privileges, education, the Church, sexual roles and language, and also tells us that appearances are deceitful. Cecily and Gwendolen rebel against sexual roles by mastering the language and being witty—qualities often associated with men—but in fact, they talk nonsense. They are also conceited and vain and ready to change quickly their affections, firstly to a man really named Ernest, showing that they cannot understand real passion, and secondly to one another—they call each other sisters at first, then hate each other. These qualities are often associated with women who are supposed to be volatile and not able to experience friendship like men—women are seen as rivals, which is a conformist view. Miss Prism and Canon Chasuble pretend to be religious, serious and pure but the former is easily distracted (she lost a baby, often quits her

9. Judith Butler, *Gender Trouble*, Routledge, Londres, 1990, p. 73.
1. S. Phelan (ed), *Playing with Fire: Queer Politics, Queer Theories*, Routledge, New York, 1997.
2. Oscar Wilde, *op. cit.*, p. 52.

job as a tutor to go on walks with Chasuble) and the latter adapts one single sermon to all the different occasions; moreover, they both have sexual desires that they express awkwardly through slips of the tongue, for instance when Chasuble says "Were I fortunate enough to be Miss Prism's pupil I would hang upon her lips" [26]. Lady Bracknell is portrayed as a greedy and arrogant aristocrat. At the same time we know that she wasn't born an aristocrat and that she became one by imitating the customs and integrating the values of the upper class. In Act III she says "When I married Lord Bracknell I had no fortune of any kind. But I never dreamed for a moment of allowing that to stand in my way" [51]. On the one hand, she has learned the dress and language codes and the values of the aristocracy and in that way, she conforms to what the audience expects from a person of her rank. On the other hand, nothing is trustworthy about her because she uses clothes as would an actress to fit her role, talks nonsense, however with the right kind of accent, and can utter the most cruel things but in a very proper language. Therefore, Oscar Wilde rebels against the artificial and hypocritical social codes of his class and suggests that anybody can pass for an aristocrat with a bit of practice. Lady Bracknell also plays the role of a father when she interviews Jack to find out whether he would be an "eligible young man" [52] to marry her daughter, "a girl brought up with the utmost care" [20]. Lord Bracknell is blatantly absent from the play, is referred to as a sick man, almost an invalid, and plays in fact the role of the mother. Here it has to be said that a lot of Victorian women had psychosomatic diseases—like Lord Bracknell who has little appetite and often retires to his bedroom— mostly because they were unhappy and frustrated by their assigned impotent roles as daughters, wives and mothers. As for Lady Bracknell she has the power of decision, the power of money and the power of language. Maybe influenced by Ibsen's *Doll's House* published earlier (1879), Oscar Wilde wanted people to reflect on the relations between the sexes, which was also a very topical issue for his contemporaries known as the 'separate sphere debate.' The play makes extensive reference both implicitly and explicitly to this debate, thus conforming to the fashionable discussion of his time. But at the same time it resists the traditional notions that govern men's and women's lives and supports equality between the sexes. For example, at the end of the play, Jack says: "Why should there be one law for men, and another law for women?" [57]. Indeed, the second half of the 19th century saw women begin to organise themselves in pressure groups in England; the Sheffield Association for Female Franchise held its first meeting in 1851. In 1867, when the Conservatives gave the right to vote to workers in Britain, John Stuart Mill, who was elected to Westminster, moved an amendment to Disraeli's Representation of the People Act in which he proposed to replace the word "man" by the word "person." It was defeated by 194 votes to 73,[3] showing that men were more afraid of women than of the "dangerous classes"—Queen Victoria herself was against female suffrage. Two years later J. S. Mill, who hadn't given up on the idea of promoting equality between men and women, published his essay *The Subjection of Women* (1869). Oscar Wilde, who was well educated, had probably read it or at least heard about it. In 1888 unmarried women were allowed to vote for the new county and borough councils for the first time. Finally, in 1894, one year before the play was published, a quarter of a million women signed the petition for the right to vote for women.

However, having stated that women do not enjoy the position that they deserve in society doesn't mean that Oscar Wilde finds women superior to men and that society would benefit from their presence in the public sphere. In the play, Algy and Jack are idle and lazy, but morally the women are not better than them: like them, they are idle, lie, cheat and are interested in money. Lady Bracknell is indeed an assertive woman, but a terrifying "Gorgon" (Jack's expression). Actually, the play portrays real anxiety about gender because it raises the difficult question about the meaning of masculinity and femininity, yet always in an ironical and derisive tone. For instance, when Lady Bracknell interviews Jack she is glad to hear that Jack smokes because 'a man should always have an occupation of some kind' [17]. It is a reversal of stereotypes about women's activities. Upper-class women were idle but sometimes did some volunteer work or some craftswork at home. It was assumed that they had "an occupation of some kind." But what do we know about what men and women are supposed to do, like and dislike? What are men's and women's preferences supposed to be? Gwendolen says in Act II that 'the home seems to be the proper sphere for the man,' which might have sounded funny and absurd to a Victorian audience, although less so to a modern one. Therefore, if it is ridiculous to state that for men, why shouldn't it be equally ridiculous to state that for women? Gwendolen then continues "And certainly once a man begins to neglect his domestic duties he becomes painfully effeminate, does he not? And I don't like that." So just as Gwendolen, heterosexual women are not supposed to like effeminate men (whereas homosexual men might). Yet, she then adds unexpectedly: "It makes them so very attractive," hinting that a male chauvinist may not be what women prefer. Here Oscar Wilde used a paradoxical punchline to explode the myths about gendered fixed identities and preferences.

3. Monica Charlot, *The Road to Universal Suffrage (1832–1928)*, Didier Erudition, CNED, 1995, pp. 124–125.

I mentioned earlier that the play was subtitled "A trivial comedy for serious people." If it is destined for serious people this implies that serious people might find an interest in it. Indeed, there are serious themes in the play but Oscar Wilde does not treat them seriously, thus debunking the very notion of seriousness. Then, why not play with this subtitle and reverse it? What if, in fact, it were a serious play for trivial people? In that case it would mean that Wilde chose to tackle serious subjects but that he did not believe his public would understand his attempts at turning traditions and preconceived notions upside down. One can also wonder whether he really cares about those notions. Is he really aware of his own discourse on gender? If he is, he does not seem to want to push it too far. Is it because he is afraid of losing his readership and audience? In fact, we do not really know the intentions of Oscar Wilde, except perhaps that, and to paraphrase Jack in the play, when he is in town he amuses himself [7].

William Archer, one of the critics, wrote about the play in 1895:

> It is delightful to see, it sends wave after wave of laughter . . . but as a text for criticism it is barren and delusive . . . it is intangible, it eludes your grasp. What can a poor critic do with a play which raises no principle, whether of art or morals, creates its own canons and conventions, and is nothing but an absolutely willful expression of irrepressibly witty personality.[4]

He appears to have been seduced by the play but a little puzzled and unable to analyse it very well. More reviews of that time would be required in order to determine if other critics were also ill-at-ease when they saw the play. On the whole we know that there were positive reviews and *Earnest* could have expected an extended run in the St James's Theatre followed by a popular tour in the provinces. However, only a few weeks after its opening, Oscar Wilde was involved in the scandal that led him to prison. For two generations Wilde's name was mud. The audience that had laughed so much during the performances shunned his company and work. Equally, it would have been interesting to have interviews of members of the audience to find out why they had enjoyed the play. Was it because they had chosen to overlook the questionings of the play or simply because they had completely misunderstood the undertones in the first place? Later, why did they really turn away from Oscar Wilde? Was it because they were really shocked by his homosexuality or just to conform to the new trend that was to despise him? Just as

---

4. *World Magazine*, 20/2/1895, cited by Ruth Robbins, *York Notes Advanced on The Importance of Being Earnest*, Longman, 2005, p. 6. [Archer's review is reprinted on pp. 107–08 of this Norton Critical Edition—*Editor*.]

Gwendolen says to Cecily in Act II that cake is rarely seen in the best houses nowadays, Oscar Wilde was rarely talked about in the best houses after the trial that he lost.

More seriously, what people maybe did not understand and forgive him was that by making his "coming out" during the trial he had disrupted the social and gender order. The latter concept did not exist in Wilde's time and was first developed by Jill Matthews in 1984 in her study of the historical construction of femininity.[5] According to her, "the idea of gender order gives recognition to the fact that every known society distinguishes between women and men, while allowing for variations in the nature of the distinctions drawn."[6] This approach emphasizes the idea that patriarchy may not be universal and leaves room for transformation of gender relations because they are regarded as a process subject to resistance as well as conformity. This way of viewing things seems to suggest that the gender order may be disrupted and changed, and Oscar Wilde was certainly one of the first ones to do so in his life and by using theatre as a means of expression for his questioning and mockery of both the social and gender orders.

As far as the staging of the play was concerned, conformity was the rule for Victorian directors, who chose a naturalist setting and realistic costumes made in London or Paris. When the public saw the actors and actresses on stage they underwent an identification process because they lived in the same flats, wore the same clothes and spoke the same apparent language. The Victorian audience then laughed at itself. Or did it? The scenes would have seemed so exaggerated that they could not possibly have recognized themselves and have taken the play seriously. They actually laughed at social and sexual relationships that, as far as they were concerned, could not exist. Exaggeration and nonsensical dialogues probably helped Wilde get away with the more troubling questions he raised.

* * *

Any writer, male or female, can find it hard to work outside the conventions, practices and aspirations of his/her predecessors. Can we then say that Oscar Wilde paved the way for contemporary authors like Frank McGuinness for example? According to Eamonn Jordan, McGuinness's dramas, for example, "set specific challenges, especially when it comes to female characters. Of all the male playwrights writing today in Irish theatre, McGuinness consistently

5. Jill Matthews, *Good and Mad Women: The Historical construction of femininity in Twentieth Century Australia*, George Allen and Unwin, Sydney, 1984.
6. Jane Pilchner and Imelda Whelehan (eds), *Fifty Key Concepts in Gender Studies*, Sage, Londres, 2004, p. 61.

confronts romanticized, conventionalized and stereotypical gendered roles and imperatives."[7]

On the other hand more recent critics have perhaps put too much
emphasis on the subversive nature of the play and a re-appraisal
might be needed. After all, Wilde himself never considered it as his
best work, describing it as "written by a butterfly for butterflies."
However, butterflies are short-lived whereas his play has survived
for more than a hundred years so far, conforming to the tastes of
many different people and resisting both time and analysis.

EIBHEAR WALSHE

A Wilde Irish Rebel: Queerness Versus Nationalism in Irish Imaginative Presentations of Wilde[†1]

One way or another, the figure of Oscar Wilde has always represented a challenge, if not a difficulty, within Irish cultural discourse. For a start, Wilde's homosexuality has been contested and
debated in twentieth-century Ireland, and this contestation often
downplayed potentially subversive elements within his writings and
his public persona. In this essay, I want to consider two key elements within Irish cultural perceptions of Oscar Wilde. Firstly I
want to trace the ways in which the figure of Wilde in the dock in
the Old Bailey was re-appropriated for a particular tradition of
rebellious Irish nationalism after his trials in 1895, and then I want
to suggest that this nationalist re-appropriation submerged or denied
the radical or 'queer' potential for Wilde's transgressive persona. I
want to suggest a tension between notions of Wilde the Irish rebel
and Wilde the decadent queer prophet of sin.

By examining the influence of Wilde on Irish writers like Joyce,
Yeats and later on contemporary writers like Seamus Heaney, Tom
Paulin, Colm Tóibín and Jamie O'Neill, I intend to tease out the
implication of this tension. Also Wilde's position as a writer of
'foreign' or decadent literature in his own lifetime now means that

---

7. Eamonn Jordan, "Meta-physicality: Women Characters in the plays of Frank McGuinness," *Women in Irish Drama, A Century of Authorship and Representation,* edited by
Melissa Sihra, Palgrave Macmillan, 2007, p. 130.
† From *Canadian Journal of Irish Studies* 36.1 (Spring 2010): 45–69. Reprinted with
permission of the publisher. Notes are by the author.
1. This essay is drawn from my book *Oscar's Shadow,* published by Cork University Press in
2011. I would like to thank Seán Kennedy, Margot Backus, Ed Madden, Joseph Bristow
and Joseph Valente for valuable feedback. I am also indebted to Noreen Doody and her
essay "Performance and Place: Oscar Wilde and the Irish National Interest," in *The Reception of Oscar Wilde in Europe,* ed. Stefano Evangelista (London: Continuum, 2010), 51–64.

he has a kind of symbolic resonance with contemporary Irish literary notions of 'queer' as disruptive and subversive. I illustrate the
ways in which an Irish nationalist Wilde became the dominant perception, often as a way of neutralising this decadence. In one text,
the 1989 play *Saint Oscar* by the English writer Terry Eagleton, I
discern a collision, a kind of irreconcilable contraction between
these two potential versions of Wilde, and I examine the ways in
which Eagleton's text attempts to celebrate Wilde's erotic subversiveness within a contradictory trope of nationalistic defiance.
Finally Joyce's interpretation of Wildean sin as redemptive and
enabling has now, I suggest, been reclaimed in the works of contemporary gay writers like Colm Tóibín and Jamie O'Neill, at a time
when queer Irishness has been identified as possible and visible
and thus Wilde figured as both queer and rebel.

To provide a context for Ireland, it is worth remembering that
Wilde's three trials of 1895 took place at a crucial juncture in the
making of the modern idea of the homosexual. In Ireland, as in
other societies towards the end of the nineteenth century, modern
ideas of sexual identity began to take shape and draw meaning from
visible mainstream cultural events. Jeffrey Weeks writes:

> Homosexuality moved from being a category of sin to become
> a psychological disposition . . . but the idea that there is such a
> thing as *the* homosexual person is a relatively new one. All the
> evidence suggests that before the eighteenth century homo-
> sexuality, interpreted in its broadest sense as involving erotic
> activities between people of the same gender, certainly existed,
> 'homosexuals' did not.[2]

To be more precise in terms of a timeframe, Matt Cook, writing
about London from 1885 to the outbreak of the First World War,
suggests that:

> These years were marked by burgeoning debate and concern
> about homosexuality and came towards the end of a half century
> of massive upheaval in the rapidly expanding British capital.
> Following Michel Foucault and Jeffrey Weeks's pioneering work
> in the 1970s, literary and lesbian and gay scholars have variously
> examined the significance of the law, newspapers, sexology, aes-
> theticism and decadence and Hellenism to shifting ideas of
> homosexuality during the period of discussion here. This field
> of debate and writing provided distinctive frames of reference
> through which homosexual relations were experienced, con-
> demned and celebrated.[3]

2. Jeffrey Weeks, *Sexuality* (London: Routledge, 2002), 33.
3. Matt Cook, *London and the Culture of Homosexuality, 1885–1914* (Cambridge: Cambridge University Press, 2003), 3. See also the very useful work by Alan Sinfield in *The*

Connected to this, Ireland was also undergoing a period of radical self-fashioning in the years after Wilde's disgrace, particularly in the years before political independence in 1922, and therefore attitudes towards his name and his sexuality became implicated in this time of flux, this cultural volatility. Furthermore, Wilde's own writings and his interconnected public persona were much more complex than any of his Irish contemporaries like Yeats and Shaw and others, because of the ambivalent strategies of self-representation he deployed around his homosexuality. Wilde's writings create a kind of imaginative mutability, both hinting at and then containing his hidden sexuality.[4] For Ireland, at this time of crucial self-fashioning, Wilde was an ambiguous figure, particularly with his perceived 'foreignness' and perceptions of his links to French decadence. Matthew Sturgis argues that "although decadence in England during the 1890s never quite managed to refine itself into a movement, it did create a pungent and distinctive flavour."[5] He discerns a "distrust of Victorian confidence in society's common aims and standards—both artistic and moral: belief in the essential loneliness of the individual consciousness and the consolation of aesthetic impressions; belief too in art's superiority to nature—and to life."[6] Wilde embodied many of these qualities, in a kind of proto-queerness, and so when he was brought to trial his connections with French decadent writing became a focus for attack. Xenophobia, as well as homophobia, prompted attacks on Wilde's decadent foreignness, but his 'French' decadence rather than his Irish unruliness fuelled public attacks in Britain. Foldy points out that Wilde:

> represented a frightening constellation of threats which conflated all these disparate elements and associations: he represented foreign vice, foreign art and indirectly, the legacy of foreign rulers . . . thus when the newspapers attacked Wilde and condemned his foreign vice, they were also expressing their xenophobic fear of foreigners and foreign influences, their hatred of a useless and parasitic aristocracy, and their intolerance for useless artists and for anyone who would actively try to subvert the status quo.[7]

Wilde Century: Effeminacy, Oscar Wilde and the Queer Moment (London: Cassells, 1994); Joseph Bristow's valuable work in studies like *Effeminate England* (New York: Columbia University Press, 1995) and *Oscar Wilde and Modern Culture* (Athens: Ohio University Press, 2008) is crucial in this context and informs much of my thought here.

4. I am grateful to Graham Allen for this interesting point.
5. Matthew Sturgis, *Passionate Attitudes: The English Decadence of the 1890s* (London: MacMillan, 1995), 299.
6. Ibid.
7. Michael S. Foldy, *The Trials of Oscar Wilde: Deviance, Morality and Late-Victorian Society* (New Haven: Yale University Press, 1997), 150.

Wilde, the decadent, proto-queer was a difficult persona for Irish public discourse and I have argued elsewhere that Irish sources found that the best way to accommodate him was within a nationalist discourse. At the historical moment in European culture when the idea of the homosexual as a dangerous type was evolving, nationalist discourse was deployed in Ireland to downplay Wilde's decadence, and to rescue and absolve him from this aberrant sexual identity.[8] There was a surprisingly reticent, even tolerant, attitude evident towards Wilde in many of the mainstream Irish newspapers, and this reticence stands in marked contrast to the energetic homophobia of the English newspapers. For example, the *Cork Constitution* commented sympathetically on the prospect of "[s]uch a life, even for two brief years, to a man of luxurious habits." Highlighting the "exacting toil and shameful degradation" of his imprisonment, they observed: "A leper would not exchange places with Wilde."[9]

This sympathy also contrasts with the Irish media coverage of two other homosexual scandals in Dublin: the 1884 Dublin Castle scandal and the 1907 stealing of the Irish Crown jewels, where opportunistic nationalist anger against Crown administrators was expressed in virulently homophobic newspaper outpourings. Connected to this, some subsequent Irish writers, many of them Anglo-Irish, saw Wilde as a disruptive figure of anti-colonial resistance, and this reconstruction, in some ways, mitigated his aberrant homosexuality for those writers and indeed for their society. Even the powerfully homophobic culture that twentieth-century Ireland was to become invented strategies by which the 'unspeakable' Oscar could be reclaimed as Wilde the Irish rebel.

Linked to this circumspection in the Irish newspapers at the time was a tendency within later Irish sources to interpret Wilde's behavior in the courtroom of the Old Bailey as heroic and politicized. In other words, Wilde's defense against the charge of homosexuality and gross indecency was later claimed for the tradition of Irish republican defiance in the face of British injustice. In particular, when, during the trial, Wilde was asked to define the exact nature of 'the love that dare not speak its name,' a coded poem about homosexuality by Lord Alfred 'Bosie' Douglas, his response would be seen as one of the great Irish anti-imperialist speeches from the dock. Seamus Heaney asserted a full century after Wilde's ordeal that "during his trials in 1895, Wilde had been magnificent

8. See my "The First Gay Irishman?: Ireland and the Wilde Trials," *Éire-Ireland* 40, no. 3–4 (2005): 38–57, where I trace the process by which Wilde could be commandeered into the acceptable mode of the Irish rebel in the aftermath of his public disgrace.
9. Cork *Constitution*, May 27, 1895.

in the dock and conducted himself with as much dramatic style as any Irish patriot ever did."[1]

Wilde the rebel was perhaps not as forthright a figure as Heaney suggests. Lucy McDiarmid argues that "In truth, Wilde wasn't exactly being truthful and certainly not being patriotic when he denied the sexual element in the love that dare not speak its name, but his declaration broke the wall of public silence about homosexuality when he brought it to a point of public utterance."[2] I would suggest that his homosexual love *did* have to speak its name when the law demanded an answer, however partial that answer would be. The simple fact that he made such a profession of ennobling same-sex love is in itself precisely the factor that provoked public disturbance and debate. The vital importance here is the implication of Wilde's articulation of the homoerotic for Irish public discourse, a defining queer moment.

Martyrs and figures of political rebellion are often constructed retrospectively and this was the case with Wilde in Ireland. Shaw, Yeats and others would interpret Wilde's downfall in the light of the literary and political career of his mother, Speranza, a view aligning him with the rhetorical traditions of nineteenth-century Protestant Irish republicanism and, indirectly, with the many impassioned speeches made by Irish activists in English courtrooms during the nineteenth century.

In the Irish newspapers, issues of unease and sexual phobia are evident as Wilde's body featured as a site for contested meaning, a means by which his sexuality could be indirectly named. But in Ireland this unease becomes ambivalent, undermined by public resentment of British imperialism. Subsequent Irish accounts of the trials and of the convicted man's decision to face arrest afterwards seized upon Wilde's national pride and sense of honour as motivating his behavior. Irish sources came to lionize Wilde for his racial difference, his Anglo-Irish pride and old-fashioned chivalry. Why was the Irish press so discreet in the coverage of the Wilde trials? Several factors may have accounted for such discretion, one being the republican legacy of his mother. More crucially, the political climate in Dublin—with the growing pressure in southern Ireland for political autonomy—may well have muted any condemnation of an Irishman at odds with the British legal and political establishment. In the earlier Dublin Castle scandal of 1884, the investigation reflected not just homophobic unease with same-sex activities,

1. Seamus Heaney, "Speranza in Reading: On 'The Ballad of Reading Gaol,'" in *The Redress of Poetry* (London: Faber and Faber, 1995), 95.
2. Lucy McDiarmid, "Oscar Wilde's Speech from the Dock," in *The Wilde Legacy*, ed. Eiléan Ní Chuilleanáin (Dublin: Four Courts, 2003), 113–135. See this for an excellent and convincing argument against the idea of Wilde as an Irish patriot in the Old Bailey.

but the antipathy Irish nationalist politicians felt towards colonial administrators.

The years after Wilde's death in 1900, and up to the foundation and consolidation of the new Irish state in the late 1920s, consti-tuted a period of intense debate over political self-definition in Ire-land, as outlined, for example, by Lucy McDiarmid in her study *The Irish Art of Controversy.*[3] Wilde's reputation and the contesta-tion of his racial and sexual identity became part of this larger debate, this moment of national remaking. Roy Foster writes that:

> The Boer War at the beginning of the century focused much moderate Irish opinion into an anti-imperial mould and pro-vided a mobilising 'cause' against the government; the Euro-pean War of 1914–18 altered the condition of Irish politics beyond recognition. The radicalisation of Irish politics (and to a certain extent, Irish society) took place between these two events and largely because of them.[4]

Wilde's posthumous reputation was implicated in this radicaliza-tion, to his benefit. In England after the trials, as Alan Sinfield notes, "Wilde's name had become forbidden and silenced, and yet, somehow, he was made even more visible by virtue of being silenced."[5] In Ireland in the years after his death, Wilde was far from invisible, with productions of his plays in mainstream the-atres, reviews of his writings and constant mentions in the national newspapers, as well as in interviews and memoirs. Most striking was the way in which Wilde was commandeered by fellow Anglo-Irish writers to become part of a particular tradition of Irish nation-alist discourse.

In the first decades of the twentieth century, then, Wilde was "nationalized,"[6] and claimed as a figure of transgressive aesthetic empowerment by Yeats, Joyce, Shaw and other Anglo-Irish writers central to debates about Irish cultural nationalism in this period. Wilde came to be read subsequently as heroic in his 'sinfulness,' a disruptive figure of anti-colonial resistance; and this reconstruc-tion in some ways mitigated his aberrant homosexuality for those writers and indeed for their society. This process of nationalisation derived partly from James Joyce, writing in 1909 in Trieste to cele-brate the poet of Salome as the prophet of sin, and partly from the accounts of Shaw and Yeats casting Wilde as the tragic hero. Wilde

3. Lucy McDiarmid, *The Irish Art of Controversy* (Dublin: Lilliput, 2005).
4. Roy Foster, *Modern Ireland, 1600–1972* (London: Penguin, 1988), 433.
5. Alan Sinfield, *The Wilde Century: Effeminacy, Oscar Wilde and the Queer Moment* (London: Cassells, 1994), 124.
6. A phrase from Margot Norris. See her "A Walk on the Wild(e) Side: The Doubled Read-ing of 'An Encounter,'" in *Quare Joyce*, ed. Joseph Valente (Ann Arbor: University of Michigan Press, 1998), 19–33.

became a figure of profound emblematic and aesthetic empowerment for both Joyce and Yeats and thus was a powerful shadow
for the two most influential Irish writers of the twentieth century.
Wilde's contemporary Shaw cited his Anglo-Irish pride as a key
support for his heroic stance, and when *The Importance of Being
Earnest* was staged in the Abbey Theatre in 1926, Lady Augusta
Gregory reflected in her journals on Wilde's poetry and on his tragic
stature.[7] His Protestant Anglo-Irish identity became an important
protection for his homosexuality, as it was intertwined in these
accounts with his mother's status as a nationalist poet. Common to
many of these accounts of Oscar the Irish rebel is a need to situate
his homosexuality within discourses of Anglo-Irish feudal pride,
and Speranza, Lady Wilde, is seen as central to any account of
Oscar the rebel.

James Joyce was a key figure in reconstructions of Wilde and one
of the few Irish interpreters to see him as prophet of decadence. His
appropriation of Wilde as a symbolic figure of sin and dissidence is
a vital one for his presence in twentieth-century Ireland. Catholic by
upbringing and education, Joyce was thirteen when Wilde's trials
took place and eighteen when Wilde died, and so his view of Wilde
is constructed very much at a distance, both temporally and spa-
tially. He was reading *The Picture of Dorian Gray* in Rome 1906
when he was writing *A Portrait of the Artist as a Young Man*, and
wrote to his brother Stan that it would have been a better book if
Wilde had had the courage to develop its allusions.[8] In March 1909,
Joyce published an article called "Oscar Wilde: The Poet of Salome,"
in a newspaper in Trieste to mark a performance of Richard Strauss's
opera *Salome*. In this article, the question of Wilde's homosexuality
is tackled directly with Joyce's characteristic forthrightness, made
possible only by the fact that he was writing outside Ireland. Joyce
makes the radical point that Wilde destabilised the widespread
homosocial structures underpinning Victorian British male culture
by bringing his sexuality into the open, however unwittingly. Joyce
identifies precisely the homophobic panic that Wilde's 'outing'
unleashed in the male social structures of his time: "Anyone who follows closely the life and language of men, whether in soldiers' barracks
or in the great commercial houses, will hesitate to believe that all
those who threw stones at Wilde were themselves spotless."[9] The
consequent rage against Wilde in Britain was the rage of a society

---

7. See Stanley Weintraub, ed., *The Playwright and the Pirate: Bernard Shaw and Frank
   Harris, A Correspondence* (Gerrards Cross: Colin Smythe, 1982), 33; Augusta Gregory,
   The Journals, vol. 2 (February 21, 1925–May 29, 1932), ed. Daniel J. Murphy (Gerrards
   Cross: Colin Smythe, 1987), 241.
8. Richard Ellmann, *James Joyce* (Oxford: Oxford University Press 1959), 233.
9. James Joyce, "Oscar Wilde: The Poet of Salome," in *The Critical Writings of James
   Joyce*, ed. John Mason and Richard Ellmann (London: Faber, 1959), 204.

recognising itself. "What Dorian Gray's sin was no one says and no one knows. Anyone who has recognised it has committed it."[1] At this very early point, Joyce was making the enlightened point that homophobia is produced as a support and a counter-discourse against which heterosexuality could define and thus assure itself of its own naturalness and centrality.

The exiled Joyce needed to reconstruct Wilde as an artist who challenged the political and moral hegemony of the British Empire; Joyce begets him, as it were, as a precursor for his own aesthetic of exile, disgrace and defiance. Again, there is little sense of Wilde's actual motives in bringing the case against Queensbury; merely a kind of retroactive mythologising in the light of Joyce's own aesthetic needs: "Here we touch the pulse of Wilde's art—sin. He deceived himself into believing that he was the bearer of good news of neo-paganism to an enslaved people."[2] Thus Joyce saw Wilde as an exemplar, refashioned in his own likeness as a subversive and a rebel, affording him both a counter-tradition of Irish dissent and also an attack against Ireland and Britain. What is also worth noting is that Joyce writes of Wilde in quasi-religious terms and thus borrows the language of Catholic belief from his own Jesuit education in Dublin to validate Wildean sin.

Margot Backus considers that "Wilde's general makeover from English pervert to Irish martyr" in Joyce's essay, "while certainly inaccurate," is "both complex and revealing,"[3] and signifies "a space of unrepresentability that Irish culture and homosexuals share relative to mainstream British scandal culture."[4] The Wilde that Joyce celebrates in this essay is simply a "heroised" version of himself, and, as Backus comments, "Joyce's transfusion of wild Irishness into his representation of Wilde is thus an ostentatiously textual construct, stemming from a particular agenda of Joyce's connected to his own self-representation as a persecuted artist liable to be silenced and dismissed owing to his Irish subject position."[5] Backus argues that, as a result, references to the Wilde trials underpin *Ulysses* as much as the Parnell divorce case, and supply Joyce with a crucial metaphor for an idea of scandal in the "Circe" episode of *Ulysses*, a point not much noticed in Joycean criticism.

Other critics have observed the role of Wilde's fate in Joyce's rebellion against the constraints of his own country and have

1. Ibid.
2. Ibid.
3. Margot Backus, "'Odd Jobs': James Joyce, Oscar Wilde, and the Scandal Fragment," in *Joyce Studies Annual* (2008): 113.
4. Ibid., 117.
5. Ibid., 124.

commented on the very partial Joycean re-construction of Wilde.
Joseph Valente writes:

> Mediated by his compatriot Wilde, Oxford Hellenism afforded
> Joyce a script to be performed or mimicked in his youth and a
> narrative code to be implemented and manipulated in his fictive
> representations of that youth. It lent the lived and the written
> story a shared ideological basis, a discourse of individual self-
> development that could address and resist in concerted fashion
> the main intellectual, sexual and aesthetic constraints of Irish
> catholic life and the political inequalities of British colonial life.[6]

The importance of Joyce's version of Wilde, however, is the link
made between the institutional homophobia at the centre of the
trials and a critique of British imperialism, a nascent disruptive
queer version of Wilde to be found in the fictions of Jamie O'Neill
and Colm Tóibín. The cultural moment in Ireland where Wilde
could be claimed by some as a rebel was a temporary moment.
Recent studies like Diarmaid Ferriter's *Occasions of Sin* suggest an
increasingly repressive and conservative societal approach to all
public discourse around sexuality from the foundation of the new
state onwards.[7] Thus Wilde's name, like that of other problemati-
cally 'queer' figures like Roger Casement[8] and Padraig Pearse, was
gradually shifted outside mainstream discourse. This was particularly true after the foundation of the Irish state in 1922, and was a
result of the increasing conservatism of the largely Catholic political majority from the late 1920s onwards. In fact, I would argue
that Wilde the Irishman disappeared from popular culture from
1922 right up to the early 1960s. By the 1930s, those writers who
had validated Wilde in the aftermath of his trials were those outside the centres of power in the new Irish state. Within an independent Irish state, Wilde's Anglo-Irish pride and his homosexuality
were moved to the margin. It would take cultural change in the late
twentieth century to re-nationalise Wilde, and this is when the difficulty of queer Wilde becomes more acute.[9]

6. Joseph Valente, "Joyce's Sexual Choices: An Overview," in Valente, *Quare Joyce*, 11.
7. Diarmaid Ferriter, *Occasions of Sin: Sex and Society in Modern Ireland* (London: Profile, 2009).
8. See McDiarmid, *Irish Art of Controversy*; and Jeffrey Dudgeon, *Roger Casement: The
   Black Diaries* (Belfast: Belfast Press, 2002) for excellent discussions on Casement's
   problematical status as both Irish nationalist and queer Irishman, paralleling Wilde
   and others.
9. An exception is the work of Richard Pine in his *Oscar Wilde* (Dublin: Gill and Macmillan, 1983) and *The Thief of Reason: Oscar Wilde and Modern Ireland* (Dublin: Gill and
   Macmillan, 1995), where he makes the vital and revealing link between Wilde's Irishness and his sexuality.

The recovery of Wilde as rebel martyr in contemporary Ireland can be seen, for example, when Seamus Heaney introduced *The Ballad of Reading Gaol* on RTÉ Radio in 1992 in these terms:

> At this distance, in that particular light, there is indeed a way of seeing Oscar Wilde as another felon of our land, another prisoner in an English jail, so that the ballad then becomes the link in the chain including John Mitchell's *Jail Journal* and Brendan Behan's *The Quare Fella*, prison literature. This poem written by the son of Speranza . . . may be devoid of Irish nationalist political intent but it is full of subversive anti-Establishment sentiment. It has about it a kind of high banshee lament, the voice of one crying in the wilderness.[1]

Likewise, on BBC Radio in 2000, the poet Tom Paulin characterised Wilde in familiar terms:

> His mother was a leading Irish nationalist poet, really he was programmed to take the trajectory that is part of the culture and that is to end up in the dock, be sentenced, taken to jail, make a brilliant series of speeches from the dock, and to be remembered as a martyr. Now he is a great gay martyr but he is also following the trajectory of so many Irish republicans.[2]

But can Wilde be a gay martyr and also a nationalist poet? In his dedication speech in Westminster Abbey on February 14, 1995, Heaney takes up this theme again:

> The cry of hurt is every bit as audible in the *Ballad of Reading Gaol* as it is in the song of St James's Infirmary although the provenance of Wilde's chain-gang poem is Irish rather than American and looks back to all the convict ballads, gaol journals and political poetry of Irish nationalist literature in the nineteenth-century—a literature in which Wilde's mother famously contributed under the pseudonym of Speranza. But if it looks back to Irish patriots in the dock for felony in Dublin and an Irish playwright in the dock for homosexuality in London, it also looked forward to English soldier-poets in the trenches in Flanders.[3]

The problem with this re-nationalising of Wilde is the sidelining of his queerness, a silencing hierarchy of appropriate Irish public discourses at work to undermine any unsettling sexual otherness. In

---

1. Seamus Heaney, RTÉ Radio, 1992. Quoted in David Coakley, *Oscar Wilde: The Importance of Being Irish* (Dublin: Townhouse, 1994), 212.
2. Quoted in McDiarmid, "Oscar Wilde's Speech," 115.
3. Seamus Heaney, "Oscar Wilde dedication: Westminster Abbey, 14 February 1995," in *Wilde the Irishman*, ed. Jerusha McCormack (New Haven: Yale University Press, 1998), 174–75.

this section of my essay, I want to examine this collision between public and private, between appropriate and queer, by examining an adaptation of Wilde's life written for the Irish stage: Terry Eagleton's *Saint Oscar*. Peter Dickinson has written that Oscar Wilde has "repeatedly been subjected to posthumous conscription [. . .] as the exemplary literary, sexual, and national outlaw,"[4] and I want to examine the way in which this conscription of Wilde's life finds itself caught between the contradictions between Wilde's potential as republican icon and the unruly nature of Wilde's sexual otherness.

In *Saint Oscar*, a play produced by Field Day—a company with a clear political connection with Irish cultural nationalism—Eagleton brings Wilde back to life, and the links between dissident sexuality and colonial subversion are explored as the drama unfolds. As Lucia Kramer comments, Eagleton's play "dispenses with historical details almost altogether and concentrates instead on theoretical issues."[5] The English-born Eagleton writes of Wilde from a position of identification with Ireland, and his play was produced within an Irish context. In an article in the *Irish Times*, it is explained that '[w]hile he [Eagleton] didn't set out to write an allegory of the present-day Anglo-Irish situation, he found it impossible to write about past conflicts between England and Ireland without reflecting them, if only indirectly, to what is happening today. . . . Words he put in Oscar's mouth have a pert and ironic ring in the post-Guilford haze."[6] Eagleton himself writes in his introduction that "Wilde's treatment at the hands of a brutal, arrogant British establishment is being acted out once more in Ireland today."[7]

With this political foregrounding, Eagleton dispenses with linear progression, and indeed with dramatic tension. Here, Wilde arbitrarily discourses with those central to his life—Speranza, Bosie and Edward Carson. *Saint Oscar* represents Wilde's homosexuality in a much more direct way, reflecting societal changes in Ireland in the late 1980s and Eagleton's own interest in Wilde is promising in terms of a fusion of sexuality and radical political potential. In the introduction he identifies "[t]wo factors that had triggered my

4. Peter Dickinson, "Oscar Wilde: Reading the Life After the Life," *Biography* 28, no. 3 (2005): 416.
5. Lucia Kramer, "Of doormats and iced champagne: The Wilde Trials in Fictional Biography," in *The Importance of Reinventing Oscar*, ed. Uwe Boker, Richard Corballis, and Julie A. Hibbard (Amsterdam: Rodopi, 2002), 202.
6. *Irish Times*, November 1, 1989, 12. The Guildford pub bombings occurred on October 5, 1974, when the IRA planted two bombs in Guildford. The bombings occurred at the height of 'the Troubles' in Northern Ireland, and in December 1974 the police arrested Gerry Conlon, Paul Hill, Patrick Armstrong and Carole Richardson, later to be known as the Guildford Four. They were released fifteen years later and had their convictions overturned.
7. Terry Eagleton, *Saint Oscar* (Derry: Field Day, 1989), xi. Subsequent references will be given parenthetically in the text.

fascination with Wilde—his Irishness and his remarkable antici-
pation of some present-day theory" (*vii*), and goes on to mention
Foucault. However Eagleton's other comments in his introduction
signal an authorial distancing from Wilde's sexuality:

> Much previous work on Wilde has centred on his homo-
> sexuality . . . but if I have tried to avoid writing a gay play about
> him, this is not only because as a heterosexual I am inevitably
> something of an outsider in such matters but because it seems
> to me vital to put that particular ambiguity or doubleness back
> in the context of a much wider span of ambivalence. (*x–xi*)

This lively and engaging drama is direct and even celebratory of
Wilde's subversive status as a colonial jester in London—"a parodist and parasite" (*viii*)—yet Wilde's undermining of British cultural imperialism is the main focus. Eagleton's bawdy, often witty,
sexually explicit directness is demonstrated by the opening ballad:
"The moral of our tale is plain for to tell: / Unnatural practices land
you in hell / If you're Quare and you're Irish and wear a daft hat /
Don't go screwing the son of an aristocrat" (6). This ambivalence
towards Wilde's sexuality permeates the play and reflects the
ways in which rebel Wilde always subsumes the spectre of queer
Wilde.

Much of the play celebrates Wilde as a playful political subversive in his discussions with Richard Wallace and Edward Carson,
and, in his encounters with Carson, Eagleton anticipates the founding of the state of Northern Ireland. As Peter Dickinson writes,
"[in] Eagleton's construction of him, Oscar thus joins a long list of
Irish writers, orators, and politicians brought down by a British cultural oligarchy that saw the seductiveness of their language and
message as threatening and subversive."[8] However, this construction of victim of British justice is at odds with his representation of
Wilde's sexuality, and it is significant that all dramatic discussion
and debate around the 'cause' and origin of his sexual nature are
confined to Wilde's first encounter, that with his mother.

This opening scene is in line with many earlier, more hostile versions of Wilde's life, where the over-mothering of Speranza is held
accountable for the 'unnatural' homosexuality of her son. In an
effort to come to terms with Wilde's sexuality, Eagleton relies on an
androgynous notion of sexuality and in doing so he falls back on a
retrograde feminizing of the homoerotic and a discourse of the monstrous to represent sexual otherness. Right at the opening of the play,
Wilde describes his birth as "a monstrous birth. When they pulled
me out they screamed and tried to kill me on the spot. A cock and a

---

8. Dickinson, "Oscar Wilde," 418.

cunt together, the one tucked neatly within the other" (6). In the play, it is the mother, Speranza, who is blamed for this hermaphroditic birth, as Wilde accuses her, "who was it unmanned me?" and he goes on to explain: "Don't you see, mother, something went awry with me within the furry walls of your womb. Your little boy is flawed, botched, unfinished. I had my own body but I was too greedy for flesh. I wanted yours, too. The two don't mix well" (13–17). The play thus falls back on the conservative notion that to be homosexual, other, subaltern, all gay men must somehow want to be female, conflating notions of transgendering with the homoerotic.

In the play, there is a problematic disjunction between the celebration of Wilde's political potential for radicalism and the representation of his unnatural sexuality, the subversiveness of one being undermined by the regressive gendering of the other. Connected with this is Eagleton's unequivocal portrayal of Bosie as a pernicious influence on Wilde—"I love him . . . as Saint Sebastian loved the arrows" (23)—but he is even-handed in demonstrating Wilde's own deliberate courting of his trials and his fall from grace. As Eagleton constructs Wilde, disgrace was the only place for him to go, the only logical end to his stance of transgression and subversion. Eagleton finds a kind of gallows humour in all this and celebrates Wilde's sabotaging of British imperialism but he still draws on traditional and limiting notions of sexual difference. As in all texts about Wilde written in the tradition of Irish nationalist history, Oscar the rebel predominates, though it is to Eagleton's credit that in 1989, when homosexuality was still criminalised in Ireland, he attempts to celebrate the subversive queerness of Wilde. The disjunction between his representation of his sexuality and of his politics is, in fact, an inevitable consequence of the tradition in which he is writing, a nationalist discourse when the erotic is always subaltern, always suspect. In the *Irish Times*, David Nowlan says: "Mr Eagleton has tried to personify Wilde the person outcast from family, nation and sex, the nation-victim of another establishment. But the parable does not work dramatically."[9] It does not work because there is no place for a progressive queer Wilde within an Irish nationalist tradition.

Finally I want to conclude by considering two texts where the gap between rebel Wilde and queer Wilde is fruitfully exploited. Matt Cook has written that "[b]oth Wilde and Wildean strategies were increasingly seen as ways of thinking about the constitution and malleability of homosexual identity in the 1880s and the 1890s and also as a means of self-invention, affirmation and endurance in the

9. David Nowlan, *Irish Times*, October 10, 1997, 1.

present."[1] Both of the contemporary gay novelists Colm Tóibín and Jamie O'Neill deploy the iconic figure of Wilde as a means of affirmation and endurance for a contemporary gay identity, and do so by fusing his nationalism with the potentially subversive nature of his sexual dissidence. In this instance, Annemarie Jogose's definition of "the queer" is most useful: "[b]roadly speaking queer describes those gestures or analytical models which dramatise incoherencies in the allegedly stable relations between chromosomal sex, gender and sexual desire. Resisting that model of stability—which claims heterosexuality as it origins when it is more properly its effect— queer focuses on mismatches between sex, gender and desire."[2] As well as linking with Wilde's earlier decadence, queerness and the resisting of models of stability like that of Irish nationalism are made possible in the broader Irish culture of the 2000s. In his introduction to *Queer Notions* (2010), Fintan Walsh describes the timeframe in which these queer plays were created in Ireland: "Written and performed between 2000 and 2010, the pieces both challenge, but also strive to imagine alternative ways of being with others, and being in the world. The works are queer in so far as they explore tensions surrounding sexual difference in the broadest sense, in a manner that illuminates and interrogates issues that affect a wide range of people, including those who identify as neither Irish nor queer."[3]

Thus, the last years of the twentieth century saw a remaking of the ways in which Ireland defined itself as a newly wealthy Europeanised liberal society. This remaking or dislocation, depending on how it is viewed, led to an expansion of the acceptable areas for mainstream creativity within Irish writing, a movement into previously unexplored imaginative territories reflecting this social and cultural change. Fintan O'Toole writes: "In the last decade of the century, the Republic embraced another form of globalisation so thoroughly that it came to represent an extreme manifestation of the phenomenon."[4] In Irish writings, marginal discourses, homosexuality for one, now became much more public and central as the law and the economy changed and, as the critic Linden Peach suggests, "previously marginalized groups, albeit not entirely free of

1. Matt Cook, "Wilde Lives: Derek Jarman and the Queer Eighties," in *Oscar Wilde and Modern Culture*, ed. Joseph Bristow (Athens: Ohio University Press, 2008), 286.
2. Annamarie Jagose, *Queer Theory: An Introduction* (Melbourne: Melbourne University Press, 1996), 3.
3. Fintan Walsh, *Queer Notions: New Plays and Performances from Ireland* (Cork: Cork University Press, 2010), 4.
4. Fintan O'Toole, "Irish Literature in English in the New Millennium," in *The Cambridge History of Irish Literature*, Volume II, 1890–2000, ed. Margaret Kelleher and Philip O'Leary (Cambridge: Cambridge University Press, 2006), 629.

their marginalized social, physical and cultural status, bring about a revisioning of the nations map in terms of margins and centres."[5] This revisioning of the nation's map meant that key figures of difficulty like Wilde were now re-appropriated as new symbols of unreflective modernity and post-imperialism within Irish writing.

Novels, in particular historical novels, can destabilise. In Jamie O'Neills 2002 novel *At Swim, Two Boys,* a narrative of homoerotic love and romance set around the Easter Rising of 1916, the figure of Oscar Wilde functions as both iconic queer and symbol of patriotic rebellion, and each version empowers and fuses with the other.[6] One of the central characters, Anthony MacMurrough, is directly figured as a Wildean transgressor, as he has also been imprisoned for gross indecency and has served the full sentence of two years hard labour. MacMurrough constantly invokes the shade of the now dead, queer Wilde in this time of nationalist agitation. At one point, MacMurrough is on a tour of Dublin with his aunt, a tour given by a nationalist Irish priest. They arrive in Merrion Square: "'I don't believe I know,' the priest remarked, 'any patriot associated with Merrion Square.'"[7] MacMurrough, to annoy his aunt, intervenes and tells the priest:

> "There was one Irishman associated with Merrion Square," he said.
>
> "Yes, the English put him on trial."
>
> "It was ever the way," the priest complacently affirmed.
>
> "Three trials, in fact. On the first he had the wit to proclaim, I am the prosecutor in this case!"
>
> "I see, yes, very good. For all his country's wrongs."
>
> "I need hardly tell you, Father Taylor, of the desertion by his friends, of witnesses bullied and corrupted, of the agitation against him got up by the newspapers."
>
> "It was ever the Saxon sneaking way." [. . .]
>
> "His conviction was inevitable. But from the dock he gave a celebrated speech that defied to the heavens the traductions of his adversaries."
>
> "A speech from the dock! I have heard it said, and have said it myself; the speech from the dock is the only truly Irish drama. Three patriots may not gather but a rendition of Emmett or of Tone will edify the occasion. It is a form peculiarly suited

---

5. Linden Peach, *The Contemporary Irish Novel: Critical Readings* (London: Palgrave Macmillan, 2004), 9.
6. For a revealing context to the novel, Tom Inglis, *Lessons in Irish Sexuality* (Dublin: UCD Press, 1998), is worth considering.
7. Jamie O'Neill, *At Swim, Two Boys* (London: Scribner, 2001), 436. Subsequent references will be given parenthetically in the text.

to the Irish temperament. And what did this speech from the
dock say?"

"The jury was unmoved, the judge called for order but still
the gallery cheered." (436–437)

The priest never finds out the name of this great Irish patriot. Mac-
Murrough's aunt intervenes before Wilde's unmentionable name
can be mentioned, but the whole Irish patriot reincarnation of
Wilde is being teased and undermined by O'Neill. MacMurrough's
aunt reproves him:

"Are you really so lunatic . . . that you were about to give Oscar
Wilde's name to the parish curate?" . . .

"Well," said MacMurrough, "and was he not an Irishman?
And did his speech not bring the gallery to its feet?"

"You refer to the eulogium on illicit love?"

"The love that dares not speak its name."

"Its name," she said, "is buggery. Any soul in the three king-
doms might have told him." (438)

In this tale of love between Irish men in time of war, the image of
Wilde presides, even to a point of parody and farce when, at one
point, MacMurrough rescues a man in difficulty swimming in
Dublin Bay and on discovering that he has actually rescued Edward
Carson, insists on giving him a full-on kiss, just to revenge himself
for Wilde's sake. At another point, the Irish patriot Tom Kettle,
here presented as an old schoolfriend of MacMurrough, asks,
appalled, when confronted with MacMurrough's homosexuality,
"Dammit, MacMurrough, are you telling me that you are an
unspeakable of the Oscar Wilde sort?" "If you mean, am I Irish, the
answer is yes" (309). For O'Neill, as for Joyce, another direct influence on this novel, the figure of Wilde can be deployed as an
empowering prophet of sin. In a perceptive review of the novel,
David Halperin argues that:

One of O'Neill's most breathtaking accomplishments in *At
Swim, Two Boys* is to cross the codes of Irish identity and gay
identity, making each into a figure for the other, thereby producing at one stroke a gay genealogy of Irishness as well as a
specifically Irish image of male homosexuality—a romantic
vision of the gay male world as 'a nation of the heart.' [. . .]
O'Neill's novel deliberately takes its reader back to the pivotal
era when gayness and Irishness alike were under vigorous construction. . . . Little wonder, then, that the plot of *At Swim,
Two Boys* hurtles relentlessly towards Easter 1916: both Irish
nationalism and queer nationalism locate their mythological
origins in an urban riot. Impertinent as it might seem to claim

the Irish Rebellion as a prototype of Stonewall, O'Neill—who
is not above making obscene puns on Ireland's 'rising'—does
finally invite us to view Stonewall as a latter-day gay replica of
Easter 1916.[8]

As Halperin suggests, the novel fuses the two possible kinds of
Irish Wilde, and its queerness destabilises the hithertofore hetero-
normativity of Irish republican discourse. Also the novelist Colm
Tóibín constructs Wilde as an Irish gay icon, an empowering presence in contemporary Irish writing, in his essay on Wilde in *Love in
a Dark Time: Gay Lives from Wilde to Almodóvar* (2002). In this
collection, Tóibín links his own recognition of himself as a gay man
with his reclaiming of Wilde as a crucial point of reference. His
essay is perhaps the most direct account of the importance of Wilde's
sexuality from a contemporary Irish gay literary and cultural perspective, and he opens with the question "Why should it matter? It
matters because as gay readers and writers become more visible
and confidant, and gay politics more settled and serious, gay history
becomes a vital element in gay identity, just as Irish history does in
Ireland, or Jewish history amongst Jewish people."[9] "The gay past is
not pure (as the Irish past can often seem too pure); it is duplicitous
and slippy" (14). Tóibín makes the link between unhappy, despair-
ing gay writing of the past and the unhappy Irish domestic writing,
but, unusually for an Irish commentator writing on Wilde, he cites
Sir William as the crucial parental influence that made Wilde
decide to prosecute Queensbury. "The Wilde's were part of a small
breed of Irish Protestants. . . . Their addiction to the cause of Irish
freedom gave them an edge, lifted them out of their own circumstances and gave them astonishing individuality, and independence
of mind" (46). Unlike Eagleton, Tóibín records Wilde's respect for
Speranza, much needed after all the sneering or grotesque accounts
of his mother that appeared in earlier Irish biographies of Wilde:
"In all of Oscar Wilde's letters in which he refers to his mother,
there is not one word of mockery or disloyalty. Mostly he refers to
her not as his mother but as Lady Wilde" (51). He also stresses that
all grotesque accounts of Speranza happen after Wilde's trials and
disgrace and that before 1895 all the contemporary accounts of her
are respectful and admiring, her reputation as a writer suffering as
a consequence with his downfall.

Tóibín is refreshingly perceptive on the idea of how gay men
approach sexual relationships, using Wilde and Douglas as his exem-
plars and deconstructing the prejudices of previous biographers:

8. David Halperin, "Pal o' Me Heart." *London Review of Books*, May 22, 2003, 32–33.
9. Colm Tóibín, *Love in a Dark Time: Gay Lives from Wilde to Almodóvar* (London: Picador, 2003), 7. Subsequent references will be given parenthetically in the text.

[quoting Richard Ellmann] "Since neither Wilde nor Douglas practised or expected sexual fidelity, money was the stamp and seal of their love." That last sentence, so full of judgement and certainty shows us perhaps more about Ellmann than it does about Wilde or Douglas. It suggests that 'since' they were not faithful to each other, they could not properly love each other; he suggests that 'since' this is the case, then the stamp and seal of their love would have to be something profane and abject and wrong. It is much more likely that the stamp and seal of their love came from their enormous attraction to each other, their need for each other, and something difficult to define and explain which is at the core of homosexual experience in the era before gay liberation and perhaps to some extent, in the era afterwards. (60)

Tóibín treats their relationship with a real respect for its authentic emotional bonding:

In most societies, most gay people go through adolescence believing that the fulfilment of physical desire would not be matched by emotional attachment. For straight people, the eventual matching of the two is part of the deal, a happy aspect of normality But if this occurs for gay people, it is capable of taking on an extraordinarily powerful emotional force, and the resulting attachment, even if the physical part fizzles out, or even if the relationship makes no sense to the outside world, is likely to be fierce and enduring. [. . .] This, more likely, was the stamp and seal of the love between Oscar Wilde and Alfred Douglas. (61)

As Tóibín puts it: "The personal became political because an Irishman in London pushed his luck" (80).

How does this essay impact on his fictive representations of Wilde? In his novel *The Master* (2004) as with the O'Neill novel, Wilde has a crucial symbolic role, the dangerous 'other' figure for the closeted and cautious Henry James, the master of the title. The turning point in James's life in London comes in April and May 1895 during the Wilde trials. Wilde obsesses James, a nightmare counterpart, a dreaded anti-self, publicly exposed and forced to defend his homosexuality in a courtroom, and as can be seen in this excerpt, Tóibín aligns Wilde's dangerous sexuality with his national identity: "Everything about Wilde, from the moment Henry had first seen him, even when he had met him in Washington in the house of Clover Adams, suggested deep levels and layers of hiddenness. . . . He remembered something vague being told to him about Wilde's parents, his mother's madness, or her revolutionary spirit, or both, and his father's philandering or perhaps, indeed, his

revolutionary spirit. Ireland, he supposed, was too small for someone like Wilde, yet he had always carried a threat of Ireland with
him."[1]

James is fascinated and also terrified by Wilde and by any supposed connection that might be made between the two men.
(James, like Wilde, was of Irish Protestant stock, but James keeps
his Irish ancestry quiet.) The lesson of Wilde's disgrace drives
James most decisively back into further closeted self-denial, but by
implication, the figure of Wilde acts as a kind of destabilising force
within the novel, the subversive Irishman willing to confront public
homophobia, a sexual rebel in a way that the repressed James can
never emulate:

> The story of Wilde filled Henry's days now. He read whatever
> came into print about the case and waited for news. He wrote
> to William about the trial, making clear that he had no respect
> for Wilde; he disliked both his work and his activities on the
> stage of London society. Wilde, he insisted, had never been
> interesting to him, but now, as Wilde threw caution away and
> seemed ready to make himself into a public martyr, the Irish
> playwright began to interest him enormously. (72–73)

Wilde becomes an other self for James, a liberated, visible, Irish
queer man, everything that fascinated and also repelled him, and
this episode is seen as crucial in the lifelong closetry and sexual
timidity of the novelist.

To conclude, I want to refer to a moment in Irish public discourse
that highlights continuing ambivalent public perceptions around
Wilde in contemporary Ireland. On December 1, 2000, President
Mary McAleese visited a centenary exhibition on Wilde in the British Library, and the Irish Times described her speech as "reflecting on a 'hesitancy' of ownership of Wilde in Ireland and Britain.
Mrs McAleese said that on the anniversary of his death, Ireland
was 'justly, joyfully' celebrating his work and life but in the past, as
she points out, with a refreshing honesty, 'Irish people have sometimes been unsure how to regard him.'"[2] There have been excep-
tions to this. Throughout the first decade of the twenty-first century
both gay and straight Irish culture sought to appropriate Wilde as a
potent symbol of affirmation and a signal for a re-invented Irish
cultural openess and modernity. In 2007, in line with their policy of
naming their ferries for Irish literary figures, Irish Ferries christened their most recently acquired luxury cruise ship, which sails
between Ireland and France, the Oscar Wilde. Witness also the

1. Colm Tóibín, The Master (London: Picador, 2004), 71. Subsequent references will be
   given parenthetically in the text.
2. Irish Times, December 1, 2000, 9.

logo of the Dublin Gay Theatre Festival, a festival that began in 2004, where Wilde is a central figure, the symbol of a contemporary gay forum. However, at the end of this decade, when it might seem as if a queer Wilde has been recovered, another moment of public unease surfaced when a proposal to rename Merrion Square Park as Oscar Wilde Gardens was rejected by Dublin City Council (the park, the site of the Wilde statue, had officially been called Archbishop Ryan Park but this name was dropped in the light of revelations about clerical abuse in the Dublin Diocese). In a letter to the *Irish Times*, Ross Higgins wrote that he was

> deeply disappointed to hear of the decision of the councillors representing Dublin South East to recommend to the Dublin City Council that Archbishop Ryan Park be renamed Merrion Square Park rather than Oscar Wilde Gardens. There was an extensive consultation process with 567 submissions received by the City Council, with 219 in favour of renaming the park Oscar Wilde Gardens and only 45 in favour of calling it Merrion Square. The park itself is the site of the only public memorial to Oscar Wilde and there is no public amenity in the city named after him. This represents an opportunity to change this. I have heard it said that since the park is commonly referred to as Merrion Square, so why not make the name official? The problem is that names matter, and symbolism matters. After all, this is why the name of the park is being changed in the first place. The councillors, in overturning the clear response of the consultation process, are making a statement: That 110 years after his death Dublin should still be ashamed of one of its most gifted sons.[3]

Clearly Wilde still troubles the waters of Irish public discourse.

MANECK H. DARUWALA

Wilde in Earnest[†]

For Dev

Algernon. How are you, my dear Ernest? What brings you up to town? Jack. Oh, pleasure, pleasure! What else should bring one anywhere?
—Oscar Wilde, *The Importance of Being Earnest*

---

3. *Irish Times*, May 14, 2010.
† Written for this Norton Critical Edition. Page numbers in square brackets refer to this volume.

"There is one story and one story only," says Robert Graves, although some writers of fiction concede that there may be two. What dominates Oscar Wilde's work, his most dazzling wit and outrageous paradoxes, and perhaps his life, is the infinitely creative tension and dialogue between two stories or ideas. These include the interplay between the concepts of truth and beauty in their many incarnations, life and art, the world as it is and a world remade nearer to the heart's desire, the public life and the private life—or the idea of the double life. As Wilde put it, "To most of us the real life is the life we do not lead" (*Essays and Lectures*, 88). But it is not till the tragic peak and end of Wilde's career that these contraries merge in the perfect progression and identity that is *The Importance of Being Earnest*. In *Earnest* the two stories, the real life and the imagined life, become one; modeled on the *Oedipus* of Sophocles and its tragic pursuit of the truth, *Earnest* gives us a glimpse of what a world might be if beauty were truth, truth beauty.

In unfolding the origins of Ernest, *Earnest* tells us the story of its own origins. It has long been acknowledged that *Earnest* shares its plot, the child lost and found, with perhaps the most talked-about classical tragedy of all, the *Oedipus Tyrannos*—or, as Wilde prefers to call it, *Oedipus Rex*. *Earnest* was at least partly modeled on a play supposed to have been set and performed during a plague and a political crisis. These associations were apparently the reason why Sophocles did not win the first prize at the city Dionysia in Athens. Western critics, philosophers, and theorists from Aristotle to Wilde, and to our own time, have pondered the value of tragedy, although to the Greeks it implied a serious handling of the subject, of course, not an unhappy ending. Why, in a world full of misery, would you pack a theater to weep over the imaginary misfortunes of people who never existed? Or why in a time of political or economic or humanitarian crisis, in the midst of the sixth great extinction of species, when earnestness and truth are critical to survival, would a play as apparently frivolous as *Earnest* continue to be so popular? Curve Leicester and the Birmingham Rep streamed it free in 2020, and the Harlem Renaissance Virtual Salon presented it "in celebration of the 100th Anniversary of the Harlem Renaissance." In brief, what is the value of a play that professes to have no use and to teach nothing in the worst as in the best of times?

At the end of that famous drinking party, Plato's *Symposium*, Aristodemus wakes up at daybreak to catch the end of Socrates' discourse compelling the half-asleep Aristophanes and Agathon to agree that the genius of comedy and the genius of tragedy are essentially the same. In what is apparently an enigmatic and

comic insight even in the original Greek, everything but the conclusion is lost, no one really follows the argument, and almost
everyone is asleep at the end. Perhaps it was not till Wilde produced *The Importance of Being Earnest*, almost twenty-three centuries later, that unintoxicated readers finally understood what
this passage might mean. In Aristotle's *Poetics*, tragedy and comedy are distinguished by the attitude to or handling of a subject,
not the ending. And Wilde's subtitle, "A Trivial Comedy for Serious People," seems to hint at that. *Earnest* not only uses and parodies the usual structures and strategies of tragic and comic drama
like anagnorisis and perepetia, but, as critics like Richard Ellmann
and Rodney Shewan have demonstrated, parodies and dissolves
Wilde's own favorite destructive and tragic themes into utopian
comedy.

It is an appropriate paradox that a play which is considered the
pinnacle of English comedy was composed by an Irishman and modeled after a Greek tragedy. Analyses of Wilde's fascination with and
transformations of Greek culture, literature, and philosophy (especially the Platonic dialogues and Aristotle's *Poetics*) have been rather
sweeping. According to Stefano Evangelista, "Ancient Greece is the
foundation on which Wilde's identity as aesthete, critic, and writer
is built" (125). For Wilde, the Greek context also had an added attraction: the love that dared not speak its name in English could find
some expression in a Greek allusion.

Wilde's identity also draws on other literary sources, but the similarities between *Oedipus* and *Earnest* extend beyond the plot, and
classicists who know the play in the original (which is Greek to me)
have detailed, for example, the marvelous use of stychomachia
in each play. Aristotle cites *Oedipus* as a model repeatedly in the
Poetics; it is apparently the most wittily structured and intellectual—
that is, the most Aristotelian—of the plays he mentions, even
though he acknowledges Euripides, who breaks all the rules, as the
most tragic of poets (XIII). Wilde excelled in Greek at Oxford, and
his review of the 1887 Cambridge production of *Oedipus* describes
it as "one of the greatest plays ever written. As ethical as *Hamlet*, as
passionate as *Lear*, and as finely constructed as *Macbeth*" (Foster
124). Wilde had also pointed out in 1882 that "'not only in its plot,
but in its construction, dramatic conception and effect,' Sophocles'
Oedipus 'gives one an excellent motive for a modern play'" (Foster
124). Plot rules, according to the *Poetics*, yet in *Oedipus* character
and language are destiny.

Earnest not only parallels the brilliant ingenuity and wit of language and construction of *Oedipus*, but may even parody its
cast. Lady Bracknell, "a monster, without being a myth" [20], who

interrogates the hero and sets him a riddle far more profound, gene-
alogical, and ambiguous than is apparent at face value, is an obvious parallel to the Sphinx. (For Knox the answer to the Sphinx's
riddle, never specified in the play, is not only "Man" but "Oedipus,"
as a baby, as a young man, and later at Colonus.) Ernest, like Oedipus, is both the riddle and the answer. Dr. Chasuble may be the
representative of religion, but it is Gwendolen who like Tiresias is
never wrong (or so she claims). Like a Greek actor who played multiple roles (perhaps performing both Antigone and Haemon), Miss
Prism is the origin of the action, exchanging the baby and the
manuscript, nature and art, at a terminus. She is also Cecily's tutor,
and the chorus. The chorus, the origin of Greek drama and often the
performer of ecstatically beautiful and moving lyrics, may sometimes
be seen as the voice of society and common sense, if occasionally offi-
cious, judgmental, and full of unwelcome advice. Miss Prism offers
moral comment, often verging on the censorious. Despite her benevo-
lence, she is not always empathetic. When Jack informs her that Earnest has perished in Paris, her response is: "What a lesson for him! I
trust he will profit by it" [30].

The ingenuity of *Oedipus* is stunning, as Bernard Knox discussed
in his *Oedipus at Thebes*. Oedipus is the pursuer and the pursued,
the detective and the criminal, the physician and the disease, the
man who actually happens to be looking for himself when he finds
himself. The play mirrors a scientific exploration and the judicial
process. Oedipus has three interrogations of witnesses (Knox 19);
Lady Bracknell not only undertakes two interviews of suitors—
Jack and Cecily—but also interrogates the messenger of this story,
Miss Prism. Miss Prism, like the shepherd messenger of *Oedipus*, is
of course the key to Jack's identity. Jack, in turn, argues his own case
against muffin-devouring Algernon, who relishes the idea that "the
truth is rarely pure and never simple" [11]. The truth does not always
redeem, as Tiresias and the audience already know, and Tiresias
does not want Oedipus to pursue it: "How dreadful knowledge
of the truth can be / When there's no help in truth!" (Fitts and
Fitzgerald, lines 304–05). Wilde's play undercuts Victorian expectations of gender roles. But it is literal gender fluidity—having been
both male and female—that is the source of Tiresias's wisdom and
his misfortune.

But if Oedipus has led more lives than one, Jocasta too has a
hidden life, grieving for the baby she thinks Laius has killed, and
grieving again when he is recovered. The plays of Sophocles and
Euripides do not seem to share but reflect on the deep misogyny
of Athenian society. Oedipus is in serial conflict with almost every
male character in the play, but he loves his daughters and for
Jocasta he has both love and respect.

JOCASTA   Oedipus, tell me too, what is it? For the love of god,
     why this rage? You're so unbending.
OEDIPUS   I will tell you. I respect you, Jocasta, much more
     than these men here. . . . (Sophocles, *The Theban Plays*
     768–70)

Even accounting for the ambiguous nature of their relationship, in
this play Jocasta has no more problem ordering the men of her family
around than Gwendolen or Lady Bracknell might. In a scene that
triggers her retelling of the past, she emerges from the palace to
break up a bitter quarrel between Oedipus and Creon, scolding them
like misbehaving children:

JOCASTA   Have you no sense? Poor misguided men, such
     shouting—why this public outburst? Aren't you ashamed,
     with the land so sick, to stir up private quarrels?
To OEDIPUS   Into the palace now. And Creon, you go home.
     (709–12)

In *Earnest* the selfless desire to become Ernest motivated by love—
by a proposal, not a plague—leads to the unfolding of a beautiful
truth that brings them all together. Oedipus pursues the truth, but
Jack is more pursued by it in the form of several demanding women.
In the play's performance of gender, the men are more earnest than
the women. But the women of the play are more determined (something drastic may have to be done, says Gwendolen) and wittier—
in their encounters with the men. Lady Bracknell, snobbishly
obsessed with origins, demands that Jack produce one parent of
either sex before the social season is quite over. But origin is not
necessarily identity, and identity in *Earnest* is no more fixed than
the species are, though of course on a different chronological scale.
Gwendolen demands that Jack be or become Ernest (she accepts the
creative solution of christening), and Cecily, charmed, like Desde-
mona or Niamh by the stories she has heard about Ernest, accepts
that she has fallen in love with an Algernon instead, although she
still demands some authenticity:

ALGERNON   Oh! I am not really wicked at all, Cousin Cecily.
     You mustn't think that I am wicked.
CECILY   If you are not, then you have certainly been deceiving
     us all in a very inexcusable manner. I hope you have not
     been leading a double life, pretending to be wicked and
     being really good all the time. That would be hypoc-
     risy. [27–28]

So *Earnest*, like *Oedipus*, is about the pursuit of truth—which in this
case is also the pursuit of pleasure—or happiness. Because despite

all the emphasis on classicism, Wilde began his literary career as a
Romantic poet in the Keatsian tradition of luxury and the pleasures
of bursting joy's grape against a fine palate with a strenuous tongue
("Ode on Melancholy").

Successor to Sophocles, Wilde in *Earnest* presents surprisingly
similar strategies for pursuing the truth. The power of *Oedipus* lies
not only in the shocking truth, never in doubt for the audience, but
in the taut beauty of its unfolding dialogue and construction. *Oedipus* and *Earnest* share a dazzling intellectual vitality, a confidence
in the power of human intelligence and wit. Apollo is the presiding
deity of Oedipus—in this play Ares not Apollo sends the plague
(Knox 99–100). The "Know Thyself" inscribed at the entrance to his
temple at Delos is the overarching theme of *Oedipus* (Knox 183).
Apollo is the god of the sun, of knowledge and of science, but also
the beautiful god of poetry and music: he is both truth and beauty.
But he is, as Swinburne put it in his "Hymn to Proserpine" (lines
8–9), "A bitter God to follow, a beautiful God to behold." In *Oedipus*, the pursuit of truth saves the city but destroys the family. For
Aristotle's favorite example of a tragic plot in the *Poetics*, it is remarkably character-driven. Oedipus could have refused to pursue the
truth or continued to rule, as in other versions of the story, or simply dismissed the oracle or his discovery as fake news and let his
people continue to die.

One of the joys of reading Wilde is in remembering what a great
artist conveniently remembers to forget. Of course *Earnest* has a
long ancestry, including Plautus and Shakespeare, but it is an
intellectual comedy just as *Oedipus* is an intellectual tragedy. Its
great passion is language itself. Like Oedipus, despite the different
consequences, it celebrates the power of human consciousness. *Earnest* brings to mind T. S. Eliot's famous remark about how good
writers steal where others merely borrow. The purloined plot is the
basis of some of the best plays we have. The play draws on tragedy,
comedy, and romance, on myth and legend and fairy tale and the
ancient theme of the child lost and found, with an abandon and
excess that verge on parody. It is this combination of self-conscious
structural and linguistic wit and ingenuity—its sheer delight in
the power of its own dazzling language—that makes *Earnest* an
archetype of the perfect comedy, and, supposedly, the most quoted
comedy in English. Repetition is part of its delight, which no
amount of familiarity can wither or stale. "Yet one had ancestors in
literature, as well as in one's own race, nearer perhaps in type and
temperament, many of them, and certainly with an influence of
which one was more absolutely conscious" (Wilde, *Dorian Gray*
121). Wilde toured America preaching his Keatsian gospel of

beauty, but he was also a highly self-aware successor to Sophocles and a contemporary of Charles Darwin. Darwin's theories of evolution did not just disrupt Victorian society, they transformed humanity's perception of itself and its place in the natural world. And *On the Origin of Species* and *The Descent of Man* may also be links to the origins of *Earnest*. *The Importance of Being Earnest* reads like an unlikely blend of Sophocles mediated by Keats and Darwin.

The more Wilde's paradoxes juxtapose the oppositions of truth and beauty, art and life, the more inextricable they seem. The interrelationship of *Earnest* with *Oedipus*, Keatsian aesthetics, and Darwin's suppressed theory of female sexual selection in *The Descent of Man* (as analyzed and interpreted in recent works like Richard O. Prum's *The Evolution of Beauty* and David Rothenberg's *Survival of the Beautiful*) is much more specific than this, and also relates to the play's enduring appeal.

David Clifford points out that Wilde admired Darwin and was aware that ideas about evolution and progress had shaped his own critical and political thought (211). Caroline Sumpter cites Wilde at his most Darwinian:

> "There is no mode of action, no form of emotion, that we do not share with the lower animals" (137). This evolutionary claim is attributable not to Darwin but to Wilde, who allows Gilbert to voice this bold assertion in "The True Function of Criticism." (1)

However, discussing the influence of evolutionary theory on Wilde's criticism, Sumpter says that

> [a]lthough Wilde is known to have owned *On the Origin of Species* and *The Descent of Man*, it is evolutionary arguments mediated via writers such as W. K. Clifford, Huxley and Spencer—figures who were also high-profile debaters in the nineteenth century—that are cited directly in his Oxford notebook and commonplace book, rather than Darwin himself. (6)

Whatever Wilde's acknowledged interpretation of Darwin might have been, *The Importance of Being Earnest* demonstrates a much more modern and at the same time more Darwinian philosophy than that which held the stage for much of the nineteenth and some of the twentieth century. Or one may look at it as a blend of Darwin and Keats (whose profession was medicine); Wilde knew his Darwin and explicitly draws upon his theories of natural and of sexual selection, for example in Gilbert's argument in "The True Function of Criticism" (which later became "The Critic as Artist"):

> Aesthetics, in fact, are to Ethics, in the sphere of human civili-
> sation, what, in the sphere of the external world, Sexual is to
> Natural Selection. Ethics, like Natural Selection, make exis-
> tence possible. Aesthetics, like Sexual Selection, make life
> lovely and wonderful, fill it with new forms, give it progress, and
> variety, and change. (quoted by Sumpter 15)

Ethics make life possible but Aesthetics make it worth living. In 1871, twelve years after publishing *On the Origin of Species*, Darwin "boldly addressed both the problem of human origins and the evolution of beauty" (Prum 25) in *The Descent of Man, and Selection in Relation to Sex*. Darwin did not claim that natural selection explained all evolutionary change or variation. But he could not reconcile the truth of his theory of evolution with the beauty of evolution, with the exuberant, extravagant, gorgeousness of the natural world, the apparently spendthrift extravagance of peacock tails or the creation of beautiful bowers, the arbitrary whims or sophisticated aesthetics of female choice. (Though peahens also display.)

> CECILY   Miss Prism says that all good looks are a snare.
> ALGERNON   They are a snare that every sensible man would
>   like to be caught in.
> CECILY   Oh, I don't think I would care to catch a sensible
>   man. [29]

Whether or not this is true of sensible men or women, Darwin seems to have been deeply troubled by its relevance to peahens. "The sight of a feather in a peacock's tail, whenever I gaze at it, makes me sick" (Prum, 25, *Darwin Correspondence Project to Asa Gray*, 3 April 1860). Ultimately, Darwin could not pursue the truth of evolution without pursuing the beauty of evolution. The peacock and the peacock's tail are the favorite emblem of Aestheticism and Art Nouveau, and Darwin's own contemporaries were deeply trou-bled about the uses of art, as were Wilde's two major influences, Pater and Ruskin. But although birds and animals may have been earlier practitioners of "Art for Art's Sake" (and for love's sake), Wilde was its most famous Victorian advocate, explaining at some length why "All art is quite useless" (*DG* Preface) in the dialogues of *Intentions* (*Complete Works*), and Yeats continues the tradition:

> . . . whatever they do or have must be a means to something
> else, and they have so little belief that anything can be an end
> in itself that they cannot understand you if you say, "All the
> most valuable things are useless." They prefer the stalk to the
> flower, and believe that painting and poetry exist that there may

> be instruction, and love that there may be children . . . ("Poetry
> and Tradition," 1907; *Essays and Introductions* 251)

The argument that art and beauty are "useless" can be a useful,
even invaluable, and sometimes disingenuous defense against an
insistence on being immediately profitable or politically useful. Not
that art should not be political (politics and the remaking of Ireland
through literature are central Yeatsian themes), but it cannot be
required by definition to serve other ends: "The poet is indispens-
able, though nobody knows for what" (Cocteau). The argument
about the uselessness of art is an argument for the disinterestedness
and freedom of art. W. H. Auden's elegy on Yeats, which famously
claims that "poetry makes nothing happen," goes on to demand that
it transform the human heart and the world: "In the deserts of the
heart / Let the healing fountain start" (248–49).

But while much of the popular and perhaps scientific interpretation of Darwinian evolutionary theory in the nineteenth and twentieth centuries set up a dichotomy between beauty and utility and
emphasized force and a practical survival of the fittest, considering
beauty a mere proxy for physical fitness and leaving little room for
it or sexual fluidity, Wilde may be said to embody the aesthetic wing
of Darwinian evolutionary theory, or what is now called Evolutionary Aesthetics.

> Now, nearly 150 years later, a new generation of biologists is
> reviving Darwin's neglected brainchild. Beauty, they say,
> does not have to be a proxy for health or advantageous genes.
> Sometimes beauty is the glorious but meaningless flowering
> of arbitrary preference. . . . These biologists are not only rewrit-
> ing the standard explanation for how beauty evolves; they
> are also changing the way we think about evolution itself. . . .
> To solve the enigma of beauty, to fully understand evolu-
> tion, we must uncover the hidden links between those two
> worlds. (Jabr)

Prum's influential *The Evolution of Beauty: How Darwin's Forgotten Theory of Mate Choice Shapes the Animal World—and Us*, drawing upon a wide range of disciplines and decades of observation,
eloquently presents what he calls this "Beauty Happens" followed
by the "Pleasure Happens" thesis, with its emphasis on mate
choice and female autonomy. Described as Darwin's most dangerous idea, it is a more feminist, queerer theory of evolution.
(Of course, the concept of beauty, like any other, can be perverted
or misused, and even Darwin did not account for the fact that one
predatory species could wipe out the rest.) Beauty, like art or pure
mathematics, may seem superfluous or useless at first glance. But

features that first evolved for beauty may not only attract individual members of a species, they may evolve unpredictable uses or functions that save an entire species from extinction. According to contemporary evolutionary biologists, feathers evolved for beauty, which led to flight, which enabled an escape from the fifth great extinction of species. Beauty saved the birds, our only surviving dinosaurs.

Even here, Wilde had a predecessor in Keats as well as Darwin. In Keats's *Hyperion*, which he composed and abandoned at twenty-three while nursing his teenage brother through his last illness, we have a theory of evolution where ethics and aesthetics are inseparable. Here, as Wilde says, the great events of the world happen in the human mind, gods die and are replaced as the mind evolves, and divine beauty is a manifestation of a finer, more just, more egalitarian consciousness. As Keats's Oceanus explains his version of the Big Bang theory and evolution:

> We fall by course of Nature's law, not force . . .
>
> And first, as thou wast not the first of powers,
> So art thou not the last; it cannot be:
> Thou art not the beginning nor the end.
> From chaos and parental darkness came
> Light, . . .
>
>   The ripe hour came,
> And with it light, and light, engendering
> Upon its own producer, forthwith touch'd
> The whole enormous matter into life. . . .
> Now comes the pain of truth, to whom 'tis pain;
> O folly! for to bear all naked truths,
> And to envisage circumstance, all calm,
> That is the top of sovereignty. Mark well!
> As Heaven and Earth are fairer, fairer far
> Than Chaos and blank Darkness, though once chiefs;
> And as we show beyond that Heaven and Earth
> In form and shape compact and beautiful,
> In will, in action free, companionship,
> And thousand other signs of purer life;
> So on our heels a fresh perfection treads,
> A power more strong in beauty, born of us
> And fated to excel us, as we pass
> In glory that old Darkness: nor are we
> Thereby more conquer'd . . .

We are such forest-trees, and our fair boughs
Have bred forth, not pale solitary doves,
But eagles golden-feather'd, who do tower
Above us in their beauty, and must reign
In right thereof; for 'tis the eternal law
That first in beauty should be first in might . . .

Have ye beheld the young God of the Seas,
My dispossessor? Have ye seen his face?

(*Hyperion* II, 180, 188–92, 194–97, 202–16, 224–29,
   232–33)

But the struggle between the Olympians and Titans in both *Hyperion* (1818) and *The Fall of Hyperion* (1819) is an entirely masculine business, like the "rebellion / Of son against sire" (*Hyperion* I, 321–22). Although there are great goddesses among the Titans, the principle "That first in beauty should be first in might" (*Hyperion* II, 229) seems illustrated by gods alone and goddesses are not involved in this beauty contest except perhaps as judges. Even the young androgynous Apollo apparently has no part in it—he is the protégé of a goddess. It may seem that the goddesses play supporting roles on the borders of male conflict. But although gods are replaced by other, more beautiful gods in the mind, the goddess as muse endures; and neither Apollo nor the poet can achieve immortality without the intervention of a goddess (Daruwala, "Strange Bedfellows" 125). As for the presiding muses of the *Hyperion*, Mnemosyne, "supreme shape" (III, 161), describes herself to Apollo as "an ancient Power / Who hath forsaken old and sacred thrones / For prophecies of thee, and for the sake / Of loveliness new born" (III, 76–79). And Moneta, an ancient muse who looks forward to new beauty and new art, is defined by more—and less—than her beauty. For Keats the pursuit of beauty cannot be disentangled from that of truth and the human condition: "None can usurp this height, return'd that shade, / But those to whom the miseries of the world / Are misery, and will not let them rest" (*The Fall of Hyperion* I, 149–51).

Wilde, in *Earnest,* performs the utopian version of that pursuit because the opposition between constructs like truth and beauty may be an artificial one. According to Pater in his review of *Dorian Gray,* to lose the moral sense is a flaw in true Epicureanism. Or as Dorian might have put it, in a slightly twisted and belated interpretation, it is better to be good than ugly. *Earnest* dissolves the artificial opposition between truth and beauty or ethics and

aesthetics, and the pursuit of truth and the pursuit of beauty are
not always distinguishable. Cecily's expectations of her education
take the path of an aesthetic and more Romantic Darwinism than
Miss Prism's stern emphasis on utility and the fall of the rupee,
and her diary may be seen as the pursuit or creation of a better
world. After all, as Elaine Scarry puts it, "This willingness con-
tinually to revise one's own location in order to place oneself in
the path of beauty is the basic impulse underlying education" (7).
This is not so different from Gilbert's interpretation of Plato in
Wilde's "The Decay of Lying," and the emphasis on an education

> so that the beauty of material things may prepare his soul for
> the reception of the beauty that is spiritual. Insensibly, and
> without knowing the reason why, he is to develop that real love
> of beauty which, as Plato is never weary of reminding us, is
> the true aim of education. By slow degrees there is to be
> engendered in him such a temperament as will lead him natu-
> rally and simply to choose the good in preference to the bad.
> (CW 1049)

As Gilbert puts it rather sweepingly, it was Plato who "stirred in
the soul of man, that desire we have not yet satisfied, the desire to
know the connection between beauty and truth, and the place of
beauty in the moral and intellectual order of the Kosmos" (CW
1018).

Nor is Miss Prism herself immune to the call of the unreal—it is
after all her fateful confusion of art and reality, of a manuscript and
a baby, that sets the whole unlikely story in motion. And she has
her romantic side—a three-volume novel of perhaps revolting sentimentality in her past, Dr. Chasuble in her future, and a dramatic, perhaps overly dramatic, imagination. As she says to Cecily,
"you will read your Political Economy in my absence. The chapter
on the Fall of the Rupee you may omit. It is somewhat too sensational. Even these metallic problems have their melodramatic
side'" [27].

Both *Earnest* and *Oedipus* revolve around names that matter to
their bearers even before they realize their significance. "You all
know me, the world knows my fame: / I am Oedipus"—the opening
lines illustrate the famous irony which permeates the play (*Three
Theban Plays*). Oedipus is a *basileus* (ruler by inheritance) who
thinks he is a *tyrannos* (a ruler not by inheritance, not necessarily
pejorative). Ernest, as the first act establishes, thinks he is Jack pretending to be Ernest. *The Importance of Being Earnest* satirizes
Victorian society; but Oedipus himself, though ostensibly Theban,
is the Athens of Sophocles, embodying all its contradictions (Knox
53–106).

Sincerity or earnestness was a highly prized Victorian quality, and it is a paradoxical catalyst of the action that Gwendolen, who believes that "[i]n matters of grave importance, style, not sincerity is the vital thing" (47), should be so enamored of "Ernest." The exaggeration of a Victorian earnestness into the desire to marry a man named Ernest is an arbitrary and absurd ideal, the pursuit of a whimsical pleasure: "It is a divine name. It has a music of its own. It produces vibrations," says Gwendolen (15). But whether it is the shimmer of a peacock's tail producing vibrations that can be felt by the admiring or indifferent object of the display, or the vibrations of the name "Ernest," the desire for beauty reshapes the world. What Gwendolen and Cecily desire can be accomplished by creativity and christening—an enthusiastic and earnest willingness on the part of Jack and Algernon to become Ernest. But the gender roles of the play are not essentialist. While Jack and Algernon compete to be Ernest, Cecily and Gwendolyn have their own battle of wits for Ernest over tea and cake.

Wilde's appearance, the infinite variety of the fashions he adopted, was itself part of the performance. But despite his devotion to the visible beauty of the world, the ultimate Wildean equivalent of the shimmer of a peacock's tail is dialogue. Wilde aspired to look like a Roman but talk like a Greek. He had his hair curled in the Roman fashion, but his art was based on the Greek art of dialogue, which is also a dramatic form as practiced by Plato. In Wilde's earlier works the turning point of the action, the most powerful and beautiful seduction, was the human voice. Talking of Milton, Gilbert comments: "everyone should compose with the voice purely. . . . Yes: writing has done much harm to writers. We must return to the voice" (CW 1016–17). Wilde himself claimed that he had put his genius into his life and only his talent into his writing, and Yeats, in his Autobiography, says: "My first meeting with Oscar Wilde was an astonishment. I had never before heard a man talking with perfect sentences, as if he had written them all overnight with labour and yet all spontaneous" (87). It may seem absurd to stress the importance of dialogue while discussing a play. But for Wilde, the entire art of literature—and of life—is based on the individual human voice. "Ultimately, the bond of all companionship, whether in marriage or in friendship, is conversation" (CW, De Profundis 880). And the human voice is the turning point, the pivot of works like Dorian Gray and Salomé, the most powerful instrument of enchantment— and disenchantment—in these stories. Words alone, even Shakespeare's, are not enough: Sybil's voice after her awakening into love "was exquisite, but from the point of view of tone it was absolutely false" (71). The awakening—or creation or fall—of Dorian Gray is accomplished entirely by language and by a voice that evokes "vibrations" in his mind even as he is told that the great events—and great sins—of the world take place in the brain (Daruwala, "Discerning Flame" 159). Dorian Gray is a twin—he and his picture come into consciousness together. "Your voice and the voice of Sibyl Vane are two things that I shall never forget. When I close my eyes, I hear them, and each of them says something different. I don't know which to follow" (216). "There was something in his low languid voice that was absolutely fascinating." But Dorian is Wilde's Mona Lisa, not Pater's, and words matter:

> For nearly ten minutes he stood there, motionless, with parted lips and eyes strangely bright. He was dimly conscious that entirely fresh influences were at work within him. Yet they seemed to him to have come really from himself. The few words that Basil's friend had said to him—words spoken by chance, no doubt, and with willful paradox in them—had touched some secret chord that had never been touched before, but that he felt was now vibrating and throbbing to curious pulses. . . .
> And yet what a subtle magic there was in them! They seemed to be able to give a plastic form to formless things, and to have a music of their own as sweet as that of viol or of lute. Mere words! Was there anything so real as words? (*DP* 20)

By the time we get to *Salomé* the voice and the words are divorced—or at least in conflict. But in Wilde's final play, this enchantment with the human voice and the magic word as the absolute expression of individual personality is distilled into a single name, "Ernest," whose vibrations set in motion the rest of the action:

> GWENDOLEN   It suits you perfectly. It is a divine name. It has a music of its own. It produces vibrations. [15]

Finally, an earnest is also a pledge or a promise, and the play, the height of Wildean success just preceding tragedy, demonstrates a Romantic confidence about the power and autonomy of the imagination to reshape the world, the promise or earnest that this is possible: "In their own hearts the earnest of the hope / Which made them great the good will ever find," writes Shelley in *Laon and Cythna* (canto IX, stanza 27). Or, as Wilde puts it, "Those whom the gods love grow young" (*CW* 1204). Finally, the major appeal of *Earnest* is a *sprezzatura* or lightness of touch that is anything but earnest. (Arthur Symons reports that Wilde's great influence, Walter Pater, regarded "undue earnestness as bad form" [Daruwala, *"Discerning Flame"* 116].) In this ideal world, as in some French translations of the Bible, the "debonair" would inherit the earth. Here the ethical balance of Wilde's theme of the double life has been reversed. Here it seems Algernon has been rather good, as Cecily suspects. Here he who lives more lives than one may discover that the real life and the imagined life are identical; here you can eat your muffin and have it too, can butter your muffin on both sides and not have it run down your cuffs. One gets the drift.

To call *Earnest* a utopian play in a dystopian time is not to suggest that it presents an ideal society. Michael Patrick Gillespie, in his close reading of *Earnest* in *Branding Oscar Wilde*, performs a thorough and illuminating exploration of the class dynamics of the play and their relevance to the central question of identity. *Earnest* satirizes and sabotages the rules and institutional structures of the society it occupies, and its oppressive gender, class, and family expectations. But all these issues connect, ultimately, to the question of identity. To the Greek "Know thyself," perhaps an impossible if profound demand, Wilde's thought-provoking response in "Phrases and Philosophies for the Young" is "Only the shallow know themselves" (CW 1205). In *Earnest*, knowing yourself and your name is also confirming or newly discovering your relationship to yourself and your world. At the end of the world *Earnest* constructs, unlike its witty predecessors among comedies of manners, or even Shakespearean romance, no one is excluded from its circle of love. And despite the explosive end of the imaginary Bunbury, it is not clear that anyone at the end of *Earnest* sacrifices any pleasures, homosocial or otherwise, or succumbs to domesticity. Given all the puns, sexual allusions, and innuendo so wittily demonstrated in Christopher Craft's ingenious "Alias Bunbury," *Earnest* remains a curiously elusive play where gender seems not only fluid but irrelevant or interchangeable. Part of the delight of *Earnest*, in fact, is the queering of all class, gender and generational expectations, and ultimately even those of Wilde's earlier works, if that is possible.

Oedipus, *Dorian Gray*, and *Earnest* are all legends of identity. To Oedipus the burden of identity is a curse, handed down from generation to generation, which one cannot escape even through self-mutilation; nor can Dorian escape identity through murder, or a murder that becomes a suicide. But in *Earnest* identity is a glorious discovery, personal and communal. The famous tragic irony of *Oedipus* is comic irony here. Oedipus, fleeing his home to escape the prophecy of parricide and incest, kills his biological father in apparent self-defense. In the amazing *Oedipus at Colonus*, Oedipus, with no less fire but a lot more retrospective insight, argues convincingly that he cannot be judged a guilty or an evil man. He is both a parricide and innocent, and not just innocent but holy—like Tiresias, whose insight also comes with a tragic blindness. Oedipus unknowingly kills the father who tried to kill him and is ultimately in bitter conflict with his sons, who destroy each other. And he is in conflict with an increasingly callous Creon. The relationships between the males in the Theban plays are infanticidal, filicidal, parricidal, and fratricidal.

Jack, traveling to his house in the country, kills an imaginary brother, Ernest, in a premeditated act of fratricide that merely turns out to be an unsuccessful attempt at Algeicide. The killing is not only imaginary but energetically and indignantly denied by its resurrected and muffin-devouring subject, who turns out to be his real brother. And Algy, in turn, kills the imaginary Bunbury, who is no longer necessary to a world made nearer to the desires of the heart. These are the happier interpretations of "he who lives more lives than one," of Wilde's enduring theme of the double or hidden life, and Algy's hidden self is better than his public persona. If "each man kills the thing he loves," in *Dorian Gray* or *Salomé* it is because the thingness of love is the fatal objectification of love. In fact, unless one counts narcissism, these works are about an absence or deficiency of love. Nobody weeps at the end of *Salomé* and perhaps of *Dorian Gray*. Comedy and tragedy share many themes, but among the greatest of these is love. Oedipus, in his pursuit of the truth, loves and saves his city, but destroys his family and himself. And Antigone dies for love.

Earnest, first performed on Valentine's Day, 1895, does not plumb the profundities of love, but it does skim its complexities. It mocks the Victorian institution of marriage—in many cases the antithesis of love. Wilde was both a member of that society and an outsider—in his wit, his Irishness, and his sexual orientation. And Wilde in *Earnest* puts the elaborate rituals and institutions of that society on display almost as an anthropologist or an ornithologist might.

But it is in the pursuit of love that the characters of Wilde's play discover themselves, and it dissolves all contraries. It is the essence of the play's merging of truth and beauty that the person you seem to be and the person you want to be turn out to be one. The logic is the logic of fairy tales, not that of Sophoclean tragedy, and in the end *Earnest* is Wilde's greatest fairy tale. *Earnest* flaunts the humor and *sprezzatura* of a Celtic fairy tale and the virtues of its characters are the fairy-tale virtues: lightheartedness, resourcefulness, a willingness to travel to new adventure and a refusal to be daunted by monsters even if they are not myths. The foundling who aspires to the hand of the princess who is his lover goes through the trial of confronting the mother or monster who is guarding the princess; he is set an impossible task which he accomplishes; finally, in the transformative spirit of a fairy tale, the foundling is revealed as the heir to a kingdom, the princess is a cousin he can marry after all, and the monster becomes an aunt one is invited to kiss. And in true fairy tale fashion, everything is repeated or happens in triplicate. And the magic word that unlocks this world is "Ernest."

In *Earnest*, each character's imagination writes the script.

> Oh, write no more the tale of Troy,
>   If earth Death's scroll must be!
> Nor mix with Laian rage the joy
>   Which dawns upon the free:
> Although a subtler Sphinx renew
> Riddles of death Thebes never knew.
>   (Shelley, *Hellas*; p. 461,
>   lines 1078–83)

In the middle of tragedy art brings us new myths to sweeten the imagination of humanity; not a post-truth consciousness but a snail-horn perception of beauty (as Keats calls it), which can distinguish between lies and the truths of the imagination. And sometimes it brings a cathartic humor and wit. The dramatic and sexually fluid counterpart of the theory of sexual selection and female aesthetic choice and desire which Darwin could not get his scientific contemporaries to consider has proved irresistible to audiences and readers from India to Africa for over a hundred years, been translated into hundreds of languages and cultures, and performed on innumerable high-school stages. Wilde is an international cultural icon and the things he said or might have said or did not say are universally quoted and "borrowed." So, as Dorothy Parker suggests, there is no point in trying to take credit for anything clever: "We all assume that Oscar said it." After various plays about a woman—or a man—with a past, Wilde gives us one about a man without a past who is instructed to acquire one before the season quite ends. In actual life, where one thinks of lost babies and bereft parents, of love lost and time lost, this would be bittersweet at best. One also thinks of the drama unfolding behind the scenes in Wilde's own life. In Sophocles violence happens offstage, and the fourth choric ode of *Oedipus* weeps "the world's outcast." But the one preceding that is a song of joyful expectation at the brink of unrealized tragedy. On stage at least, *Earnest* remains Wilde's greatest triumph; with the rediscovery of the accidental substitution of art for life, with the recovery of baby, handbag, and an extended family, all losses are restored and sorrows—such as they are in *Earnest*—end.

WORKS CITED

Aristotle. *Aristotle's Poetics*. Trans. James Hutton. Norton, 1982.

Auden, W. H. *Collected Poems*. Ed. Edward Mendelson. Vintage, 1991.

Clifford, David. "Wilde and Evolution." In *Oscar Wilde in Context*. Ed. Kerry Powell and Peter Raby. Cambridge University Press, 2013, pp. 211–19.

Cocteau, Jean. *The Testament of Orpheus*. Dir. Cocteau and Auric, 1960.

Craft, Christopher. "Alias Bunbury." In *Another Kind of Love: Male Homosexual Desire in English Discourse, 1850–1920*. University of California Press, 1994. 106–39.

Daruwala, Maneck H. "The Discerning Flame: Of Pater and *The Renaissance*." *Victorians Institute Journal* 16 (1988): 85–128.

———. "Strange Bedfellows: Keats and Wollstonecraft, *Lamia* and *Berwick*." *The Keats-Shelley Review* 11.1 (1997): 83–132.

Darwin, Charles. The *Darwin Correspondence Project*. University of Cambridge. www.darwinproject.ac.uk/letter/DCP-LETT-2743.xml.

———. *Darwin Online*. http://darwin-online.org.uk.

Ellmann, Richard. *Oscar Wilde*. Vintage, 1987.

Evangelista, Stefano. "The Greek Life of Oscar Wilde." In *British Aestheticism and Ancient Greece*. Palgrave Macmillan, 2009. 125–57.

Foster, Clare L. E. "Wilde and the Emergence of Literary Drama, 1880–1895." In *Oscar Wilde and Classical Antiquity*. Ed. Kathleen Riley et al. Oxford, 2018. 107–26.

Gillespie, Michael Patrick. *Branding Oscar Wilde*. Routledge, 2017.

Graves, Robert. "To Juan at the Winter Solistice," *Complete Poems*, Vol. 2. Ed. Beryl Graves and Dunstan Ward. Carcanet, 1997.

Jabr, Ferris. "How Beauty Is Making Scientists Rethink Evolution." *The New York Times*. Jan. 9, 2019. 22.

Keats, John. *Complete Poems*. Ed. Jack Stillinger. Harvard University Press, 1978, 1982.

Knox, Bernard. *Oedipus at Thebes: Sophocles' Tragic Hero and His Time*. Norton, 1971.

Plato. *Plato's Symposium*. Trans. Seth Benardete. Commentary by Allan Bloom and Seth Bernardete. University of Chicago Press, 1986, 1993, 2001.

Prum, Richard O. *The Evolution of Beauty: How Darwin's Forgotten Theory of Mate Choice Shapes the Animal World—and Us*. Doubleday, 2017.

Rothenberg, David. *Survival of the Beautiful: Art, Science and Evolution*. Bloomsbury, 2011.

Scarry, Elaine. *On Beauty and Being Just*. Princeton University Press, 1999.

Shelley, Percy Bysshe. *Shelley's Poetry and Prose*, 2nd ed. Ed. Donald H. Reiman and Neil Fraistat. Norton, 2000.

Shewan, Rodney. *Oscar Wilde: Art and Egoism*. Barnes & Noble, 1977.

Sophocles. *The Theban Cycle*. Trans. Dudley Fitts and Robert Fitzgerald. Harcourt, Brace Jovanovich, 1977.

————. *The Three Theban Plays.* Trans. Robert Fagles, Introduction by Bernard Knox. Viking Penguin, 1982, 1984.

Sumpter, Caroline. "'No Artist Has Ethical Sympathies': Oscar Wilde, Aesthetics, and Moral Evolution." *Victorian Literature and Culture* 44.3 (2016): 623–40.

Wilde, Oscar. *The Complete Works of Oscar Wilde.* Ed. Vyvyan Holland. Harper & Row, 1989.

————. "The English Renaissance of Art." In *Essays and Lectures.* www.gutenberg.org/ebooks/774.

————. *The Picture of Dorian Gray.* 3rd ed. Ed. Michael Patrick Gillespie. Norton, 2020.

Yeats, William Butler. The *Autobiography of William Butler Yeats.* Collier Macmillan, 1965.

————. *Essays and Introductions.* Macmillan, 1961.

Oscar Wilde: A Chronology

1854	Oscar Fingal O'Flahertie Wills Wilde is born in Dublin at 21 Westland Row on October 16. He is the second child of Dr. (later Sir) William Wilde, noted oculist, aural surgeon, and author of medical texts, travel books, and antiquarian studies of Irish folklore and custom, and Jane Francesca Elgee Wilde, a fervent Irish nationalist who had published political pamphlets under the pen name Speranza.
1857	Wilde's younger sister, Isola Francesca Emily Wilde, is born on April 2.
1864	William Wilde receives his knighthood.
1864–71	Oscar Wilde attends the Portora Royal School at Enniskillen. Upon leaving, he is awarded the Portora Gold Medal as best classical scholar.
1867	Isola Wilde dies on February 23. Wilde writes the poem "Requiescat" to commemorate her passing.
1871–74	Wilde receives a scholarship to Trinity College, Dublin, where he wins the Berkeley Gold Medal for his study of Greek.
1874–78	After winning a demyship (a form of scholarship), Wilde enters Magdalen College, Oxford, in October 1874. He studies with the writer and critic John Ruskin and Walter Pater, the essayist and chief proponent of "art for art's sake" Aestheticism. Wilde distinguishes himself as a scholar, poet, and dandy.
1876	Wilde's father dies on April 19, and his mother moves to England.
1878	Wilde wins the Newdigate Prize for his poem *Ravenna*. It is subsequently published by Thomas Shrimpton & Son, Oxford. He also completes his degree, earning rare double first in his final examinations.
1879	After an unsuccessful attempt to secure a position as a fellow at Oxford, Wilde settles in London and begins to work to secure a place in society.
1880	Wilde privately publishes his first play, *Vera, or the Nihilists*.

1881   Wilde commissions David Boque to publish his first volume of verse, *Poems.* He also becomes the subject of a series of cartoons in *Punch* satirizing the "art for art's sake" movement. The Gilbert and Sullivan light opera *Patience* is produced; it contains a character, Bunthorne, based on Wilde.

1882   Wilde arrives in New York on January 2 and begins a highly successful lecture tour of the United States and Canada. He departs for England on December 27.

1883   In Paris, Wilde completes his second play, *The Duchess of Padua,* and has it privately printed. A production of *Vera* is staged in New York but withdrawn after one week.

1883–84   On September 24, Wilde begins a successful lecture tour of the United Kingdom that carries over into the next year.

1884   On May 29, Wilde marries Constance Lloyd, the daughter of a Dublin barrister and a woman with financial resources.

1885   On January 1, Wilde takes a house at 16 Tite Street in Chelsea, an artistic section of London. The Wildes' son Cyril is born June 5. Wilde becomes book review editor of the *Pall Mall Gazette.*

1886   The Wildes' second son, Vyvyan, is born November 3. Wilde begins a friendship with Robbie Ross that will last the rest of his life; Ross later acts as Wilde's literary executor.

1887–89   Wilde edits *Woman's World,* bringing notoriety to the magazine by securing contributions from a number of well-known women.

1888   *The Happy Prince and Other Tales*, a collection of fairy tales that Wilde originally composed for his sons, appears.

1889   Wilde publishes "Pen, Pencil and Poison" in *The Fortnightly Review,* "The Decay of Lying" in *Nineteenth Century,* and "The Portrait of Mr. W.H." in *Blackwood's Edinburgh Magazine.*

1890   "The Picture of Dorian Gray" appears in novella form in the July issue of *Lippincott's Monthly Magazine.* It arouses a storm of controversy in the English press.

1891   Wilde publishes "The Soul of Man under Socialism" in the *Fortnightly Review* and *Intentions,* a collection of essays. Together they offer important insights into Wilde's aesthetic philosophy. He also brings out *Lord Arthur Savile's Crime and Other Stories* and *A House of*

Pomegranates, two collections of short stories, and a novel-length version of *The Picture of Dorian Gray* (which produces none of the uproar that the novella caused). Wilde also begins his doomed friendship with Lord Alfred Douglas, nicknamed "Bosie."

1892   *Lady Windermere's Fan* is staged at the St. James's Theatre to great popular acclaim. On opening night, Wilde is reintroduced to Lord Alfred Douglas, with whom he begins a tempestuous affair that will ultimately end in scandal. Wilde writes (in French) *Salomé*. The London production is prohibited because of the invocation of a little-known and rarely enforced English law forbidding theatrical depiction of biblical characters.

1893   *A Woman of No Importance* is staged at the Theatre Royal. *Lady Windermere's Fan* and *Salomé* (French version) are published.

1894   Wilde publishes *Salomé* in English translation with illustrations by Aubrey Beardsley. He also publishes *The Sphinx*, a long poem, and *A Woman of No Importance*, a play. He writes *The Importance of Being Earnest*.

1895   *An Ideal Husband* opens on January 3 at the Haymarket Theatre and *The Importance of Being Earnest* opens on February 14 at the St. James's Theatre. Both plays are popular and critical hits. Wilde's increasingly reckless behavior draws public criticism from the Marquess of Queensberry, Lord Douglas's father. Wilde sues for libel but loses the case. Evidence from this trial leads to Wilde's arrest for homosexual offenses. After a hung jury on his first trial, Wilde is found guilty in the second. On May 25, he is sentenced to two years at hard labor. He is originally imprisoned in Pentonville and on November 20 is transferred to H.M. Prison, Reading.

1895–97 While in prison, Wilde writes *De Profundis*, a sometimes moving description of his spiritual progress and a sometimes violent castigation of Bosie's behavior during their affair. On his release from prison, Wilde goes to the Continent. For the next three years he lives primarily in France, often subsisting on the charity of friends.

1898   Wilde anonymously publishes his best-known poem, *The Ballad of Reading Gaol*, on February 13. He also publishes two letters on prison reform. His wife, Constance, dies in Genoa on April 7.

1899   Leonard Smithers publishes *The Importance of Being Earnest*.

1900   On November 30, after being received into the Roman
         Catholic Church, Wilde dies of cerebral meningitis at
         the Hotel d'Alsace, Paris. He is buried at the British
         Cemetery in Bagneaux, France.
1909   At the direction of Robert Ross, Wilde's literary execu-
         tor; his remains are moved to to a tomb designed by
         Jacob Epstein at Père Lachaise Cemetery, Paris.

Selected Bibliography

I have listed only Wilde's book-length publications. Over his lifetime, he wrote a great many articles and reviews. One may find reference to these works in the Mason and Mikhail bibliographies listed below.

• indicates works included or excerpted in this Norton Critical Edition.

WORKS

Ravenna (Newdigate Prize Poem). Oxford: Thomas Shrimpton & Son, 1878.
Vera, or the Nihilists. London: Ranken, 1880.
Poems. London: Bogue; Boston: Roberts, 1881.
The Duchess of Padua: A Tragedy of the XVI Century Written in Paris in the XIX Century. New York: privately printed, 1883.
The Happy Prince and Other Tales. London: Nutt; Boston: Roberts, 1888.
"The Picture of Dorian Gray." (Novella.) *Lippincott's Monthly Magazine* 46 (July 1890): 3–100.
The Picture of Dorian Gray. (Novel.) London: Ward, Lock, 1891.
Intentions. London: Osgood, McIlvaine; New York: Dodd, Mead, 1891.
Lord Arthur Savile's Crime and Other Stories. London: Osgood, McIlvaine; New York: Dodd, Mead, 1891.
A House of Pomegranates. London: Osgood, McIlvaine, 1891; New York: Dodd, Mead, 1892.
Salomé: Drama en un acte. Paris: Librairie de l'Art Indépendent; London: Elkin Mathews and John Lane, 1893.
Lady Windermere's Fan. London: Mathews and Lane, 1893.
Salomé. Trans. Lord Alfred Douglas. Ill. Aubrey Beardsley. London: Mathews and Lane; Boston: Copeland and Day, 1894.
The Sphinx. London: Mathews and Lane; Boston: Copeland and Day, 1894.
A Woman of No Importance. London: Mathews and Lane, 1894.
The Soul of Man under Socialism. London: privately printed, 1985.
The Ballad of Reading Gaol. London: Smithers, 1898.
The Importance of Being Earnest. London: Smithers, 1899.
An Ideal Husband. London: Smithers, 1898.
De Profundis. London: Methuen; New York: Putnam, 1905.
Impressions of America. Sunderland: Keystone Press, 1906.
Poems. London: Methuen, 1908.
De Profundis [with Additional Matter]. London: Methuen, 1908.
Reviews. London: Methuen, 1908.
Miscellanies. London: Methuen, 1908.
The Suppressed Portion of "De Profundis." New York: Reynolds, 1913.
Essays of Oscar Wilde. London: Methuen, 1950.
The Importance of Being Earnest: A Trivial Comedy for Serious People in Four Acts as Originally Written by Oscar Wilde. The New York Public Library, 1956.
Literary Criticism of Oscar Wilde. Ed. Stanley Weintraub. Lincoln: U of Nebraska P, 1968.

LETTERS

Hart-Davis, Rupert, ed. *Selected Letters of Oscar Wilde*. Oxford: Oxford UP, 1979.
———. *The Letters of Oscar Wilde*. New York: Harcourt, 1962.
Holland, Vyvyan, Merlin Holland, and Rupert Hart-Davis, eds. *The Complete Letters of Oscar Wilde*. New York: Holt, 2000.

BIBLIOGRAPHIES

Beckson, Karl. *Oscar Wilde: The Critical Heritage*. New York: Barnes & Noble, 1970.
Fletcher, Ian, and John Stokes. "Oscar Wilde." *Recent Research on Anglo-Irish Writers*. Ed. Richard Finneran. New York: MLA, 1983.
Mason, Stuart [pseud. Christopher S. Millard]. *Bibliography of Oscar Wilde*. London: Laurie, 1914; rpt. London: Rota, 1967.
Mikhail, E. H. *Oscar Wilde: An Annotated Bibliography of Criticism*. London: Macmillan, 1978.
Small, Ian. *Oscar Wilde: Recent Research*. Greensboro, NC: ELT, 2000.

BIOGRAPHIES

Cohen, Ed. "Laughing in Earnest: The Trying Context of Wilde's 'Trivial' Comedy." *Literature, Interpretation, Theory: LIT* 3.1 (1991): 57–64.
Ellmann, Richard. *Oscar Wilde*. New York: Vintage, 1987.
Friedman, David. *Wilde in America: Oscar Wilde and the Invention of Celebrity*. New York: W. W. Norton, 2014.
Harris, Frank. *The Life and Confessions of Oscar Wilde*. New York: Duffield, 1914.
Hofer, Matthew, and Gary Scharnhorst, eds. *Oscar Wilde in America: The Interviews*. Urbana and Chicago: U of Illinois P, 2010.
Holland, Merlin, ed. *Oscar Wilde: A Life in Letters*. New York: Carroll and Graf, 2003.
Hyde, H. Montgomery. *Oscar Wilde: A Biography*. New York: Harcourt (Farrar, Straus, & Giroux), 1975.
Lewis, Lloyd, and Henry Justin Smith. *Oscar Wilde Discovers America*. New York: Harcourt Brace, 1936.
Mikhail, E. H. *Oscar Wilde: Interviews and Recollections*. New York: Harper & Row, 1979.
Morris, Roy, Jr. *Declaring His Genius: Oscar Wilde in North America*. Cambridge, MA: Harvard UP, 2013.
Pearson, Hesketh. *Oscar Wilde*. New York: Farrar, 1975.
Ricketts, Charles. *Recollections of Oscar Wilde*. London: Nonesuch, 1932.
Sherard, Robert. *The Life of Oscar Wilde*. London: Laurie, 1905.

CRITICISM

• Bastiat, Brigitte. "*The Importance of Being Earnest* by Oscar Wilde: Conformity and Resistance in Victorian Society." *Cahiers victoriens et édouardiens* 72 (Oct. 2010): 53–63.
Craft, Christopher. "Alias Bunbury: Desire and Termination in *The Importance of Being Earnest*." *Representations* 31 (Summer 1990): 19–46.
Donohue, Joseph. "Wilde and the Idea of a Theatre." In *Rediscovering Oscar Wilde*, C. George Sandulescu, ed. Gerrards Cross: Colin Smythe, 1994.
Eltis, Sos. *Revising Wilde: Society and Subversion in the Plays of Oscar Wilde*. Oxford, England: Clarendon, 1997.

Gillespie, Michael Patrick. *Oscar Wilde and the Poetics of Ambiguity.* Gainesville: UP of Florida, 1996.

• ———. "The Branding of Oscar Wilde." *Études Anglaises* 69.1 (Jan.–
March 2016): 23–35.

———. *Branding Oscar Wilde.* New York: Routledge, 2017.

Gupta, Nikhil. "Oscar Wilde's Hair: Phobic Reactions and Novel Self-Fashioning
at the Turn of the Century." *Modernism/modernity* 25.1 (January 2018): 73–91.

Hall, Jean Graham. "Oscar Wilde: The Tragedy of Being Earnest: Some Legal
Aspects." *The Wildean: The Journal of the Oscar Wilde Society* 19 (2001):
35–42.

Haslam, Richard. "Oscar Wilde and the Imagination of the Celt." *Irish Studies
Review* 11 (Summer 1995): 2–5.

Kaplan, Joel, and Sheila Stowell. "The Dandy and the Dowager: Oscar Wilde
and Audience Resistance." *New Theatre Quarterly* 15.4 (60) (1999): 318–31.

Knowles, Ronald. "Bunburying with Bakhtin: A Carnavalesque Reading of *The
Importance of Being Earnest.*" *Essays in Poetics: The Journal of the British
Neo-Formalist Circle* 20 (Autumn 1995): 170–81.

Kohl, Norbert. *Oscar Wilde: The Works of a Conformist Rebel.* Trans. David
Henry Wilson. Cambridge: Cambridge UP, 1989.

Lalonde, Jeremy. "A 'Revolutionary Outrage': *The Importance of Being Earnest*
as Social Criticism." *Modern Drama* 48.4 (Winter 2005): 659–76.

Mackie, Gregory. "The Function of Decorum at the Present Time: Manners,
Moral Language, and Modernity in 'an Oscar Wilde Play.'" *Modern Drama*
52.2 (Summer 2009): 145–67.

Mackie, W. Craven. "Bunbury Pure and Simple." *Modern Drama* 41.2 (1998):
327–30.

McCormack, Jerusha, ed. *Wilde the Irishman.* New Haven and London: Yale
UP, 1998.

• Mikhail, E. H. "The Four-Act Version of *The Importance of Being Earnest.*"
Modern Drama 11 (1968): 263–66.

• Nassaar, Christopher S. "Some Remarks on 'Parody, Paradox and Play in *The
Importance of Being Earnest.*'" *Connotations* 14.1–3 (2004–05): 173–76.

• Niederhoff, Burkhard. "Parody, Paradox and Play in *The Importance of Being
Earnest.*" *Connotations* 13.1–2 (2003–04): 32–55.

Nunokawa, Jeff. *Tame Passions of Wilde: The Styles of Manageable Desire.*
Princeton: Princeton UP, 2003.

Paglia, Camille A. "Oscar Wilde and the English Epicene." *Raritan: A Quarterly Review* 4.3 (Winter 1985): 85–109.

Powell, Kerry. *Oscar Wilde and the Theatre of the 1890s.* Cambridge: Cambridge UP, 1990.

Ransome, Arthur. *Oscar Wilde: A Critical Study.* London: Martin Secker; New
York: Mitchell Kennerlye, 1912.

Roditi, Edouard. *Oscar Wilde.* Norfolk, CT: New Directions Books, 1947.

Rose, David. *Oscar Wilde's Elegant Republic: Transformation and Fantasy in Fin
de Siècle Paris.* Newcastle-upon-Tyne: Cambridge Scholars Publishing, 2015.

Sinfield, Alan. *The Wilde Century: Effeminacy, Oscar Wilde and the Queer
Moment.* New York: Columbia UP, 1994.

Smith, Philip E., II, and Michael S. Helfand, eds. *Oscar Wilde's Oxford Note-
books: A Portrait of Mind in the Making.* New York: Oxford UP, 1989.

• Snider, Clifton. "Synchronicity and the Trickster in *The Importance of Being
Earnest.*" *The Wildean: Journal of the Oscar Wilde Society* 27 (2005): 55–63.

Thienpont, Eva. "From Faltering Arrow to Pistol Shot: *The Importance of Being
Earnest.*" *Cambridge Quarterly* 33.3 (2004): 245–55.

Walkowitz, Rebecca L. "Ethical Criticism: *The Importance of Being Earnest.*"
Contemporary Literature 43.1 (2002): 187–93.

• Walshe, Eibhear. "A Wilde Irish Rebel: Queerness Versus Nationalism in Irish
Imaginative Presentations of Wilde." *The Canadian Journal of Irish Studies*
36.1 (2010): 45–67.